Charlotte in Love

Charlotte in Love

The Courtship and Marriage
of Charlotte Brontë

Brian Wilks

Michael O'Mara Books Ltd

First published in Great Britain in 1998 by
Michael O'Mara Books Limited
9 Lion Yard
Tremadoc Road
London SW4 7NQ

A CIP catalogue record for this book is available from the British Library

ISBN 1-85479-315-2

1 3 5 7 9 10 8 6 4 2

Designed and typeset by Keystroke, Jacaranda Lodge, Wolverhampton

Printed and bound in England by Clays Ltd, St Ives plc

'There is occasions and causes why and wherefore in all things.'

(William Shakespeare, *Henry V* Act V, Scene ii)

'If any man think that he knoweth anything, he knoweth nothing yet, as he ought to know.' St Bernard of Clairvaux

(The first entry in Arthur Nicholls's commonplace book)

To my granddaughter **Tessa**,
who reminded me what fun words are.
And to the memory of **Fizzy**, gentle
and devoted companion to us all.

Contents

Preface

ᔥ

The Brontë family is remembered for the two great love stories concocted in the dining room of Haworth Parsonage, *Jane Eyre* and *Wuthering Heights*, but there exist two perhaps even greater love stories connected with the same place, neither of them fiction, and both belonging to creatures of flesh and blood.

The love letters between the Reverend Patrick Brontë and Maria Branwell during their courtship in 1812 tell a tale of a joyful, impatient passion and of a happiness that produced six healthy babies. All the children reached the age of ten before two daughters died of consumption. The comparatively early deaths of Maria and Elizabeth Brontë, at twelve and eleven respectively, must be seen in context as infant mortality in England was high in the first quarter of the nineteenth century. It is, however, a tale that is tragic in its brevity. Married in 1812, Maria died of cancer in great suffering in 1820, having enjoyed only eight years with her husband, and even fewer with their children. The marriage of Charlotte Brontë to Arthur Nicholls in 1854 did not last a year, yet throughout its nine months' progress Charlotte protested her happiness. What tragedy that family knew, how the stark sadness and poignancy of the true stories challenge the imagined fables of *Jane Eyre* and *Wuthering Heights*. The story of vulnerability and common human suffering engages us, lacking the anaesthetising effect of art that can make suffering bearable. The story moves us because we recognise it from our own experience of life's mixed cup: we know it to be true, for it happened to people, not creatures of the imagination.

The Brontë family was driven by two forces: the need for affection and the need for an audience. The former was sought mostly from the other members of the closely knit family; the latter from the world, through writing and publication. All the Brontë family passionately sought both. Nothing else would do. Just as they needed each other's love, so, through a shared intuitive grasp of the magical power of words, they craved the ability to write and to have their writings read.

At first the children were each other's audience, but in time, like their father, they came to desire a wider public.

Just as Patrick Brontë all his life wrote for newspapers, scribbled poetry, attempted novels and issued pamphlets, so were his children would-be chroniclers of life. Charlotte and Emily matured to write novels of genius, but the novels are works of fiction, their characters merely 'inhabitants of dreamland'. The story of Charlotte Brontë's courtship and marriage is a true one, for while its joys, its tortured course, its fulfilment and the pathos of its sudden and bitter curtailment may read like a novel, these events really happened.

The courageous commitment shown by Charlotte, and her husband Arthur, in risking all for love, in surrendering a manageable, predictable comfort for an uncertain and untried partnership, was no aberrant impulsive act. It was the necessary and longed-for fulfilment of all that Charlotte Brontë had hoped would be possible in life: no cold intellectual activity of the spirit, but a response to the impulses of flesh and blood.

Prologue

C harlotte Brontë was not afraid to talk about love. In her life and her writing love was a consuming fire of passion. She received four proposals of marriage, and was not afraid to reject them all. Only the fourth received any kind of reconsideration after months of agonising doubt. In declining one in 1851 she told her friend Ellen Nussey that 'each moment he came near me – and that I could see his eyes fastened upon me – my veins ran ice . . . were I to marry him – my heart would bleed – in pain and humiliation'. In rejecting Ellen's brother's proposal some twelve years earlier she had protested that she had been forced to ask herself two questions:

> *Do I love him as much as woman ought to love the man she marries ?*
> *Am I the person best qualified to make him happy ? Alas, Ellen, my*
> *conscience answered no to both these questions . . . I had not, and could*
> *not have, that intense attachment which would make me willing to die*
> *for him; and if ever I marry, it must be in the light of adoration that I*
> *will regard my husband . . .*
> (Charlotte Brontë [CB] to Ellen Nussey, 12 March 1839)

Elsewhere, Charlotte claimed that to show true love one should be prepared to offer one's breast to the hoofs of a kicking horse – such was her belief in the power of human affection and the nature of love's sacrifice. Tragically, in the event Charlotte Brontë's marriage to Arthur Bell Nicholls in 1854 led almost at once to her death, the famous woman of independent means dying six months pregnant, aged thirty-eight, before she had been married twelve months.

Charlotte Brontë died for her belief that love between human beings was beyond reason, that whatever benefits and comforts life offered none could moderate the effect of that mutual need for shared affection which we all possess. Fame as an author was not enough. Charlotte Brontë longed for affection, never abandoning the hope of finding physical fulfilment with someone who would value her for herself beyond all others. Much as she joked about being an old maid – ' . . . I am certainly doomed to be an old maid. Never mind, I made up my mind to that fate ever since I was twelve years old . . . ' (CB to Ellen Nussey, 4 August 1839) the reverse was true, for she was too lonely all her adult life ever to accept a single existence as sufficient. How could it be otherwise for the creator of the passionate Jane Eyre ? If there is any coherent theme in Charlotte Brontë's novels it is the search for love, for the passionate enfolding of a lover's arms, the physical comfort lovers bring to each other. In one of his stories, her father, Patrick Brontë, advised young couples contemplating marriage, 'Let each look upon the other as the best earthly friend.' (Patrick Brontë [PB], 'The Maid of Killarney', 1818) Earthly comfort, a passionate love, was something Patrick Brontë knew about. Some surviving love letters that Maria Branwell wrote to him during a brief courtship, in which he is addressed as 'Dear Saucy Pat', bear witness to a full-blooded and exciting relationship.

In all, Charlotte had three serious proposals of marriage before the one she accepted from Arthur Bell Nicholls, her father's curate, in December 1854. All three she had dismissed without hesitation. Why then did she accept the fourth? Was Arthur Nicholls the man she was best qualified to make happy? Would he make her happy? Would he be prepared to die for her? Was she prepared to die for him? Did she see him with 'the light of adoration'? Could he call out in the night and be heard, like Mr Rochester, over many miles? Nothing in life is quite that simple, however. Arthur Nicholls's declaration of love, the pouring out of his distress over and deep feelings towards Charlotte, came as a complete surprise to her. In her father, the same evening, it induced a near apoplectic fit: Arthur Bell Nicholls, the impoverished curate, was, it seems, no better than a bounty hunter, a turncoat, an impertinent upstart whom she should send packing.

Perhaps her father's unreasonable outrage, his unequivocal reminder that at thirty-six she was surely irrevocably 'on the shelf', was too blunt, too near the truth. Agreeing that she would of course refuse the proposal, there was nevertheless something in her that was ready to respond to Nicholls's manifest suffering. Charlotte Brontë's astonishment gave way, perhaps, to curiosity, and then to an understanding of just how deeply and truly the man was in love with her. Arthur Nicholls, often described as cold and rather aloof, in this case at least proved unable to hide or even disguise his feelings. Resigning from his post as Patrick Brontë's curate, he lived out the days before he left the parish a picture of abject misery. Wild and desperate gestures such as applying to be a missionary overseas gave way to less dramatic arrangements, which meant that he could at least write letters to Charlotte, even if he could not see her. In time, however, matters worked out, somehow. They were married in St Michael's Church, Haworth, on 29 June 1854 – a wedding service that the parson father refused to attend even though it was held in his own church.

In *Jane Eyre*, Charlotte Brontë created one of the world's most memorable love stories. The tale of the orphaned girl's bitter loneliness in a cold unfeeling world where her relatives scorn, shun and bully her; of the deprivations of her schooldays and of her painfully slow realisation that her life has no meaning at all; seems to have cast a hypnotic spell over readers for more than a hundred and fifty years. The insignificant governess's courtship with and marriage to the maimed Mr Rochester is one of the world's great love stories, and 'Reader; I married him' must be among the best-known lines in literature.

And yet, when all is said and done, *Jane Eyre* is fiction. Jane is, as Charlotte Brontë warned, 'an inhabitant of dreamland', her story often very far removed from reality however much it derived from Charlotte's own remembered experience of her schooldays. The consummation of Jane and Rochester's passionate love, which made her 'bone of his bone, flesh of his flesh', is an artistic fulfilment which satisfies the fancy, providing the happy ending that life so often withholds. Charlotte Brontë's own love story has a very different ending. Life seldom displays the apt completeness or serenity of art.

Creating the great romance of *Jane Eyre*, and writing three other love stories of equal power, Charlotte Brontë at the same time lived her own romance, at first in her imagination and finally in a loving relationship with a man. The story of her own life, as her novelist friend – and, after her death, biographer – Elizabeth Gaskell was quick to realise, contained all the ingredients of a compelling fiction. History has been unjust in seeing her marriage as an unfortunate tragedy, a loss to the world of literature, to the extent that her suitor and, in the end, husband, Arthur Nicholls, has been on the one hand vilified as the selfish brute who arrested the pen of a woman of genius, and on the other, written out of history as a mere cipher, a dull curate with no claim to consideration at all. Little notice has been taken of him, which is a pity, for Charlotte was prepared to risk all in becoming, of her own choice, this humble clergyman's wife.

Such misunderstanding is not only simplistic, but unjust both to the couple and to their memory. Charlotte Brontë was well aware of what she was doing when she married Arthur Nicholls, and lived long enough to record her happiness as his wife. He, for his part, adored her, mourned her death and honoured his promise to care for her old and bereft father for the rest of his long life.

This is the story of Charlotte's growing understanding of the nature of human love and devotion as she experienced them, and of a relationship that grew from aquaintanceship to friendship, to admiration and respect, through sympathy and understanding to love – a love that Charlotte said gave her 'the best earthly comfort a woman ever had'. It is a true tale of love which, in its tragic outcome, moves us to sadness and pity as surely as Shakespeare's *Romeo and Juliet*.

The account of the courtship, wedding and honeymoon tour is Charlotte Brontë's own love story, a tale full of surprises and unexpected comforts, and the beginning of a marriage that promised a true happiness for a woman who, while she had endured much suffering in her family circumstances, had found an international audience for her writings. It is, however, easy to forget that it was also Arthur Nicholls's wedding and honeymoon tour. For too long the bridegroom has been overshadowed by the bride's fame, the celebrated author's reputation consigning her husband to obscurity.

We must find room for Arthur Nicholls, and for a balanced exploration of all that his relationship with Charlotte Brontë came to mean, from their first meeting through to the sad separation at her death, before the first anniversary of their quiet, hopeful marriage.

Acknowledgements

T his is not another biography of Charlotte Brontë. Why and when Patrick O'Prunty (if that ever was his name) adopted the spelling Brontë, whether Anne Brontë was in love with William Weightman, are not this book's concern, nor is it concerned with the autobiographical impulse behind Charlotte Brontë's art as a novelist. This is a love story about a woman who wrote some of the most moving and enduring love stories in the world's literature. I hope that it will persuade readers to peer into the shadows cast by Charlotte Brontë's towering genius to discern the figure of her husband, whose personality has for so long been overshadowed by her writings and by the chance survival of many of her letters.

The quotations from the letters of Charlotte Brontë and other members of the Brontë family are taken from T.J. Wise and J.A. Symington (eds), *The Shakespeare Head Edition in Four Volumes: The Brontës, Their Lives, Friendships and Correspondence* (Blackwell, 1932), with the benefit of Margaret Smith's edition of Charlotte's letters, *The Letters of Charlotte Brontë*, Vol. 1 (Oxford University Press, 1995), with its informative and helpful notes for the earlier years.

In common with all who now write on the Brontës I have gratefully made use of Juliet Barker's impressive *The Brontës* (Weidenfeld & Nicolson, 1994), together with many volumes of the Brontë Society Transactions. For information about Trinity College, Dublin, I am grateful to Mary B. Higgins, who also sent me information about the Royal School at Banagher. I am grateful to the Thomand Archaeological Society, Eire, for permission to quote from the article 'Banagher Royal School' by Michael Quane (*North Munster Antiquarian Journal*, Vol. 10 (2), 1967).

Ten years directing the Brontë Scholars' Conferences at Leeds University were a good apprenticeship, from which I gained many insights. I am indebted to the Church of England Archives, East Bermondsey, for the help I have had in researching the National Society records of the Church School at Haworth over many years.

Sally Shuttleworth's *Charlotte Brontë and Victorian Psychology* (Cambridge University Press, 1996) has begun the study of Charlotte as a *woman* responding to her circumstances, while the fullest discussion of the question of Charlotte Brontë's pregnancy, or otherwise, is to be found in John Maynard's *Charlotte Brontë and Sexuality* (Cambridge University Press, 1984). As ever, the staff of the Parsonage Museum at Haworth have been patiently helpful and generous with their time and assistance.

We shall never know the full story of Charlotte's courtship – the passage of some one hundred and fifty years muddies the waters of history – but the least we can do is recognise that it takes two to make a marriage, and that for every Mrs Nicholls there is a Mr Nicholls. Charlotte Brontë's eloquence should not be allowed to deny her husband some consideration. For too long her version of events has gone unchallenged. I hope that others better qualified than I will be able to continue the exploration of Arthur Nicholls and his Ireland, a story waiting to be told, and one that has more than a passing relevance to the last months of Charlotte's life. I should add that this book is a personal exploration the inadequacies of which, despite the assistance of a most diligent editor in Toby Buchan, rest with me. I must also thank Elise Dillsworth for her patient and steady advice through all the stages of the book's progress.

In his *I Can't Stay Long* (1975), Laurie Lee eloquently describes the limits of and constraints upon biographical study, something which all who venture to write of the Brontë family must acknowledge.

Seven brothers and sisters shared my early years, and we lived on top of each other. If they had all written of those days, each account would have been different and each one true. We saw the same events at different heights, at different levels of mood and hunger – one suppressing an incident as too much to bear, another building it large around him, each reflecting one world according to the temper of the day, his age, the chance heat of his blood. Recalling it differently, as we are bound to do, what was it, in fact, we saw? Which one among us has the truth of it now? And which one shall be the judge? The truth is, of course, that there is no pure truth, only the moody accounts of witnesses.

I am naturally grateful to my wife Sue, who not only undertook to retrace with me Charlotte's honeymoon journey, including the trek through the Gap of Dunloe, but who also kept the idea of a book about Charlotte's marriage and honeymoon alive for more than ten years, finally encouraging me at a dispiriting moment to send the idea out one more time.

BRIAN WILKS

Far Headingley, January 1998

Chapter One

❦

First Meeting

'Papa has got a new Curate lately a Mr Nicholls from
Ireland . . . he appears a respectable young man, reads well,
and I hope will give satisfaction.'
(CB to Mrs Ebenezer Rand, 26 May 1845)

The lovers in this story are a celebrated novelist and a poor
curate of the Church of England. Despite having known each
other for some nine years, their courtship only began towards
the end of their acquaintance. It was one-sided. The curate fell in love
with the novelist: she had hardly noticed him. Eventually she agreed to
marry him, scattering reservations to all her friends that she did not
expect to 'love her husband'. She was thirty-eight years old when they
married, he thirty-six. Both declared that they were wonderfully happy
in their married life together. Sadly, before they could celebrate a single
anniversary of their wedding she was dead.

What made this mature woman decide to take the risk of marrying?
Who was this man who succeeded where three others had failed? What
had the creator of Jane Eyre hoped for with him? How did her father
feel as his last surviving child (five others and his wife were already
dead) contemplated the irrevocable step into wedlock? These are the
questions raised by the odd courtship, and by the circumstances that
guided Charlotte and Arthur to marriage, honeymoon and a tragically
brief life together. If some of these questions present us with a mystery,
there is a yet more curious twist, for there exists no objective account of
the courtship, or even of Arthur Nicholls's proposal. The whole story
comes from the pen of the novelist herself. What she said, what her
father said, what Arthur said and did, all this is to be found only in her
letters to friends. There is no way of testing her veracity. For more than
a hundred years her biographers, without exception, have taken her

1

version of events as the truth. If she says that her father had an apoplectic fit when Arthur proposed to her, then we have all believed her; if she writes that Arthur was refusing meals and pining for her, equally we believe that. We learn from her breathless gossiping in letters to her intimate friend Ellen Nussey of the daily progress of the 'objectionable business', but nowhere other than in the slow unfolding of events can we see what is really happening. If we pause to consider that we cannot possibly have all the correspondence that took place – we have not one of Arthur's letters to Charlotte, for example – and then reflect on the inadequacy of a purely subjective narration, we are compelled to realise that we have had a very biased account of the whole proceedings. It only remains for us to acknowledge that the account we have, and which has so seduced biographers, was set down by one of the finest storytellers in English, to realise that we may have been misled. It is difficult not to be beguiled by Charlotte Brontë's narrative skill even when it is her own life she is writing about. Nor is it really any wonder that generations of biographers, historians and commentators, quite apart from merely interested readers, have all believed her story.

Unlike fiction, however, life has other versions: there may be only one rendering of the events in *Jane Eyre*, but there are other versions of the courtship and marriage of Charlotte Brontë. Arthur Nicholls would have had his own tale to tell, which would necessarily have been quite different from his wife's account. Although little is known of his thoughts and feelings, nor of his version of events, Charlotte's husband was no mere cipher. Before we accept her account as true, therefore, we must at least consider his side of things, even though Charlotte's was authorised by Elizabeth Gaskell and set in stone by subsequent biographers.

The players in the drama are three: Charlotte, Arthur and Charlotte's father, Patrick Brontë. The story begins with Arthur's arrival in Haworth, newly ordained as a deacon of the Church of England, the first step towards becoming a priest in Holy Orders. We do not know why this young Irishman decided to be ordained in England, although that was not an unusual step in itself, the Church of Ireland and the Church of England being at that time one and the same. Neither do we know how he came to apply to Haworth for his first post as curate. All we know is that he did apply, was appointed and duly arrived there in 1845, where he was given a brief mention, already quoted at the head of this chapter, in a letter Charlotte wrote to a friend: 'Papa has got a new Curate lately a Mr Nicholls from Ireland

. . . he appears a respectable young man, reads well, and I hope will give satisfaction.'

And that was that.

Whatever the twenty-seven-year-old Reverend Arthur Bell Nicholls expected when he arrived in Haworth as the new curate to Charlotte Brontë's father in May 1845, nothing could have prepared him for the reality. He had done some teaching of classics, but that apart, this was his first real job. An Irishman like his parson employer, when Nicholls arrived in the small Yorkshire township he was an outsider. There was, moreover, much for him to do. Working in a new country would have been enough to come to terms with, but the young curate found that his parson was rapidly becoming blind, and would rely more and more on him to conduct services and oversee the church schools. The Parish of St Michael and All Angels was strung out along the edge of wild moors in an infamously rugged part of Yorkshire. Its inhabitants were a strong-minded, obstinate and generally rough lot, mostly illiterate, and with appalling infant and adult mortality rates. As if this was not enough of a challenge, the parsonage was home to a bewildering group of eccentric young adults, one of history's most extraordinary families. Nor was the parish an easy one to work in. There were as many dissenters, with their own schools and chapels, as there were members of the Church of England, and consequently the role of the officiating clergy of the established Church was questioned and by no means went unopposed.

Prior to Arthur Nicholls's arrival, Patrick Brontë had eloquently and frankly described his parish and parishioners in letters, requesting grant aid from the National Society in London for the schools for the poor which he had established in Haworth and nearby Stanbury:

I have resided in Yorkshire, above thirty years, and have preached, and visited in different parishes – I have also been in Lancashire, and from my reading, personal observation, and experience, I do not hesitate to say, that the populace in general are either ignorant or wicked, and in most cases where they have a little learning it is of a schismatical, vainly philosophical or treacherously political nature . . .

(PB to the Secretary of the National Society, 4 August 1843)

It is hard to believe that he would have introduced the parish to the new curate in any different tones. He clearly had no illusions about his

3

parishioners, or about the need to enlighten them and to educate them along Christian lines. Time and again Patrick Brontë described his parish as a pagan, uncivilised place. More than once his bishop, the Bishop of Ripon, endorsed his appeals for help, agreeing that the parish was a poor and 'uncivilised' place, and that Brontë's efforts at civilising the parish needed every help.

The parishioners were poor, uneducated and suffered endemic ill health and poor living conditions. The poverty and squalor of the homes of quarrymen, weavers and wool-combers would not have been unfamiliar to the young Irishman. He had seen the misery of poverty and epidemic illness, as well as the dispossession of cottagers by landlords, back in the town of Banagher in Ireland, where he was brought up and educated by his aunt and uncle. Nothing, however, could have prepared him for the experiences of the first three years of his early ministry, years dominated by the events taking place in the parsonage as much as in the parish. Irrevocably, Arthur Nicholls would find himself caught up in the bizarre circumstances of Patrick Brontë's family for, as the parson's assistant, he could not avoid having a close knowledge of parsonage affairs. His lodgings with John Brown, the sexton, in the house next to the Brontës', would bring him as close as possible to living in the parsonage itself.

The Reverend Patrick Brontë had been born of peasant stock in the north of Ireland in 1777. By supreme efforts of self-education and application he had found his way, through village schoolteaching in Drumballyrony, to a sizarship at St John's College, Cambridge. Being a sizar meant that in return for some domestic duties in the college Patrick could attend lectures and read for a degree, and in 1806 he duly gained a BA, having won some prizes for work in Greek and Latin along the way of which he was justly proud. Cambridge must have brought him into contact with social prejudice of all kinds, his extreme poverty and lowly upbringing contrasting sharply with the lives of the predominantly aristocratic and wealthy scholars of the college. Inevitably, only teaching or ordination offered him a way forward into any kind of security or modest financial gain. His progress at Cambridge had been observed by agents eager to recruit for an evangelical ministry, however, and thus his path was cleared. In the year in which he graduated he was ordained first as deacon in the chapel of Lambeth Palace, and then, in 1807, as priest in the Chapel Royal of St James's Palace at Westminster, a remarkable progress from the peasant cottages of Ireland. His hard-won education was a prize he valued highly; it made him a highly principled, strongly opinionated yet compassionate man, with a profound belief in the power of education for all classes of people. Via curacies in Wethersfield in Essex and Wellington in Shropshire he made his way to Yorkshire, first as curate at Dewsbury, then priest in charge of Hartshead-cum-Clifton, next perpetual curate at the Old Bell Chapel, Thornton, and thence, in 1820, finally to Haworth, where he was to remain for forty-one years outliving his wife and all six of his children. While above all a parson, Patrick Brontë had always cherished the ambition to be a writer. Throughout his life he wrote and published creditable stories, poetry, and pamphlets, while passing on to his children a deep and sensitive understanding and enjoyment of literature.

By the year 1845 Patrick Brontë had held the living of St Michael and All Angels in Haworth for twenty-five years, the years in which his four surviving children Charlotte, Patrick Branwell, Emily Jane and Anne had grown to maturity. Two other daughters, Maria and Elizabeth, had died in 1808 and 1809 as children. His wife, Maria, had also died shortly after their arrival in the township of Haworth and her elder sister, Elizabeth, known to the family as 'Aunt Branwell', had agreed to live in the parsonage and help her brother-in-law raise the family of six children. This she had dutifully done, being, as Branwell said, 'as a mother to them', albeit a strict one, until her death in 1842.

By 1845 and Arthur Nicholls's arrival in the parish, all the young Brontës had made attempts to earn their living away from Haworth. All had foundered. The girls had reluctantly and protestingly been teachers and governesses, and the two elder girls, Charlotte and Emily, had even spent time as pupil-teachers at a school for girls in Brussels. Patrick Branwell, the only son, known in the family as 'Branwell' or 'Branny' in order to distinguish him from his father, had blundered his way in and out of employment – as a private tutor, and as a railway clerk, hoping to become a stationmaster – being dismissed in disgrace as often as he was employed. For a spell he had even tried to earn his living as a portrait painter in Bradford, running out of commissions and into debt in the process. Sadly, Branwell's only attributes at the time Arthur Nicholls met him were an ability to talk the hind leg off a donkey, drink deeply, run up debts, and occasionally write some moderately good poetry.

And yet, of all the Brontë children, he had shown the most promise. He had been the most precocious, writing good verse at a very early age, able to draw and to paint in watercolours and in oils. It is to him we owe the sole portrait of the three Brontë sisters, now in the National Portrait Gallery in London. He was also a musician, playing the flute, the piano and the church organ. Almost at the moment Nicholls set foot in Haworth, however, Branwell was dismissed from his latest post, that of tutor to the son of Mr and Mrs Robinson at Thorp Green Hall, near York, where Anne was also working as governess. He was dismissed, moreover, in disgrace, it now being believed that he had an affair with his employer's wife. The son of the house who had been brought up to think of himself as some kind of genius, now finally succumbed to self-pity and self-indulgence in drink, bouts of taking opium, and morbid depression from which he never recovered. His return to the parsonage heralded a three-year period of misery and despair for the whole household, as though Arthur had arrived for the start of the last act of Branwell's personal tragedy, and the onset of the most traumatic time for the parson and his family. There is no way that Arthur could have avoided knowing of – and to a degree having to cope with – the chaos and hurt that Branwell would cause the family.

Setting these domestic problems aside, Patrick Brontë's deteriorating eyesight would have ensured that he would be glad of the arrival of the young Arthur Nicholls, although we have no record of any particular welcome being offered to a fellow Irishman. Almost as soon as Arthur arrived he was busy in the churchyard conducting burials, just as his parson had begun his ministry at Haworth twenty-five years earlier. Funerals were a grim staple of a parish priest's work. The infant mortality rate in this part of Yorkshire was one of the highest in the country, 45 per cent of children never achieving six years of age, while the average lifespan for a villager was a mere twenty-five years, and as little as fourteen for a child who worked in a mill.

It is hard to envisage the task of the priest and his curate from a twentieth-century perspective. The youthful curate would spend much of his time burying those younger than himself, burying the children of those he married as well as the parents of those children. Patrick Brontë's forty-one years in the parish must have meant that he saw three generations baptised and buried, conducting funeral services for those he had baptised and in due course married.

Such was the parish to which the young Arthur had been appointed, a very modest first post. Patrick Brontë was himself known as a 'perpetual curate', the parish of Haworth belonging to the nearby Bradford Parish Church. There would be little hope of advancement in this job, but there would be an overwhelming experience of pastoral work, and little interference from Church patrons, for there were no wealthy landed families with any interest in the township, only mill owners.

As well as their ordination and their common nationality, Arthur and Patrick shared an enlightened enthusiasm. Both held the provision of education for the poor to be a prime function of the Church and of their individual ministry. Both had been youthful teachers in schools in Ireland before completing their own education, Patrick as a completely unqualified youngster at schools in Glascar and then in Drumballyrony before going to Cambridge, Arthur while still an undergraduate at Trinity College, Dublin, teaching classics in his uncle's school, the Royal School at Banagher, where he himself had been a pupil, and later in a national school near by. The two Irishmen had much in common; in exile from their own families, they were dedicated to ministering to others, to bettering their parishioners' mental and physical wellbeing as well as attending to their spiritual needs.

With his eyesight rapidly fading, Patrick Brontë was happy to let his new man undertake most of the duties of the parish. He himself would still preach his homely sermons (which he gave without notes), but increasingly he allowed Arthur to take up the reins. In this the young man proved a godsend, and one the whole Brontë family appreciated for the help that he could give 'Papa'. In this respect he did indeed give satisfaction, as Charlotte had hoped when she wrote to Mrs Rand, the wife of the former schoolmaster in Haworth, announcing the new curate's arrival. Her succinct declaration – 'Papa has got a new Curate lately a Mr Nicholls from Ireland . . . he . . . reads well, and I hope will give satisfaction' – now has a resonance she could never have foreseen. Arthur's being 'from Ireland' would in time take her to that country on a honeymoon tour, where she would meet her husband's genteel and loving family. Arthur's ability to 'read well' would be tested after her death, in the hours he spent reading her novels to her bereaved father in the loneliness of the empty parsonage. In marrying him she found that he did indeed 'give satisfaction', many times saying how happy she was. All that lay in the future, however. In 1845 Arthur Bell Nicholls was just another 'curate', something which qualified him as an object of comic scorn in the family. His predecessor, William Weightman, had been dubbed 'Miss Celia Amelia' by the sisters, and in due course Arthur would be parodied as one of the 'shower of curates' at whose expense much fun is had in the opening of Charlotte's novel *Shirley*.

A Nest of Scribblers

Considering the circumstances of the Brontë family in 1845, it is not surprising that Arthur Nicholls receives scant mention in the family chronicles. Even allowing for the fact that letters and diary entries may have disappeared over the years, the surviving documents merely record his arrival, his doing duty for Patrick Brontë, and short holidays he spent visiting his family in Ireland – the last only mentioned because of the inconvenience to Patrick Brontë and his family.

The Brontë family was a closely knit one, united not only by their love for each other, but by the irresistible compulsion to write. In securing this curacy, Arthur Nicholls had stumbled upon a nest of scribblers. Patrick Brontë had pamphlets and books weighing down his shelves – poetry for cottagers, religious texts and topical pamphlets – and he was a frequent correspondent, when his eyesight allowed, with a variety of local newspapers on topics of national as well as local importance. But whereas he was the only visible writer, all three of his children were preoccupied with writing of all kinds. Branwell had poems published in various regional newspapers, under pen-names that were transparently obvious to any member of the family other than the Reverend Brontë. This 'scribblemania', as Branwell termed it, was no new or recent thing. From the earliest days the four Brontë children had busied themselves creating volumes – indeed, little libraries – of stories written down in tiny hand-stitched booklets which they made themselves, books which, despite their size (2 inches by 1), contained thousands of words in almost microscopic print. As Charlotte always maintained, it 'had long been their ambition to be writers', an ambition in all probability caught from seeing their father's printed works on the bookshelves and from their awareness all their lives of the importance he gave to writing, his love of words in action, as both a preacher and a would-be poet, being unavoidably infectious.

Arthur could have had no idea what he had let himself in for. All he saw was an ailing old man, three plainly dressed, unfashionable daughters and a short, bespectacled, red-headed son who was as excitable and unpredictable as his father was proud and dignified. Of the crucible of creativity that quietly bubbled away in parlour and bedroom he would see nothing, even though it was nearing a critical and most productive condition.

If the secret of their writing was one preoccupation of the parsonage inhabitants, overriding this was their preoccupation with themselves. Never simple folk, each of Patrick Brontë's children was deeply introspective, nursing and feeding deep personal desires, memories, disappointments, frustrations and ambitions. Soon these were to surface in the most dramatic fashion.

Charlotte, deeply depressed, vowing that her whole life had been pointless, was pining for a lost love, drawing out her days in longing for the arrival of love letters that never came, letters never in fact written by her former teacher Constantin Heger in Brussels. Emily, who, having been born in 1818, was exactly Arthur's own age, while ostensibly – or so tradition has it – busying herself with household management, was compiling an anthology of highly imaginative and passionate lyric verse. Anne, the youngest, born in 1820, was writing verse and gathering her experiences as a governess into material for two major novels. Branwell, younger only than Charlotte, was in the middle of an affair with his employer's wife that lifted him to euphoria, only subsequently to plunge him into a terminal despair that led almost directly to his abuse of alcohol and laudanum (tincture of opium) and an early death.

When Arthur Nicholls arrived in Haworth the scene was already set for the beginning of a drama that equals any in the Brontë sisters' novels. There was, however, little on the surface to give any warning of what was about to happen. He could not in his wildest imaginings have envisaged what the future held for him and this family; indeed, not even the Brontës themselves, the main players in the drama, could foresee what the next year would bring. Nothing of their past life had prepared them for the storm that was about to break, and which would irrevocably, albeit incidentally, link Arthur Nicholls with the family in a way that no other outsider other than the family servants would ever be linked.

All, however, was not yet doom and gloom, a redeeming characteristic of the Brontës being their sense of fun. Arthur, the new curate, would be looked over and summed up, a fate that awaited all clergy who passed through Haworth parsonage door, which included 'fat little bishops' from time to time.

Arthur's arrival coincided with the culmination of Patrick Brontë's successful campaign to augment the three bells in the church tower with another three to make a peal. The tower was duly raised in height to provide room for a ringing chamber, the new bells were installed and celebratory changes rung, Charlotte wryly commenting that living so close to the church (the tower is virtually in their front garden), they had the benefit of the tones of the peals. The coincidence of Arthur's middle name, Bell, and all the meetings with their talk of bells and belfries, meant that the Brontë sisters did not need to look far in seeking a collective pen name. Their poems would ring out (muffled only by the pseudonym) as the work of the Messrs Bell when published, at their authors' expense, in 1846. Many years later, Arthur Nicholls wrote that it had never occurred to him that the girls had deliberately used his second name as the last part of their pen names; nor had he known of any family of that name in the parish.

Arthur Nicholls has been given little credit for coping so well with the conditions – indeed, the crises – in the Brontë family that greeted him on his arrival; in short, there has been an injustice in the way history has dealt with him. We all have a habit of glossing over reality in order to pursue a more dramatic story, and in this Charlotte's first biographer, Mrs Gaskell, was no different. Her *Life of Charlotte Brontë* skewed the focus of the family history, so that the effect is as if, being told so much about Charlotte, we readily accept other members of the family and their immediate circle of acquaintances as no more than a supporting cast. Such an approach can never be right, as Jane Austen was to comment, for the interiors of families are complex and interdependent. But for Arthur Nicholls's competence, the first three years of his time in the parish would have been even harder for the Brontë family. Easing his parson's burden at a time of physical weakness and family crisis, he must have become a fixture within that family, without whom the difficulties would have been even more critical. Is it too much to imagine that by his functioning so well, he ensured that the Reverend Patrick Brontë kept his job, and thereby his home for his family? When, later, Nicholls briefly left the parish having incurred his parson's wrath by having the impudence to propose marriage to his daughter, Patrick Brontë soon realised how much he had relied upon the curate's competence. That realisation must have played a large part in the eventual reconciliation between the two men that we know took place.

'Unloved – I Love; Unwept – I Weep'
(CB, from her poem 'Reason')

Arthur could not have met Charlotte Brontë at a worse time. For some months she had been obsessed with a sense of futility, for in the previous year she had found and lost a profound love, a love that she refused to forsake, despite all the evidence of its hopelessness. It was the most maturing and the most embittering of her experiences next to the deaths of her mother and older sisters many years before.

Charlotte had found a man whom she could adore, whose intellect she could respect, and at whose feet she would willingly sit in admiration. She called him her 'master', and that is precisely what he was. Who was this paragon and how did he, wittingly or unwittingly work his spell? What were the characteristics that so enchanted her?

The man was Constantin Georges Romain Heger, a professor at Brussels Athénée, who also taught at the Pensionnat Heger, a private boarding school for girls owned and run by his wife. Everything about him, perhaps not the least his virility (he fathered six children by two wives), attracted Charlotte when she first met him, and indeed went to live in the school where the thirty-three-year-old professor lived with his second wife.

Charlotte was twenty-six when she and Emily arrived at the Pensionnat Heger in Brussels in 1842. She was, moreover, an immature twenty-six, having led a very sheltered and sequestered life. She and her younger sister Emily were to be both students and teachers, having persuaded their Aunt Branwell to finance their going abroad to school in order to improve their chance of setting up their own school back in England. (In the event, their plan, when it was tried, foundered through lack of students, not a single one applying for the school when it was advertised in 1844.) Heger's influence on the Brontë sisters, his retiring and eccentric English pupils, was to be profound. For his part, he found the girls to be gifted and well worth teaching. His method of tuition, an original mixture of encouragement and the most severe criticism while making use of translation as a discipline, must be acknowledged as an essential ingredient in the Brontë sisters' creative mix. Like their father, Heger was a rhetorician, a man preoccupied both with fine style and with the importance of literature as an educational tool. Beyond that, however, he, emotionally, was to sweep Charlotte off her feet. Perhaps more than any other man, Constantin Heger was responsible for the passion, and also the frustration, which led to the creation of Jane Eyre.

Charlotte and Emily had both been governesses, and both had chafed at what they found to be a thankless drudgery. Moreover, it was without social standing, so that they were nonentities in the houses or little schools where they were employed. With their naturally retiring temperaments, the highly intelligent young women had suffered inordinately in the employ of local middle-class families whom they despised. Enslavement was their understanding of that way of earning a living; it repelled them. Yet Charlotte's plan to spend time in a school in Europe was more than a means of escaping work as a governess; it was a daring and desperate bid to look beyond Haworth, beyond Yorkshire and even England, to feed an eager imagination and to see something of the larger world. The exchange of Yorkshire for Brussels was a quite remarkable one. Comparison of the interior of their father's church in Haworth with that of the Protestant Chapel in Brussels, or with the glorious medieval interior of St Michel et Ste Gudule at the end of the rue d'Isabelle, where the sisters were to live, offers the most eloquent statement about the rite of passage implicit in that exchange. It did not suit Emily, however, who was glad to return to Haworth at her aunt's death towards the end of the year, and to allow Charlotte to go back alone for a further spell at the school. But if the elder sister never shook off the effect of her time in Brussels, neither in many respects did Emily. Monsieur Heger was an exacting but outstanding teacher. The tasks he set Emily and Charlotte honed their writing skills and gave them confidence; the practice they gained stood them in good stead when they finally came to write in earnest.

Heger's influence on Charlotte was of a different order entirely, for he was everything that she most admired. An unashamed intellectual – more so than her father, whom she admired immensely – he was also something of a hero in her eyes. Had he not taken up arms and fought on the barricades when the Belgians defied the Dutch, during which his own brother-in-law had been killed? Her father's often-mentioned military exercises while an undergraduate at Cambridge were insignificant by comparison. Furthermore, Heger had been on the payroll of the Comédie Francaise, having been educated in Paris, where his first wife and son had died of cholera.

Whatever professional attentions this fiery, eloquent, dramatic young professor showed his impressionable English pupil-teacher, she was bound to be infatuated. Charlotte was susceptible; her childhood writings, her dreamland, had been full of just such men, so that there was little that Heger could have done to prevent his pupil from falling in love with him. Indeed, it was his wife, Zoë, who seems to have realised for her own reasons that it was not wise for Charlotte to remain in the school and in his company. She saw the young English teacher off, quite literally accompanying her to the ferry bound for England, and many believe that she subsequently exerted a form of censorship over any correspondence that might have kept the relationship alive.

Charlotte was under Heger's spell for almost two years, hardly a passing infatuation. Her return to Haworth was reluctant, and it is said that as she left Madame Heger to set sail for England she shouted out in French that she 'would be revenged', perhaps feeling as ill used as Malvolio, whose line from *Twelfth Night* she used. While some believe that her love for Heger was a 'self-constructed romance', it was nevertheless real to her and, self-constructed or not, it dominated her waking and sleeping moments for the next twelve months and more. Later she writes (in French) to her 'master', from whom she has received no comforting letter, or even the briefest of notes:

Day and night I find neither rest nor peace. If I sleep I am disturbed by tormenting dreams in which I see you, always severe, always grave, always incensed against me . . . O I know that you will be irritated when you read this letter. You will say once more that I am hysterical (or neurotic) – that I have black thoughts etc. So be it . . . I submit to every sort of reproach. All I know is I cannot, that I will not, resign myself to lose wholly the friendship of my master. I would rather suffer the greatest physical pain than always have my heart lacerated by smarting regrets. If my master withdraws his friendship from me entirely I shall be altogether without hope; if he gives me a little – just a little – I shall be satisfied – happy; I shall have a reason for living on, for working.

Monsieur, the poor have not need of much to sustain them – they ask only for the crumbs that fall from the rich men's table. But if they are refused the crumbs they die of hunger. Nor do I, either, need much affection from those I love . . . you showed me of yore a little interest, when I was your pupil in Brussels, and I hold on to the maintenance of that little interest – I hold on to it as I would hold on to life.

You will tell me perhaps – 'I take not the slightest interest in you, Mademoiselle Charlotte. You are no longer an inmate of my house; I have forgotten you.'

Well, Monsieur, tell me so frankly. It will be a shock to me. It matters not. It would be less dreadful than uncertainty. I shall not re-read this letter, I send it as I have written it. Nevertheless, I have a hidden consciousness that some people, cold and common-sense, in reading it would say – 'She is talking nonsense.' I would avenge myself on such persons in no other way than by wishing them one single day of the torments which I have suffered for eight months. We should then see if they would not talk nonsense too.

One suffers in silence so long as one has the strength so to do, and when that strength gives out one speaks without too carefully measuring one's words.

I wish Monsieur happiness and prosperity.

(CB to Constantin Heger, 8 January 1845)

Self-constructed or not, Charlotte's suffering is palpable. The letter went unanswered, although we know it was delivered and, obviously, kept.

There can be little doubt that this mood of heartbreaking despair and loss preoccupied Charlotte through the first year of Arthur's work in Haworth. The letter above, written before his arrival, forms a bracket with another some months after his arrival in November of the same year. Charlotte had painfully rationed herself to writing only once every six months to ease her soul, despite the continuing silence from the recipient of her letters. Again she wrote in French, adding at the end the following poignant note in English:

Monsieur – The six months of silence have run their course . . . the summer and autumn seemed very long to me; truth to tell, it has needed painful efforts on my part to bear hitherto the self-denial which I have imposed upon myself . . . I tell you frankly that I have tried meanwhile to forget you . . . I have done everything; I have sought occupations; I have denied myself absolutely the pleasure of speaking about You – even to Emily; but I have been able to conquer neither my regrets nor my impatience. That indeed is humiliating – to be unable to control one's own thoughts, to be the slave of a regret, a memory, the slave of a fixed and dominant idea which lords it over the mind . . . to forbid me to write to you, to refuse to answer me, would be to tear from me my only joy on earth, to deprive me of my last privilege . . . so long as I have hope of receiving news from you I can be at rest and not too sad . . . when day by day I await a letter, and when day by day disappointment comes to fling me back into overwhelming sorrow, and the sweet delight of seeing your handwriting and reading your counsel escapes me as a vision that is vain, then fever claims me – I lose appetite and sleep – I pine away. May I write to you again next May ? I would rather wait a year, but it is impossible – it is too long.

(CB to Constantin Heger, 18 November 1845)

Thus Héloïse would have written to her Abelard. No wonder Charlotte hardly mentioned Arthur Nicholls in that year. How could so besotted a lover have noticed the arrival of a mere replacement curate? And yet what a passionate nature these letters signify. What depths of feeling are worn openly on the sleeve of correspondence! The short, bespectacled and plainly dressed 'T'parson's Charlotte' was clearly not all she seemed. Neither, in the long run, it must be said, was the rather reticent, orderly, correct Reverend Nicholls.

Arthur could have had no idea of the elder Miss Brontë's inner turmoil. How could he? Even her close family knew little of her secret grieving. Besides, he had a new job to master and little time to worry about his parson's moping daughters. Ellen Nussey had no inkling as to why her lifelong friend was so out of sorts for, like other friends, all she was told was that Charlotte felt trapped, 'imprisoned' at Haworth:

> *I can hardly tell you how time gets on here at Haworth – there is no event whatever to mark its progress – one day resembles another – and all have heavy, lifeless physiognomies – . . . meantime life wears away – I shall soon be thirty – and I have done nothing yet.*
>
> (CB to Ellen Nussey, 24 March 1845)

When we recall that thirty years was longer than the average lifespan of a poor inhabitant of the parish, Charlotte's complaint takes on greater meaning.

Shortly after Arthur's arrival in Haworth, however, there were to be events enough to satisfy even the low-spirited and restless Charlotte, events that began a course that was not to be fully run until four years later. In the second month of Arthur's curacy the parson's youngest daughter, Anne, resigned her job as governess at Thorp Green Hall, a post she had held successfully for five years, and came to join her sisters in their 'prison', the parsonage at Haworth. Almost at once they were joined by their brother, Branwell, who had been a tutor in the same household as Anne, but who had been summarily dismissed in disgrace for grave and insupportable misconduct. Thus abruptly began a three-year period of turmoil and confusion centred upon the young man's unpredictable behaviour and self-pitying indulgences, behaviour which, in stark contrast to Charlotte's secret suffering, was to be rehearsed in public bars and trumpeted all over the parish. As well as supporting an ailing parson, Arthur found himself, while running parish affairs, helping to keep steady a family adrift in a mêlée of misunderstandings, recriminations and, at times, bitter despair. Nor, lodging as he did with John Brown the sexton, one of Branwell's few Haworth intimates, could Arthur have avoided being party to all the gossip and conjecture abroad in the parish about the Brontë family's troubles, however proud and secretive that family might be.

Whereas Charlotte mourned in secret the loss of her 'master', her brother Branwell wailed loud and long over the loss of his 'mistress', through his being banished from the company of Mrs Robinson, his employer's wife. Branwell so wove self-pitying tales about himself that to this day it is not possible to do more than guess at the truth as to what had been happening at Thorp Green. Anne, in a diary paper, hinted tantalisingly that while working there as governess alongside her brother as tutor, she encountered 'some very unpleasant and undreamt-of experience of human nature – '.

To the family, Branwell was ill – albeit, as Charlotte bluntly said, 'so very often owing to his own fault' – and it must have seemed a mercy that as Patrick Brontë lost his sight, he was also less and less aware of the gradual deterioration that overtook his son. Whatever had happened at Thorp Green that led to Branwell's abrupt dismissal – from a post that his youngest sister seems to have procured for him in the house where she had been employed for more than four years – was merely the latest disaster in a series of failures that characterised his rather feckless attempts to earn a living. From the earliest days the only boy of the family had been led to believe he was something of a genius, and whether that was so or not, he certainly displayed more than usual creative energy in leading the children's games and dreaming up imaginative adventures. Yet despite such early promise, whatever this apple of his father's eye, and the gifted darling of the family – the one they thought so clearly marked for fame – undertook turned to ashes of recrimination, disgrace and despair. Some biographers of the family conjecture, though it cannot be proven, that away from Haworth Branwell had fathered illegitimate children. Whatever the truth of that, there is no doubt that he frequently turned to drink, ran into debt, and towards the end of his life resorted to taking laudanum. It is conceivable that Branwell's actions constituted, for him, the only possible response to the challenge of living with such a strong father. Each Brontë child had to come to terms not only with their father's character, but with what he had achieved and his continuing position in the parish, for a parish priest in early Victorian times was a man of some importance. Each child must at times have chafed at being dependent upon him under his authoritarian and judgemental eye. Charlotte, perhaps his favourite after his son, sometimes found her father an exasperatingly opinionated and difficult man. Mrs Gaskell pilloried Patrick Brontë in her biography of Charlotte, saying that he was no more than a cassocked savage who should have been taken out into the garden and shot! Clearly he was no easy father to come to terms with, nor was his own progress from peasant to parson, achieved solely by his own efforts and abilities, easy to match. Interestingly, Patrick Brontë generously forgave Mrs Gaskell though he thought her remarks were somewhat extreme. He praised her biography of his daughter and rose to her defence when others attacked her.

The new curate could have had no idea or warning of the volatile nature of the household to which he was now attached. His parson's fast-advancing blindness ensured that Arthur Nicholls would necessarily, and increasingly, come into close contact with the parsonage and much of what was happening in it. Almost at once Arthur's landlord, John Brown, was to take Branwell off for a tour of North Wales, possibly to help him to pull himself together, while at the same time removing him from the prying eyes of the curious gossips of Haworth.

There can be no doubt that Arthur Nicholls would have been well aware of much that was happening in his parson's family, and that if he possessed so much as an ounce of natural curiosity he must have been intrigued, if not alarmed, by what was being enacted before him. Branwell was, after all, his contemporary, being but a year older, and comparisons between the two would instinctively have been made. Branwell's dismissal and his three-year decline into self-indulgent remorse and despair threw the whole household in turmoil. Charlotte, nursing her own loneliness as a bitter secret, had little sympathy with her brother's flagrant flaunting of his misery. She wrote and said many harsh things about him, not the least of her complaints being a feeling that the brother who might have been relied upon to care for and protect his sisters, had in fact betrayed them. It is easily forgotten that the family were at almost constant financial risk. Their home, albeit free of rent, belonged to the Church. Had Patrick Brontë's health failed completely, his family – who had no relatives within reach or with whom they had kept in contact – would find themselves in difficulty. Proud and educated as they were, they were still vulnerable, and it was increasingly necessary to keep their father functioning in the parish, and thus keep their only home (even though a seeming prison) secure. Clearly the young man of the family was not going to provide for his sisters, or even for his father in his old age. Ironically, it was the overlooked but useful, reliable and steady Arthur Nicholls who would in the end care for the remnants of the family in their final years.

Whatever was happening in the parsonage, in the parish Arthur Nicholls was kept busy. He had the church schools to oversee, and much else towards which he felt he had a responsibility. Not the least of these concerns was his distress at the condition of the now celebrated graveyard that fronted the house and ran alongside the church (as it still does today), a graveyard overfull with graves and where an average of two burials a week took place. It was, moreover, a graveyard that was soon to be condemned by a public health inspector (one of the first in the land to be so) as particularly unhygienic and, since springs ran through it, a threat to the health of the village that huddled on the steep hillside immediately below.

A public footpath ran through the churchyard, as it does to this day. Arthur Nicholls wanted it closed, for to his horror the villagers, far from seeing the graveyard as a place where the dead might find a final peace, used it as common land. Mules grazed, pigs and hens scavenged, washing was put out to dry on the headstones, and a corner of the yard served as a privy for the bordering public house, the Black Bull. So much for quaint rural English churchyards in the days of the Brontë family. Arthur had some small success, for he managed to stop the women using the graveyard as a place to hang out their washing. Patrick Brontë, much amused, celebrated the event by writing a poem which, tongue-in-cheek, teased the proper young curate:

> *The females all routed have fled with their clothes*
> *To stackyards and backyards, and where noone knows,*
> *And loudly have sworn by the suds that they swim in,*
> *They'll wring off his head, for his warring with women.*
> *Whilst their husbands combine & roar out in their fury*
> *They'll lynch him at once, without trial by Jury.*
> *But saddest of all, their fair maidens declare,*
> *Of marriage or love he must ever despair.*
>
> (PB, 'Church Reform')

The innocent prophecy of the last line would be given an ironic denial before ten years were out, notwithstanding the parish washerwomen's scorn.

Although knowing of his parson's love of writing, and possibly something of Branwell's poems published in newspapers (and it is very difficult to believe that Branwell would have kept such publication quiet, there being not an ounce of reticence in his being), Arthur Nicholls would have known nothing of the secret industry of the Brontë sisters. He could have had no inkling of their evening writing sessions, or of their long history of making up stories for each other. What went on behind the parlour door was not open to inspection or discussion, even, it appears, with Branwell, who had once been such an energising and commanding element in their childhood games. Nicholls had to wait until the rest of the parish learnt of the novels written by the daughters of the parsonage, long after their composition and the trials of finding publishers.

His first years at Haworth, however, coincided with the crucial phase in the sisters' writing and their ambition to be published, a period when the affairs of the parish, or even beyond the parsonage windows, held little interest for the sisters. Charlotte's return from Brussels, and Anne's from Thorp Green, brought the sisters together in such a way that, unknown to the rest of the household, they encouraged, irritated and organised each other into somehow getting into print. The story is told that it was Charlotte's nosiness that led her not only to discover, but to have the impertinence to read, poems that Emily had secretly written; Charlotte herself maintained that she had found them by accident. Nothing is known for certain about the row between the sisters, only that subsequently Emily warned her elder sister never to disclose her authorship either of her poems or her novel, a warning which, true to her nature, Charlotte promptly forgot when she met George Smith, the publisher of *Jane Eyre*, in London, in July 1848.

In 1846 a small volume of the sisters' poems was published at their own expense, the three authors demurely hiding behind the odd pen names of 'Currer, Ellis and Acton Bell'. The book failed, only two copies being sold, although there was at least one quite favourable review. Where many might have been dismayed, the Brontë sisters seem to have been encouraged, for their next move was to send three complete novels out to publishers. Clearly there had been much burning of midnight oil, despite Branwell's distracting and disturbing behaviour. The completion of three manuscript novels by three different writers in a single family, whether eventually published or not, is in itself a remarkable achievement. Knowing as we do what was to follow this first stepping into print, and knowing that one of the manuscripts was *Wuthering Heights*, we also know, as no one in the parsonage did, that this was a momentous event in the history of English literature. Patrick Brontë later protested that at the time they were writing their novels he had no idea what his daughters were up to, adding, very frankly, that in any case they would hardly have benefited from the advice or criticism of an elderly clergyman. It should be remembered that the period of intense writing and publication of the novels was also the time of Patrick Brontë's blindness, a time when he had to be read to, and when he would not have been able to 'see' for himself much of what was going on around him in the parsonage. How could he have known what the girls were doing, or of Branwell's behaviour. His celebrated comment about the publication of the novels, that he had 'had no idea', may have meant just that. A man who needs a huge magnifying glass to read at all, and who was facing total blindness, would inevitably be forced in upon himself, and thus little aware of what was happening around him. The operation on one eye, in August 1846, for cataract which was to restore his sight came in the middle of the period when the three daughters were most busily engaged in writing their works and finding publishers for them. In short, a near-blind old man is unlikely to find and scrutinise his daughters' writing, or to intercept and read the letters that the post brings them.

By the end of 1847 the Brontë sisters were launched as novelists, although still sheltering behind their pen names, and thereby enjoying with relish the 'advantage of being able to walk invisible'. Whatever rejoicing there was, secret or otherwise, in the parsonage, it would have been short-lived, however, for each step they had taken toward publication had been shadowed by a further deterioration in their brother's physical and mental state. In May 1846, just as the book of his sisters' poems was published, Branwell announced to a friend that his life in the past months had been one 'of cold debauchery, the determination to see how far mind could carry body without both being chucked into hell'. Towards the end of 1847, at the time when Charlotte's *Jane Eyre*, Emily's *Wuthering Heights* and Anne's *Agnes Grey* had been printed and were in the hands of their authors, Branwell had suffered several falling fits, probably through the effect of delirium tremens. He had also once set his bedclothes on fire, from which time he had been made to sleep in his father's bedroom where he could be watched over. Life must have been wretched for all the family during these months. In his lucid moments, Branwell admitted that he was making enormous difficulties for his father and sisters. At times he would stay out drinking all night and then sleep during the day, alarming and exasperating his sisters. Perhaps the ultimate embarrassment came when Sheriff's officers arrived at the parsonage seeking a Patrick Brontë to cart him off to a debtor's prison if he could not pay what he owed. The debts were of course paid, while the family was forced to share in the ignominy of the disgrace. Life as published writers was a mixed cup for 'the Messrs Bell', as Charlotte called them.

Nor did matters improve. There can be little doubt that Arthur would by now have understood fully the difficulties that Branwell was causing the family. For his part, Branwell could have known nothing of his sisters' writing, or the publication of their books. He persisted in his self-destructive behaviour, and the family despaired of him. They were shocked, however, when in September 1848 he suddenly died, for no one had seemed to realise just how serious was the damage he had done to himself through alcohol and laudanum. Worse was to follow, however, for his was only the first of three deaths in the family. It is widely understood that Branwell knew nothing about the publishing activities of his sisters. It is possible that he was far too preoccupied with self-pity and self-abuse to care much about what was happening around him. Indeed, his surviving letters of this period are the erratic and extravagent ramblings of a drugged and deeply disturbed mind. At his funeral, Emily took cold. She never recovered, dying from consumption less than three months after her brother. In the new year Anne was ailing, and the following May she too died from consumption while on a trip to Scarborough, where she had hoped the change of air would ease her sufferings from consumption and offer a chance of recovery. These deaths reduced the Brontë family from five members to two in nine terrible months. Arthur Nicholls not only witnessed this tragedy, he was involved in the funeral services for the two who had died in Haworth (Anne was buried at Scarborough). What his feelings were as he saw the close family reel beneath this triple blow is not recorded, neither do we have any record of the address he gave at Branwell's memorial service. It is, however, unthinkable that the experience could have done other than draw him close to his parson, Arthur perhaps coming to view the latter as a father figure.

It is, perhaps, worth pausing for a moment to reflect on the situation in which the young clergyman found himself, for he must have been in a considerable dilemma. Instead of conducting Branwell's funeral service secure behind the language and procedure of the Prayer Book (the Reverend William Morgan, godfather to Charlotte and long-standing friend of their father, fulfilled that office) Nicholls was given the surely invidious task of delivering a memorial address at Branwell's funeral. Notwithstanding the conventions which require the speaker to talk only favourably of the dead, what could Arthur possible say? The villagers knew, for they had witnessed it often enough for themselves, the nature and some of the causes of Branwell's decline; after all, falling fits in public bars are hardly discreet failings. As for his family, no one knew more clearly than they the nature of his last years. We can only wonder how Arthur Nicholls balanced up truth with fitting comment, and all of it spoken in the presence of his vicar, the dead young man's father.

The task would have been quite a challenge. Knowing the history of the family as we do today, we can speak of Branwell's unfulfilled early promise, of the young artist, of the precocious poet, the stimulating and enthusiastic instigator of the juvenile imaginings and writings of a quartet of youngsters; we can remember his flute playing, his delight in the Haworth church organ. Arthur Nicholls would have known little of all this, however. Almost from the moment he met Branwell he would have seen the failing young man, the tutor returned to Haworth in disgrace. Would Nicholls have spoken of Branwell as the organist to the Masonic Lodge, or as the member of the Haworth Boxing Club? Indeed, it is unlikely that his coffin would have been borne on the shoulders of fellow pugilists. One wonders who other than the family would have attended the funeral. Any activity that Branwell undertook, any post he had filled, whether as tutor, railway clerk, or portrait painter, had ended in failure. Nicholls did not have much to go on. No comment, no service sheet survives, and perhaps it is just as well, for there are some events across which a curtain should be quietly drawn. Patrick Branwell Brontë's ignominious end and the eulogy spoken at his funeral are perhaps two of them. Whatever Arthur Nicholls was able to say about his unfortunate contemporary Patrick Branwell, compromised as he was by the public knowledge of his appalling behaviour and rapid self-inflicted decline, we can be sure that Nicholls gave no offence, for he continued to enjoy his vicar's complete trust and confidence for many years after Branwell's death.

It is not unusual, however, for a coolness to arise, between people, even between friends and relatives, who have of necessity had to work together in times of great suffering. The Brontë family were much more easily able to remember the Reverend William Weightman's time as a curate, at a period when the family was much happier, than they were Arthur Nicholls, who without any doubt had been with them through some extremely difficult times. Nor could Arthur have been blind to Charlotte Brontë's sad plight. Suddenly she was her father's only surviving child. How vulnerable she now was, for having been born the third of six children, and having, after the deaths of her two elder sisters, been for twenty-five years the oldest of four, she was now the sole survivor, left alone with her elderly father.

Arthur Nicholls not only spoke the address in Branwell's memory, he also, only months later, conducted Emily Brontë's funeral. She had been his own age, and Branwell only a year older; these were his contemporaries that he was burying. It may be that when, in 1854, Charlotte married Arthur Nicholls, his knowledge of the family, the fact that he had known her dead sisters and brother and had shared something of those dark days of grief, lent comfort and weight to the support that he could offer her. Certainly Mrs Gaskell was not alone in approving the match because Nicholls had known Charlotte's dead sisters. Far from offering little when proposing to Charlotte, Nicholls, through his proximity to and understanding of some of her suffering, offered much, and that uniquely.

Two sources confirm Nicholls's regular visits to the parsonage at this time: village gossip as reported by Charlotte's friend Ellen Nussey, and the parsonage dogs, Emily's mastiff, Keeper, and Anne's King Charles spaniel, Flossy. While the family was in crisis Nicholls had taken over exercising the dogs, a habit which continued after the deaths of the dogs' mistresses until the dogs themselves died. The village gossips, however, were hot on the trail of romance. As early as 1846, when Patrick Brontë was almost completely blind and utterly dependent on his curate in the running of the parish, a rumour was circulating that Miss Brontë (a title reserved for the eldest of any unmarried women in a family – therefore Charlotte) was going to be married to the useful and helpful curate. Ellen Nussey, perhaps teasingly, wrote to ask Charlotte whether it were true. Charlotte's reply is eloquent:

Who gravely asked you whether Miss Brontë was not going to be married to her papa's Curate?

I scarcely need say that never was rumour more unfounded – it puzzles me to think how it could possibly have originated – A cold, far-away sort of civility are the only terms on which I have ever been with Mr Nicholls – I could by no means think of mentioning such a rumour to him even as a joke – it would make me the laughing-stock of himself and his fellow curates for half a year to come – They regard me as an old maid, and I regard them, one and all, as highly uninteresting, narrow and unattractive specimens of the 'coarser' sex'.

(CB to Ellen Nussey, 10 July 1846)

The rumour was only premature by six years.

Chapter Two

❧

The Proposal: 'Perfectly Justified in His Objections'

'Agitation and Anger disproportionate to the occasion ensued – if I had loved Mr N and heard such epithets applied to him as were used – it would have transported me past patience – as it was – my blood boiled with a sense of injustice – but Papa worked himself into a state not to be trifled with – the veins on his temple started up like whip-cord – and his eyes became suddenly bloodshot – I made haste to promise that Mr Nicholls should on the morrow have a distinct refusal.'

(CB to Ellen Nussey, 15 December 1852)

'I should wish however to discharge his mind of the impression that there was any quarrel between Mr Brontë and myself – an angry or unkind word never passed between us – we parted as friends when I left Haworth – my leaving was solely my own act – I was not driven away by him. I always felt that he was perfectly justified in his objections to my union with his daughter.'

(Arthur Bell Nicholls [ABN] to Clement Shorter, 18 June 1895)

The poet and playwright Christopher Fry once remarked that considering the creative energy flying about in Haworth Parsonage it is a wonder the walls did not explode. If ever the walls were in danger of exploding, nine o'clock on the evening of 13 December 1852 was perhaps the most likely moment. When Charlotte told him that, minutes earlier, Arthur Nicholls, the curate, had proposed marriage to her, Patrick Brontë indulged in a fit of rage that not only alarmed his daughter, but gave her pause to think how unjust her father could be. The Reverend Brontë (according to the account

24

that Charlotte gave to her intimate friend, Ellen Nussey) not only railed at this nonentity's temerity in suggesting that he could ask for the hand of Charlotte Brontë, the successful and celebrated novelist, but he also fulminated upon the absurdity of his daughter marrying at all. Such an unreasonable and violent reaction to the whole idea of *any* marriage upset Charlotte. Though she did not know it at the time, it was to set her to defy her father, something which she had never before considered possible. It is as ironic that, in doing so, she was taking what would prove to be a fatal step, as it is sad that her father handled the whole business in so selfish and clumsy a manner. Eventually, perhaps for the first time in his relationship with Charlotte, he had to climb down; to accept what he believed to be wholly insupportable. Yet what are we to make of Arthur Nicholls's statement, at the time of his resignation from Haworth after Charlotte had refused him, that curate and parson had parted friends, without an angry or unkind word ever having passed between them?

Even more surprising, and neglected by other commentators and biographers, is Arthur Nicholls's belief that Patrick Brontë 'was perfectly justified in his objections' to his 'union with his daughter'. This belief runs counter to the whole tale of injustice and bitterness towards Nicholls that Charlotte herself originated in her letters to Ellen, leaving the thought that we may have been hoodwinked for all these years by her subjective version of the events of that evening in the parsonage. It is worth remembering that Arthur probably never saw the letter to Ellen, and never heard that highly charged report of what took place. Since biographers must always be on their guard, it becomes a question of whose version we should believe. Can we even trust Nicholls's claim that he and Patrick Brontë were always friends? Arthur's devotion to his father-in-law after Charlotte's death, when he cared for him for six years as his only 'son', suggests that it might well be true that he and the old man, who had shared so much even before Charlotte's death, remained amicable throughout the proposal episode. Furthermore, it is ironic that Patrick Brontë's misgivings, however badly expressed and whatever his reasons, might have been well founded. At least Nicholls confirmed that he understood and respected the objections the parson had expressed. Fears for Charlotte's health may have combined with a desperate alarm that marriage might put the life of his only surviving child at risk, a terrible thought for the old man. Marriage in the middle of the nineteenth century meant child-bearing, and in her late thirties Charlotte would therefore have been taking a considerable risk. In the event, marriage did indeed lead swiftly to her death.

It is clear from Charlotte's account that she believed her father thought she was an 'old maid', as firmly 'on the shelf' in her spinster-hood as her many-times-rejected and still-unpublished novel *The Professor* was locked away in a cupboard. Her father's certainty that marriage was not for her proved hurtful, as hearing our own secret anxieties voiced by others often does. For although Charlotte had for many years called herself an old maid, it was quite another thing to be seen as one by her father. The latter's near-apoplectic rage drove her to assure him, there and then, that Mr Nicholls would have her refusal the next day, a hasty decision, hardly made in a mood of cool reflection. The old man's prejudiced display also alarmed her; conceivably she was witnessing what lay in store for her as he grew older and perhaps became more often the volatile, bigoted bully.

As we have seen, Charlotte wrote the whole story of the proposal and its dramatic effect on her 'dear' Papa in a letter to Ellen Nussey, giving us a first-hand, although possibly biased, account of the evening's events. Two things, she said, gave her pain. The first was 'Papa's vehement antipathy to the bare thought of anyone thinking of me as a wife', which had undoubtedly stung her. The second was 'Mr Nicholls' distress':

> *Attachment to Mr N – you are aware, I never entertained – but the poignant pity inspired by his state on Monday evening – by the hurried revelation of his sufferings for many months – is something galling and irksome. That he cares something for me – and wanted me to care for him – I have long suspected – but I did not know the degree and strength of his feelings.*

> (CB to Ellen Nussey, 15 December 1852)

In this Charlotte showed herself to be both compassionate and not unsympathetic to Arthur Nicholls. More interestingly, however, it confirms that she had never really stopped believing that she would one day be someone's wife, that there was always the possibility that she would fall in love with someone. At the time of the proposal she was thirty-six years old, her increasingly irascible and dependent father seventy-five.

His proposal of marriage to Charlotte Brontë had been no easy undertaking for Arthur Nicholls. It seems that over and above an anxiety that he might be rejected was an absolute fear of broaching the subject with his employer, Charlotte's father. The letter to Ellen describing Arthur's proposal, written quickly after the event, reads as well as any episode in Charlotte Brontë's fiction, the hand of the novelist everywhere apparent:

On Monday evening – Mr N was here to tea. I vaguely felt – without clearly seeing, feverish restraint. After tea – I withdrew to the dining room as usual. As usual Mr N sat with Papa till between eight & nine o'clock. I then heard him open the parlour door as if going. I expected the clash of the front door - He stopped in the passage: he tapped: like lightning it flashed on me what was coming. He entered – he stood before me. What his words were – you can guess, his manner you can hardly realise – nor can I forget it – Shaking from head to foot, looking deadly pale, speaking low, vehemently yet with difficulty – he made me for the first time feel what it cost a man to declare affection where he doubts response.

The spectacle of one ordinarily so statue-like – thus trembling, stirred, and overcame gave me a kind of strange shock. He spoke of sufferings he had borne for months – of sufferings he could endure no longer – and craved leave for some hope. I could only entreat him to leave me then and promise a reply on the morrow. I asked him if he had spoken to Papa. He said – he dared not – I think I half-led, half put him out of the room. When he was gone I immediately went to Papa – and told him what had taken place.

(CB to Ellen Nussey, 15 December 1852)

Patrick Brontë, according to Charlotte, left his daughter in no doubt about his objections to Arthur Nicholls's proposal: ' . . . Papa thinks a little too much about his [Arthur's] want of money; he says the match would be a degradation – that I should be throwing my self away . . . ' His harshest statements, however, were reserved for his curate, whom he held in contempt.

Why did the Reverend Patrick Brontë react so violently to the news that his curate had proposed to his daughter? His extreme rage surely went beyond pique that Nicholls had broken with convention and good manners by not seeking the parent's permission before making the proposal. And yet the outcome of this breach of etiquette tells us much about both men. Nicholls clearly understood how Brontë might react, an instinct confirmed by events, hence his fear of broaching the matter with him. Perhaps the curate knew his parson only too well. Patrick Brontë, in reacting as the other feared, was certainly exposed as selfish, hasty and unreasonable. He seemed not to understand the nature of the man he was dealing with, or the situation that his daughter had sensed was developing. It seems that the old man sought to avoid change, that he could see no reason why he should not live out his days being cared for by his only surviving child, the mature and famous writer, whose success, moreover, had brought financial security – not to mention many creature comforts – to the parsonage in his old age. With Charlotte to manage his home and Arthur to run the parish, he must have had plenty of time in which to enjoy the reflected glory of his daughter's success, not the least part being the distinguished visitors who came to call. From Patrick Brontë's point of view, there was much to be said for maintaining the status quo.

One tradition, although it must remain conjecture, suggests that Patrick Brontë had taken great pains to distance himself from his Irish origins. Having been raised in true poverty, it is suggested, he may have wanted his background and his family still in Ireland to remain undiscovered. This might well have added to his dismay at the thought of his daughter being connected through marriage with Ireland and all that he had sought – successfully – to leave behind, or so the theory continues. It is true that on her honeymoon tour in her father's native country, Charlotte did not expect Ireland to be a very civilised place, looking to find 'Irish negligence' all around her, for she appears to have held a prejudiced and superficial view of the nation. Whether this came from her father or not we cannot know. It is also true that while in Ireland no suggestion was ever made, or even hinted at, that she herself had relatives, her father's kin, in the north of the country whom she and her husband might visit. The belief persists in some quarters that the Cambridge graduate was ashamed of his lowly upbringing and his family, as though that were the natural outcome of his having found himself an education. This is not necessarily the only response to moving on from humble beginnings, however. Pride in achievement and a sense of integrity of personality may well also accompany such progress. Moreover, there is no evidence that Patrick was ashamed of being Irish; quite the opposite.

Nor was Nicholls the first Irish curate to work in Patrick Brontë's parish in Haworth, so that it would be a mistake to believe that the latter was so prejudiced against his fellow countrymen.

Until the eventful evening of Arthur's proposal to his parson's daughter, the two men had worked together amicably, each apparently confident in, and supportive of, the other's work in the parish. Clearly the older man had much to respect in the fact that over seven years his curate had given no cause for complaint, even though he had several times had to shoulder the full burden of all parish duties during the

Reverend Brontë's blindness and periodic illnesses. It is impossible, however, to acquire a balanced view of the events of that evening in December 1852 without knowing more about the 'Curate of Haworth', as Arthur Nicholls styled himself in all correspondence. It is clear that once the proposal had been made battle lines were drawn up. Arthur, if we are to believe Charlotte, shrank from mentioning his intention to Patrick Brontë. Her father, as soon as he heard of the proposal, began a desperate campaign to vilify Nicholls, if not to prevent any possibility of marriage should Charlotte change her mind, something which can be verified from the content and tone of letters he wrote to Charlotte over the next weeks, when she was away from the parsonage. One of the most interesting and revealing of these was sent as if from Anne's dog, Flossy. As has been said, since the deaths of Anne and Emily, Arthur Nicholls had inherited the task of parsonage dog-walker. Patrick Brontë therefore used an underhand device to attack Nicholls in an attempt to influence and no doubt control his daughter. Charlotte, while staying in London after the incident of the proposal, had innocently sent her regards to Flossy in a letter to her father. Never slow to seize an opportunity, Patrick Brontë craftily used the dog's 'voice' to launch a vehement attack on Nicholls:

> . . . *Flossy to his much respected and beloved mistress, Miss Brontë, my kind mistress, as, having only paws I cannot write, but I can dictate, and my good master has undertaken to set down what I have to say . . . so many things are done before me, which would not be done if I could speak . . . so, I see a good deal of human nature that is hid from those who have the gift of language . . . I see people cheating one another, and yet appearing to be friends – many are the disagreeable discoveries which I make . . . one thing I have lately seen . . . no one takes me out to walk now, the weather is too cold, or too wet for my master to walk in, and my former travelling companion [Nicholls] has lost all his apparent kindness, scolds me and looks black upon me . . .*

Included with this letter, having dropped the dog conceit, was a much more open attack on Nicholls:

> . . . *You may wish to know how we have all been getting on here, especially in respect to* master *and* man; *on yesterday I preached twice, but my man, was every way very quiet – he shunned me as if I had been a Cobra de Capello – turning his head from the quarter where I was, and hustling away amongst the crowd to avoid contact – it requires no*

Lavatar to see that his countenance was strongly indicative of mortified pride and malevolent resentment – people have begun to notice these things, and various conjectures are afloat – You thought me too severe – but I was not candid enough – this conduct might have been excused by the world in a confirmed rake – or unprincipled Army officer, but in a clergyman, *it is justly chargeable with base design and inconsistency – I wish him no ill – [here Charlotte's father descended into insult] but rather good, and wish that every woman may avoid him forever, unless she should be determined on her own misery – all the produce of the Australian* diggins *[diggins; i.e. goldmines] would not make him and any wife he might have, happy . . . Ever your affectionate Father,*

P. Brontë

(PB to CB, circa 19 January 1853)

There can be little doubt that Patrick Brontë had set himself not only against the marriage, but against his curate. We are privileged to see this letter, intrusive though it may be, but Arthur Nicholls could have had no idea of the extent of his parson's active undermining of his position, and it is doubtful whether he ever saw this letter. He would, of course, read Charlotte's account of his proposal when Mrs Gaskell saw fit to publish it in her *Life of Charlotte Brontë*. Understandably, the publication of such intimate letters – in this case, Charlotte's to Ellen Nussey – caused him no little distress.

Clearly there were no holds barred in Brontë's attack on his curate's character and reputation. Vehement though it was, however, the attack failed, Charlotte eventually ignoring all her father's denigration of the man who had dared to suggest marriage to her. Yet Patrick Brontë might have prevailed had he been more subtle, for the strength of his unreasoned attack aroused in his daughter sympathy for Arthur where it had been meant to display his treachery. Charlotte was unable to dismiss the suitor as readily or as passionately as her father desired. By the following April, although she remained convinced that she could not marry him, we see the extent that her heart had warmed to the man:

I may be losing the purest gem, and to me far the most precious, life can give – genuine attachment – or I may be escaping the yoke of a morose temper. In this doubt conscience will not suffer me to take one step in opposition to Papa's will, blended as that will is with the most bitter and unreasonable prejudices.

(CB to Ellen Nussey, 6 April 1853)

It is time to look at this man who had caused such a rumpus, such a battle between father and daughter. We must now find time for the Reverend Arthur Nicholls, a man whom, almost inevitably, the world would misunderstand. His wife's early death cast him in a sombre role for literary historians; but for him, many believe, literature might have had more Jane Eyres and more Lucy Snowes!

Time for Arthur

Jane Carlyle, wife of 'The Sage of Chelsea', the writer, critic and historian Thomas Carlyle, became so tired of being seen merely as an accompaniment to her famous husband that she said she felt like the child in Goethe's *Wilhelm Meister* (which Carlyle himself had translated), who tugged at the skirt of his preoccupied mother's dress, calling out, 'I too am here.' So, in the story of the Brontë family, and certainly at the time of his marriage to Charlotte, Arthur Nicholls might have said 'I too am here'. In the many biographies of his wife he remains a shadowy figure, little care being taken to see him as an equal partner in the marriage, or even to consider that his life before his curacy at Haworth might have been of any significance. This is a great injustice, however, not only to him, but also to Charlotte in her agreement to marry him.

The argument that because Arthur Nicholls, a mere curate, was not famous before his marriage, we cannot expect to know much about him, is unworthy. Too dazzled by the swift tragedy that overtook the author of *Jane Eyre* after she married, commentators have failed to take a cool look at the whole story. Yet we must find time for Arthur if we are to have any small understanding of why Charlotte Brontë felt able to marry him, or if we wish to comprehend her father's fury, and eventually, his equally startling pleasure at the idea of Arthur as a son-in-law. It should go without saying, therefore, that the marriage cannot be understood unless both partners are given equal consideration.

In one respect, Charlotte's fame as a writer does help us know about her life. Because she became famous, her letters were, in many cases, preserved, interest in, or curiosity about, the author of *Jane Eyre* being well established during her lifetime. Above all, it is the survival of her many letters to her intimate friend Ellen Nussey that has ensured that so much is known of the family history. While there is no equal documentation of Arthur's life there is a story to be told, and facts that contribute to that story. Some of his letters have also survived, letters that have been surprisingly overlooked or ignored by biographers and commentators. Many of these are to do with school business in the parish of Haworth, and show clearly the extent to which Patrick Brontë left responsibility for running and developing the schools in his curate's hands. These letters, always courteous, brief and to the point, written in a clear, firm hand, deal soberly with church and school matters. Whatever else he may have been, Arthur was an efficient manager of school affairs and an effective letter-writer. One letter in particular gives us a flavour of the man and confirms how closely his thinking and ideas were in step with those of his incumbent. Writing to the National Society about the need for support for the church schools, he supports his case with an illustration from his own experience:

> *I asked them [two young boys of the parish] if they knew who made them? 'Nay' they replied. I asked them if they had heard of God? 'Nay' they replied, after a while one of them said he knew of a lad who had heard of God . . . he went to a methodist Sunday School.*
>
> (ABN to the National Society, January 1848)

This situation he found to be 'a disgrace in any country . . . out of 1200 there is not one *single child* at present receiving instruction in the principles of the established church.' The truth is that the two clergymen made an excellent team, as it is also true that Arthur Nicholls need not be the shadowy cipher that historians and biographers have made him, for there is enough evidence to establish an idea of his character and his qualities.

Charlotte Brontë, creator of Jane Eyre and Lucy Snowe, those lonely, longing, loving young women, chose to accept Arthur Nicholls as husband out of her need for affection and companionship, the imagined events and feelings of her fiction having little bearing upon her own real desires. Fame and an income were one thing, but books on a shelf offered little comfort on lonely nights, as an east wind rattled the windows and doors of a house where an old and increasingly difficult father limited life. Charlotte must have felt considerably strengthened once she had married Arthur Nicholls. No stranger to her family and its history, he was a very strong link with her past. Furthermore, he made no attempt to remove her from that sustaining place or from the supporting continuity of her home; on the contrary, he agreed to honour and preserve its ceremonies and remembrances. How secure she must have felt, and how much less threatening the future with her father must have seemed.

Arthur Nicholls shared much with Patrick Brontë, not least his Ulster origins. The latter had been born in 1777 in a humble cabin at Emdale, and his curate in 1818 at Kilkead, County Antrim, of Scottish descent, his father being a farmer. In common with other male offspring in what was a family of ten children, Arthur was taken to live with his aunt and uncle, Dr Alan Bell, the headmaster of the Royal School at Banagher, County Offaly, in mid-Ireland. Here he was educated and eventually – and successfully – coached by his uncle in Greek, Latin and Hebrew for entry to Trinity College, Dublin. If Arthur thrived under his uncle's supervision, he flourished in his aunt's care, becoming so devoted to her that he had her to live with him until her death in her 101st year.

Beyond the common experiences of their backgrounds, both Patrick Brontë and Arthur Nicholls benefited from help outside their own home, both grew to value education highly, both had experience of living amongst poverty, and both had come to see teaching as an important means of assisting people to cope with such conditions. Banagher was a distressed and dwindling small town which did not escape the harsh realities of the hardship caused by the potato famine and by compulsory evictions. Thus Arthur would have been well schooled in the needs and difficulties of the poor, so that Haworth in that respect would not have been unfamiliar territory. Like his parson, Arthur had also benefited from a university education, a benefit he sought to pass on to others through teaching and through his ordination into the priesthood. In the light of all they shared in outlook and experience, it should not surprise us that the two men worked well together.

While still an undergraduate, Nicholls taught classics at his uncle's school and at an endowed school nearby, where he was paid a higher wage. It may well have been this schoolteaching that prolonged his time at Trinity College, Dublin, for the register shows that he enrolled there in 1837 but did not graduate until 1844. Possibly ill health held him back, and there is a story that he was warned at an early age that he had a weak heart, and that from time to time his family would see him surreptitiously feeling his own pulse. Beyond that, however, it has been suggested that one of Patrick Brontë's objections to Arthur marrying Charlotte was due to the curate's poor health. In letters to Ellen Nussey, Charlotte indicates clearly that she also had misgivings about Arthur's health (ironically, as is often the case with this form of mild hypochondria, he lived well into his eighties).

Yet however similar Arthur Nicholls's experience was to that of

Patrick Brontë – he had, for instance, been a classics teacher at the Royal School, Banagher, Brontë a classics examiner at Woodhouse Grove School, and both parson and his curate were as familiar with school-rooms and classes as they were with liturgy and congregations – his family background may not have entirely pleased the older man. Always proud, he could not boast, as his curate could, a family of clergy and the headmaster of a noted school. Because of his blindness and the vicissitudes of his family life in the early years of Arthur's curacy, the Reverend Brontë had of necessity to rely on his assistant, who proved competent and loyal. But the curate had a clearly defined role, the limits of which were also clearly defined, and the suggestion that he might step out of his accustomed subservience upset the balance of his position in Patrick Brontë's scheme of things. To be fair to him, if his daughter was taken aback by the proposal, the old man could not have had the faintest inkling of Arthur's intentions. Furthermore, to shuffle an old adage, he stood to lose a good curate as well as a daughter if the marriage went ahead, while the pattern of his life would certainly change, and all without the slightest warning.

Surprisingly, Arthur's early life also had much in common with Charlotte's. For both, the most significant female adult in their formative years had been an aunt, by whom their respective households had been managed, for each was deprived of the comfort of their natural mother. Both were sent away from their homes for schooling, both were raised in an environment where education was seen as important, and both grew up under the influence of the Bible and orthodox Protestant teaching, with literature and cultural matters given due importance. If anything, Arthur would have had a richer cultural background and a broader horizon than Charlotte through the social round of the houses around Cuba House in Kingstown where he lived. Moreover, he would have known something of the 'society' of the day, not least because Lord Rosse, of Birr Castle, had a long-standing interest in the school that Dr Alan Bell, Arthur's uncle, ran in nearby Banagher. Both enjoyed relatively privileged positions in the imme-diate society of the small, poor townships where they lived; to some extent they were also isolated in the same way, since neither would have been able to mix as equals with the villagers around them, their contact always being of a philanthropic and, arguably, condescending nature. As a result, both grew up with the realisation that they were set apart from the common order of folk in their immediate locality. If this sense of isolation was to have a profound effect upon the works of Charlotte and her sisters, it perhaps also enhanced a sense of loneliness in her as well as in Arthur. It may be that, in the end, each responded to that loneliness in the other.

Charlotte's Predicament

However old, plain, humble, desolate, afflicted we may be, so long as our hearts preserve the feeblest spark of life, they preserve also, shining near that pale ember, a starved, ghostly longing for appreciation and affection.

(*Shirley*, Chapter 10)

When Arthur Nicholls surprised her – and ignited her father's wrath – with his proposal, Charlotte was in something of a predicament. She had recently sent the manuscript of the final chapters of her last novel, *Villette*, to her publisher, from whom she had received no response either of satisfaction or dismay. As a result she was in limbo, anxious that the ending would be accepted, for it had been completed only with great difficulty. Furthermore, while trying to finish the book she had been beset by illness, her own and her father's. Patrick Brontë had been suffering from bronchitis and periodically been bedridden, and she had been ill with headaches and a liver disorder that had led to acute depression. It had not been a happy time:

. . . oh Nell! I don't get on – I feel fettered – incapable – sometimes very low . . . it [illness] hinders me in working – depresses both power and tone of feeling . . .

(CB to Ellen Nussey, 14 September 1852)

Significantly, she and her father had only managed to keep going because Arthur Nicholls once again looked after the parish for two months, while Martha Brown, the young live-in servant, ran the house. Both these helpers knew the family intimately, and formed a team that was to stay together, as we shall see, for many years to come. Clearly the curate was an essential element in the household; indeed, perhaps was taken for granted as such. Patrick Brontë's stroke was but the latest in a series of alarms about his health, not least because his eyesight, which had been so wonderfully restored by the operation for cataract in 1847, failed from time to time. Something of a hypochondriac, his health was always a source of anxiety for Charlotte. His chest had always given him trouble, and the great white scarf wound tightly round his neck which we see in the photographs taken in these years bears witness to his fear of chills and bronchitis. In short, he was no easy person to live with, and was becoming less so.

Writing *Villette* had been a trial for Charlotte in other ways, whereas the completion of *Shirley* some years before (it had been published in 1849) had been to some degree a therapeutic undertaking after her sisters' deaths. She complained bitterly that she had never written anything without first talking it through with her sisters, and openly confessed her loneliness and her frustration. She needed her sisters' encouragement, and their rivalry, to spur her on. Mrs Gaskell, who only knew Charlotte after the death of her sisters, was quick to see the poignancy of the novelist working alone at the table where she had so often sat with Emily and Anne.

But the loneliness as a writer was nothing to the bitter loneliness of the woman as the years crept up on her. A letter to Ellen Nussey develops the theme of her predicament and gives us an insight into the state she was in when Arthur asked her to marry him:

> . . . *I am silent because I have nothing to say. I might indeed repeat over and over again that my life is a pale blank and often a weary burden – and that the future often appalls me . . . The evils that now and then wring a groan from my heart – lie in position – not that I am a single woman and likely to remain a single woman – but because I am a lonely woman and likely to be lonely.*
>
> (CB to Ellen Nussey, 24 September 1852)

If *Villette* has a single theme it is loneliness, for the novel is shot through with a bitter longing for affection that borders on de-rangement. In this novel Charlotte took a long steady look at herself, her past and her possible future. There is little of comfort in the images she saw. In the chapter 'The Fête' she rehearsed, albeit in the guise of narrator, her past experience as a governess. A pupil bluntly tells her teacher, the narrator, of her hopeless prospects:

> '*I suppose you are nobody's daughter, since you took care of little children when you first came to Villette: you have no relations; you can't call yourself young at twenty-three; you have no attractive accomplishments – no beauty. As to admirers, you hardly know what they are; you can't even talk on the subject: you sit dumb when the other teachers quote their conquests. I believe you never were in love, and never will be; you don't know the feeling: and so much the better, for though you might have your own heart broken, no living heart will you ever break . . . '*
>
> (*Villette*, Chapter 14)

This theme is the one consistent thread – indeed, a desperate concern – in all Charlotte Brontë's published stories. She felt desperately the lack of accomplishment, the lack of beauty and, by 1852, the lack of youth. A passage in the chapter 'Old Maids' in *Shirley*, published three years earlier, captures its author's very real anxiety:

> *Caroline looked at the little mirror before her, and she thought there were some signs [of her becoming an old maid]. She could see that she was altered within the last month; that the hues of her complexion were paler, her eyes changed – a wan shade seemed to circle them, her countenance was dejected: she was not, in short, so pretty or so fresh as she used to be.*
>
> (*Shirley*, Chapter 10)

Charlotte's fears, eloquently stated in this same chapter, were that her path would be one where 'Winter seemed conquering her spring: the mind's soil and its treasures were freezing gradually to barren stagnation.' It is no exaggeration to say that this fear dogged Charlotte's maturity, and is found everywhere in her letters and her writing. At first it was a joke she shared with friends, but by the time Arthur Nicholls proposed to her she was more than a little afraid of becoming a sour person with 'the vinegar discourse of a cankered old maid' (*Shirley*, Chapter 10).

How was she to avoid this fate? The answer, for Charlotte, was clear, resounding through her writing: find someone to love one, someone who would offer back the love that is given. Such is the love between William and Frances that concludes *The Professor*, such the love between Jane and Rochester at the end of *Jane Eyre*, and such between Caroline and Robert, Shirley and Louis in the pair of weddings that round off *Shirley*. It is notable, however, that such love is not present in *Villette*, the latest of all the novels; here the blessing is withheld, the emblematically named Lucy Snowe (Charlotte had considered naming her Frost) remaining alone at the end of the story.

Villette is problematical in this respect. It is a love story that tells nothing of the perfecting of a partnership. The heroine remains merely a patient observer of other marriages. Lucy Snowe is content with a single life for three years while her 'lover' is abroad; it is as if she has been 'frozen', placed in a cabinet (in fact, a school that this lover, M. Emmanuel, purchases and equips for her, though without any consultation with her), her love set in amber. Irresistibly, the lines from Shakespeare's *Twelfth Night*, 'She sat like patience on a monument', come to mind, lines that Emily used in *Wuthering Heights*. The last paragraphs of the novel are enigmatic and ambiguous, for it is left to the reader to decide whether Lucy's lover returns safely from the West Indies, or is drowned at sea. They did not appeal to the Reverend Brontë, who spoke for many when he said that he would have preferred a happy ending. Charlotte refused, holding to the image of a patient woman awaiting the return of a lover as he journeys through tempestuous seas, and preferring to let the reader's imagination offer a fitting end to the story. The tale was told and it was up to the audience to find for itself the fit conclusion, and to decide the implications for the protagonists' future.

The cool representation of love in *Villette*, indeed of loneliness in love, is a mature vision fitting Charlotte's circumstances at the time when she completed the novel in 1852. It is also the summation of her fictional depiction of love, a depiction that, from first to last, developed through many types and patterns in her writing.

Charlotte Brontë's novels are, however, an untrustworthy guide to her own idea of love. The needs of her heroines are not her needs, although they can help us to understand something of her beliefs, hopes and frustrations, in the sense that they derive from her mind and no other. If, therefore, we read the novels and her surviving letters in the context of the events of her life, we may come closer to under-standing that 'love' of which she claimed knowledge. Here, though, we must grasp the biographical nettle; the question as to just how much can we truly know of another's life. The great biographer Thomas Carlyle provides cold comfort with his bland 'Not at all.' Biography, he tells us, is a feast of empty shells, the meat having all been eaten.

The fundamental flaw in historical biography is the reliance on written words. It is easy to imagine that what a person writes is what a person means, that an account written out is a true one; that descriptions of places or persons or events can be precise and accurate. All writing is subjective, and thus influenced by personality, point of view and involuntary prejudice. Is Charlotte's account of Arthur's proposal the truth about what took place that evening in December? We have no other version to compare it with, for neither Arthur nor Patrick Brontë left their own accounts. We can be sure they would all be different, though each authentic to its author. The truth about any event is an amalgam of feelings and facts, elements that are seldom verifiable. When those events and perceptions date from nearly a hundred and fifty years ago, we must acknowledge that truth recedes, eludes our grasp as we move steadily away from the circumstances and singular preoccupations of the protagonists. When, moreover, the figure that we seek to know is a celebrated one, facts become inextricably clothed in popular tales and gossip – both from the fashionable literary circles of salons and from the marketplace and washhouse – which in turn become enshrined in myth and legend. So it is with Charlotte Brontë. Such has been the influence of her novel *Jane Eyre*, so powerfully has it worked its spell upon the imagination of the world's readers, that its author is seen to be synonymous with Jane Eyre, the orphan child-governess-bride, and her novel, at least in essence, unavoidably autobiographical: Jane's schooldays are Charlotte's.

Clearly, fictional characters derive from their author's imagination and their author's experience. It is wrong, however, to hold the naively simplistic view that Jane Eyre or Lucy Snowe speak for Charlotte Brontë. Though such characters may owe their origin in part to their author's own experience, the artistic process, however, removes them from everyday reality. The autobiographical elements of novels such as *Jane Eyre* or *The Professor* transcend the history of Charlotte Brontë, deriving their value from a distillation of her memories and imagination. Charlotte always resisted accepting that she was in any way Jane Eyre, her life being infinitively more complex than Jane's. But if they do not speak for her then for whom do they speak? In Charlotte's case, it is possible to find some firm ground in this quicksand of conjecture. It is a necessary truism to state that without Charlotte Brontë the characters would not exist. Through her imagination they have their only being, and because they are creatures of her thought processes they will naturally possess many of her own qualities. While we cannot claim that the events of the fiction are in all cases those of her life, we can note the similarities and sense the resonance between things we know Charlotte Brontë experienced or says she experienced, and their surrogate counterparts in the novels. Thus, if we are sanguine about the limitations of making such deductions, we can find patterns and preoccupations in the work that may be relevant in considering the novelist's account of her own experiences. Charlotte Brontë's joke to Ellen Nussey that she would be an old maid may be considered alongside the chapter in *Shirley* in which she describes what old maids are. Taken together, it seems fair to believe that the topic, or her anxiety about being left a spinster, was one that increasingly exercised her as the years passed. While we cannot know her state of mind when her father opposed her marriage to Arthur Nicholls, we can imagine that her age, her interest in the plight of unmarried women, the prospect of nothing more for her in the immediate future than looking after an elderly father, all combined to offer us a picture of sorts. Naturally we cannot know everything, though hindsight often betrays us into thinking we can. Always those who record events, even the protagonists themselves, engage in distillation of truth, a process of selection and rejection in order to give a comfortable, or what seems to the teller a reasonable, account.

Bearing in mind the impossibility of knowing all the circumstances that shaped Charlotte Brontë's personality, we can nevertheless piece together parts of the jigsaw puzzle. Because she was so successful as a writer in her lifetime, and because her friend Elizabeth Gaskell wrote so moving a memoir of her, we have a considerable amount of material to consider. Mrs Gaskell's bias – she did not, for instance, either like or approve of Patrick Brontë – and her own ability as a practised novelist to spin a good yarn, produced so compelling, if so slanted, a view of Charlotte's life that the original is likely to remain forever obscured. Yet by looking beyond Mrs Gaskell's polished icon, by re-reading her sources, a more balanced view may be established, one in which happiness takes its place beside the elements of melodrama and tragedy that drive Mrs Gaskell's 'defence' of her friend.

Love Begins at Home: The Parsonage Nursery

Love begins at home, fed by the life of the family and nurtured by parental care and the relationships between siblings. By the age of nine, however, Charlotte Brontë had suffered the loss of her mother and her two elder sisters, Maria and Elizabeth, and she thus from an early age clearly understood the nature of loss and grief. The death of her mother was a dreadful blow, but the deaths of her two sisters, older playmates after whom she would have run and whom she would have seen as role models, must have been devastating. Moreover, from being a secure middle child she was suddenly the eldest of four motherless children cared for by a fifty-year-old spinster aunt, a sternly dutiful woman who, holding to her own bedsitting room in the small parsonage, would argue politics with her brother-in-law and take snuff. Understandably the children clung to each other, Charlotte fulfilling the role of 'little mother' and leader, with her younger brother's bossy and precocious assistance. Undoubtedly the younger children must have come to rely on her.

As this sadness passed, the four survivors were happy together, at times deliriously so. The shared losses may well have brought them together for comfort and support, indeed to survive at all, so that over the years a bond of love was forged deriving from their minds being 'cast in the same mould', and from an exhilarating mutual love of words. Words to these children were magical things; they could be juggled with, strung together to make sentences, to make jokes, to make stories of horrible deeds and loving encounters. Words were the essential ingredients of scribbling, and scribbling together was, with drawing, what the Brontë children did best. It was storytelling that characterised not only their play, but their development. It may be that their father's love of reading and writing inspired them, and certainly their earliest mock volumes bear title pages that ape the Reverend Brontë's printed works. Tabitha Aykroyd, the cook-housekeeper who ruled the homely kitchen from 1825 to 1855, was in awe of their heady excitability, vowing that such extremes of imaginative play could 'addle bairns' brains'.

There is little doubt that the four parsonage children, left to themselves for much of the time while their father attended to parish matters and their aunt claimed hours alone for her not-so-young self, made the most of each other's company. The cellar became a dungeon, plays were written and memorised, toy soldiers were set marching in imagined kingdoms, and always there waited the great expanse of moorland immediately behind the house. Through all its seasons the moor beckoned. Winter snows giving way to flooding waterfalls in spring, whinberry picking, seas of purple heather serenaded by ascending larks or drumming snipe, all made the moor a wonderland for children. Streams and stepping stones as well as howling winds and piercing rain provided the growing children with a challenging environment, a potent mix of danger and beauty, of days of summer calm and winter hazard.

Above all, the Brontë children loved each other. Their juvenile writing bears witness to affectionate games of teasing, rebuking, parodying, but above of all of a wonderful sharing of ambition, hopes and fears. They could play elaborate games with words, games that were to be sustained throughout childhood into maturity. Theirs may in many ways have been an enviable childhood; it was certainly, as time would show, uniquely appropriate for young writers, at least for female writers of their day.

True love is full of merriment and humour. Much fun was had by Charlotte and her siblings, mischievous joking that persisted into their adulthood. Love, a deep need for certain people in particular, for their companionship and embraces, was a staple of the Brontë children's development. This love came to be associated with the house where it flourished. As children, none of the four Brontës would ever be happy away from the parsonage, for it was the nursery of their love for each other, and the proving ground of their talents. It exerted an almost magnetic pull upon them which, as the years passed, was to prove at times as debilitating as it was sustaining. Emily could not thrive away from the parsonage, while her brother and sisters seemed drawn back to it, willy-nilly. Later in life Charlotte came to view this as a kind of thraldom, seeing the deep love of the place as a binding fetter, while the adult Branwell felt smothered and imprisoned by the house.

Charlotte the Ugly Duckling

Slight of stature, shortsighted, delicate in health, her head disproportionately large, Charlotte Brontë was dogged by the idea that she was ugly. Her friends saw her as a curious creature, crippled by shyness to the point of being gauche. Clearly she suffered from a poor self-image. The writer Harriet Martineau on first meeting the mature Charlotte found her to be an odd little person, 'the smallest creature I had ever seen'. In *Jane Eyre* there is a passage that sets out the pain felt by a plain young woman, clearly drawn from Charlotte's own experience:

> *I rose, dressed myself with care . . . I ever wished to look as well as I could, and to please as much as my want of beauty would permit. I sometimes regretted that I was not handsomer: I sometimes wished to have rosy cheeks, a straight nose, and small cherry mouth: I desired to be tall, stately, and finely developed in figure; I felt it a misfortune that I was so little, so pale, and had features so irregular and so marked . . .*
> (*Jane Eyre*, Chapter 11)

Charlotte's poor eyesight, so weak that she had to hold books close to her nose in order to read at all, meant that she was to some degree isolated from what was going on around her, even from her brother and sisters. Ellen Nussey recounts how Emily would torment her older sister by leading her close to animals or the water's edge, and then tell her where she was. Moreover, even within the happy and supportive group of the four children, Charlotte could be lonely. Introspection and loneliness can attend upon poor eyesight, for such a child may tend to live in its own world if the walls of a room and everything in it are no more than a blur. For Charlotte, ball games were denied her, and she alone of the parsonage children played no musical instrument, though

Emily played the piano with some skill, Anne played too, and Branwell was a good flautist and sang competently. Perhaps Charlotte made a contribution by turning the pages of the music or by pumping the bellows for Branwell when he played the church organ? We do know that she never danced, and nowhere do we hear of her ever singing. There would have been little point in her father teaching her how to load and fire a pistol, as he did Emily. None of the family pets were considered hers. Emily had Keeper and her hawk Hero, Anne had Flossy; only after her sisters' deaths would they nominally become Charlotte's, and then it was Arthur Nicholls who exercised the two dogs. All this suggests that Charlotte was somehow at a distance from her siblings, her weak eyes perhaps contributing to that isolation. Many who knew her were to comment on how closely she would scrutinise paintings and illustrations, even with the benefit of spectacles.

If isolation was an early companion in her childhood, more galling was the sense that she was not pretty. She did not have her youngest sister Anne's curls, nor Emily's height. The passage in *Jane Eyre* where Jane compares her plain self with a society beauty is surely auto-biographical, a conjecture borne out by the cruel self-parody in a drawing which she added to the foot of a letter to Ellen Nussey:

> '*Listen, then, Jane Eyre, to your sentence: tomorrow, place the glass before you, and draw in chalk your own picture, faithfully, without softening one defect; omit no harsh line, smooth away no displeasing irregularity, write under it, "Portrait of a Governess, disconnected, poor, and plain".*
>
>   '*Afterwards take a piece of smooth ivory . . . take your palette; mix your freshest, finest, clearest tints; choose your most delicate camel-hair pencils; delineate carefully the loveliest face you can imagine; paint it in your softest shades and sweetest hues . . . call it "Blanche, an accomplished lady of rank".*'

(Jane Eyre, Chapter 16)

Poor and plain was how Charlotte always saw herself. Her friends commented that she would willingly have traded her success as a novelist to have been pretty. The evidence both from her intimates and from people she met combines with the evidence of the novels to confirm her low self-esteem. Such a sense of inadequacy begs love and affection, if only as compensation. All her life she yearned for recognition, for acceptance of her spirit and true nature despite her looks and seeming insignificance. Knowing how small she was, the scene at the school, Lowood, from *Jane Eyre*, in which the big girls elbow out the smaller from the fire in a freezing schoolroom, and the little girl has to make her way from one end of the room to the other by clambering over or creeping beneath forms and desks, becomes especially telling.

Desperation was never far from Charlotte's thinking, not least because of the recognition she constantly sought. It is therefore little wonder that Heger's acknowledgement of her serious engagement with writing, his recognition of her agile and quick mind, bowled her over, swept her into what must have been the hope, if not the real-isation, of a relationship only ever longed for and dreamed of. The most intelligent man she had ever met, even more learned than her impressive father, the celebrated Professor would sometimes give her his undivided attention, and even took lessons in English from her, again alone. This would have been heady stuff for any young woman; to Charlotte it was water on parched earth. She was clearly overwhelmed, but also released, as her friend Mary Taylor (who was in Brussels at the time) noticed, from the 'cage' of Haworth Parsonage and, we might add, released too from the cage formed by her sense of inadequacy. Having bathed in the light of such recognition, it is no surprise that she was so devastated to leave the man she saw as her 'master'. However ill founded her admiration – indeed, her love – for Heger, her suffering at leaving him was real. Heger cannot be entirely blameless in this matter, for it is not over-difficult for a gifted and flattering teacher to turn the head of an impressionable and inexperienced pupil. It is not really to be believed that a man noted for his skills as a rhetorician, who had once moved among the actors of the Comédie Française, would have been modestly correct with the young Englishwoman he taught. Having to leave him, and thereby to lose his attention to her writing, his praise and his informed criticism of her efforts, was a loss which Charlotte would mourn deeply and long:

I suffered much before I left Brussels – I think however long I live I shall never forget what the parting with Monsr Heger cost me – It grieved me much to grieve him who has been so true and kind and disinterested as a friend . . .

When do you think I shall see you Ellen – I of course have much to tell you . . . things which we should neither of us wish to commit to paper . . .

I do not know whether you feel as I do Ellen – but there are times now when it appears to me as if all my ideas and feelings except for a few

*friendships and affections are changed from what they used to be –
something in me which used to be enthusiasm is tamed and broken – I
have fewer illusions – what I wish now is active exertion – a stake in life
– Haworth seems such a lonely quiet spot, buried from the world – I no
longer regard myself as young, indeed I shall soon be 28 – and it seems
as if I ought to be working and braving the rough realities of the world
as other people do . . .*

(CB to Ellen Nussey, 23 January 1844)

This was written immediately after Charlotte's return from Brussels
– her second visit, when she had gone alone – when she was opti-
mistically expecting letters from Heger, and before she had undergone
the misery of his silence, his refusal to answer the desperate letters
she was to send him in the coming tormenting and bewildering year. It
is worth pondering her statement that Ellen would understand that
there were things she wanted to tell that they should neither of them
'wish to commit to paper', a timely reminder that an absolute reliance
on surviving letters and written accounts may be more than a little
misleading. Written accounts are not events, and only seldom are they
the truth of any human transaction. It is worth recalling Charlotte's
discretion when we too readily judge Arthur Nicholls from few and
brief surviving letters. It may be that his relationship with Charlotte
was one about which neither he nor she would have wished to commit
words to paper.

Charlotte Brontë at the age of twenty-seven knew love's suffering,
knew the wrench of leaving a man whom she adored, who nurtured her
love of writing and under whose stern influence her imagination soared
and her competence as a writer developed. She was about to endure the
bitter isolation of one whose offerings in love are ignored – not even
rebuffed or refused, but simply callously ignored, among the cruellest
of hurts that any human being can inflict upon another. The inspiration
and joy she had tasted in Brussels would now sour. In time, this
smouldering hurt would burst into the flames that would engulf
Thornfield Hall and consume the impediment of the wife who stood
between Jane Eyre and her marriage to Edward Rochester. It is
arguable, even likely, that Charlotte might have wished just such a fate
for Madame Heger.

To the loss of Heger must be added the loss of her brother as he
pursued his selfish and wasteful path to self-destruction. Coming as
they did after the deaths of her mother and two elder sisters, the brutal
silence of Heger and the death of Branwell more than any other factor

fed her increasing anger with men, men whom she admired, but who nevertheless let her down. The revenge with which she had threatened Madame Heger was soon to be turned against men, seen at once in *Jane Eyre*, where only a maimed Rochester marries his Jane. Before this unequivocal, even tough, vision was realised, however, the more anodyne and conventional story, *The Professor*, would first be told. The reasonable tale was the necessary apprentice work, completed before Branwell's worst excesses confirmed her dark view of men. It was while in the throes of her brother's infuriating self-pity, when she was having to read to and write for her blind father (who, as has been said, could not have known half of what was going on in his own home), that she conceived the story of *Jane Eyre*, with its passages of uncompromising and shocking violence. Love for Charlotte was now a tempestuous physical passion, rather than a sedate, manageable emotion. A wild anger, an irrepressible indignation, had become the chief, the most challenging and honest, ingredient of her work and of her understanding of love's power. Now it is possible to see the strength of her belief that a true lover bares his breast to the hoofs of a kicking horse for his beloved.

One of the lasting effects of Charlotte Brontë's infatuation with Constantin Heger, one that remained with her and influenced her against Arthur Nicholls, was that the former had responded to her intellect. It was to her mind, to the attention of an apt pupil, to her skill as a teacher and gifts as a writer, that he had reacted. Lacking beauty, the sensitive young woman craved intellectual recognition. Perhaps Heger reinforced this lopsidedness in her character, and certainly her criticism of Arthur Nicholls at the time of his proposal focused on his intellectual limitations; she could not see him as her intellectual equal. Could she in 1853 still be looking for her 'master' of 1843 and all that he had meant to her? In writing to Ellen Nussey in 1854, announcing her engagement to be married, there is surely a suggestion of slight regret that Nicholls was not Heger:

> . . . *I am still very calm – very – inexpectant. What taste I have of happiness is of the soberest order. I trust to love my husband – I am grateful for his tender love to me – I believe him to be an affectionate – a conscientious – a highly-principled man – and if with all this I should yield to regrets – that fine talents, congenial tastes and thoughts are not added – it seems to me I should be most presumptuous and thankless . . .*
>
> (CB to Ellen Nussey, 11 April 1854)

Love in the Novels

Charlotte Brontë's concept of love can be traced in her novels with greater assurance than it can be in her life. In the stories we have ideas she formulated, wrote down and sent forward for publication. We can borrow this comparative certainty to shed light upon her all too often intangible and elusive experience. From the earliest writings, her childhood scribblings based upon fairy tale, Arabian Nights romance and, later, the poetry of Byron, there is a steady development towards more mature attitudes, so that the thrill of conquest and the swooning rapture of the early work give way to the suffering and sacrifice that true love so often brings.

Setting aside the considerable body of juvenile writing, precocious and full of promise though it is, the published works, taken in their chronological order of writing, record a flowering of love, a sustained process of understanding that is as satisfying as it is subtle, complex and challenging. The distance from Frances Henri in *The Professor* to Lucy Snowe in *Villette* is considerable; the development of a steady vision of love's complexity is profound.

The Professor, originally entitled *The Master* (the fair copy has the latter title scored out, clearly by Charlotte), can be seen as unashamedly autobiographical. Unconvincingly disguised as a narrative of the experiences of a man (William Crimsworth), it is a love story that draws heavily upon much that happened to Charlotte in Brussels, where the novel is set. The story is gentle, the courtship between Crimsworth and Frances Henri delicate, the denouement and marriage tender and pleasantly satisfying; it is possible that the story was a palliative for the bitterness of Charlotte's disappointment when her adored 'master', Heger, refused to correspond with her and thus shut her out of his life. In *The Professor* the heroine finds her soul mate, two teachers find a compatible union and are blessed with children in a life that is little short of idyllic. The book never found a publisher in Charlotte's lifetime. The general view was that it failed because its main character was unconvincing; it may be that the transfer of the narrator's sex blunted its power. By the autumn of 1846, however, even while *The Professor* was journeying round publishers and gathering its many rejections, Charlotte was busy writing *Jane Eyre*. This time she made the narrator of the story a woman, calling up her own feelings to invest her principal character with a burning passion. *The Professor* was written after Charlotte had given up hope of ever again hearing from Heger. Her most plaintive pleas had all gone unanswered. She had endured a year of abject misery. The novel appears to have been an attempt to distance herself from her bitter experience, one in which the true depth of her feelings of hurt and disappointment were suppressed. It is as though Charlotte, capable and sensible Charlotte, was making a real attempt to present a composed piece of work that had little of her profound misery in its pages. The poems that she included in the Bells' collection of verse, which was published in 1846, were likewise insipid and artificial. In later years she came to disown them as trivial and lacking the feeling and power of her sister Emily's poems in the same volume. As for *The Professor*, little in that novel suggests the force of what was to come in *Jane Eyre*. What could have happened in the time between the completion of the first manuscript, and the starting of the second?

As we have seen, two circumstances bore upon Charlotte's creative imagination in the period when she thought of the story of *Jane Eyre*, the one her aching loneliness and despair at losing contact with a man she worshipped, the other the rapid deterioration of her brother and his palpable weakness in surrendering to largely self-inflicted misery. Charlotte clearly became angry, angry with men. Heger had without doubt hurt her badly, and all that he had once offered her had turned to ashes. Branwell's reckless imposition on his sisters and their father, which lasted almost three years, was equally a process of deep dis-illusionment for Charlotte. As she had once been utterly devoted to him as co-partner in their childhood writing games, so she was in the same measure sickened by his whining self-pity and his drunken stupors. Two of her heroes were tainted in her eyes, two of the most significant men in her life had failed her, while her father was at this time almost completely blind, and thus helpless in many respects. Had it not been for the admirably reliable curate, Arthur Nicholls, things would have been a good deal worse.

Perhaps the greatest contrast between *The Professor* and *Jane Eyre* can be seen in the treatment of the male characters. *Jane Eyre* lacks sympathetic men. Mr Reed is dead before the tale begins, his widow utterly spoils the unspeakably horrid son, John, who is violent and out of control. The Reverend Brocklehurst is clearly a cruel and pompous moral hypocrite, appearing more as a statue ('a black pillar' with a 'grim face at the top') than as a person; even the apothecary is instrumental in recommending that the little orphan girl be sent away to a charity boarding school, the infamous Lowood. In the first half of the novel the male characters are absent, depersonalised or made wildly unsympa-thetic to such an extent that Jane herself comments when she first meets Edward Rochester (also introduced – though not until Chapter 13 – as a statue, for initially he neither speaks nor moves), as if confirming the reader's alertness in noticing her treatment of men, that Rochester was the first man whose 'portrait' she hung in the gallery of her memory, the first man, who was neither brother nor father whom she had really noticed. In noticing him, it is as if Jane Eyre has suddenly grown out of her childhood relationships with men, and that this meeting signals a new stage in her life. Until this point in the story all the significant people with whom Jane has had any relationship have been women. It is women who have embraced her or rejected her, soothed her mind and combed her hair, as it was the homely, gentle Mrs Fairfax who had welcomed her to Thornfield Hall, and shown her into a large well-furnished bedroom that was, for the first time in her life, to be her own. This room has great significance, for it will be the scene of her maturing, the background for her hopefulness in the anticipation of marriage and for her desolation after the wedding has been so dramatically halted. Here she will be visited by Rochester's mad Creole wife, Bertha; from here she will be summoned to tend the wounds of the injured Mason and to quench the flames of Rochester's bed hangings; outside the door of this room a persistent, angry and distressed Rochester will keep vigil. The room is the setting for the drama of her maturing, a staging post in her journey forward to marriage and physical fulfilment.

Charlotte had vowed revenge as she left Madame Heger and Belgium, and it may be that in *Jane Eyre* she wreaked that revenge. Furthermore, the novel has all the fire (at times literally) and passion that *The Professor* lacks.

Above all, love in *Jane Eyre* is wholly different from love in *The Professor*. It is more robust, more overwhelming, more dangerous. It consumes; it is not cold, but is rather a matter of hot blood. Blood is drawn at the very start of the story when, avoiding a book thrown by her violent cousin, Jane cuts her head on a door; the blood trickles down her neck as, unjustly, she is berated by her aunt. There is no doubt that these rites of passage point towards a mature understanding of love's suffering, of what the poet W.B. Yeats called 'the mire and fury of human veins'. The fictional child is at once announced as a creature of flesh and blood who, when wounded, bleeds. She is seen in stark contrast to the illustrations of icy wastes in the book she pored over in the window-seat as the story began. Love in this story is clearly to do with life and involvement, the crying out in the darkness of the night, a longing that goes beyond rational behaviour, a love that would even come to countenance adultery, for Jane, in answering the mystical call in the night, makes her way to Rochester without knowing that his wife has died. She sets out to go to him accepting all that had been abhorrent to her at the time of the interrupted wedding. Love is now a reckless, consuming fire; it has overcome appearances and all other superficiality, so that even the unthinkable adulterous relationship can be entertained, and caution and convention thrown to the winds.

A Woman's Place

In her first completed adult novel, *The Professor*, Charlotte Brontë, wounded and vulnerable, sought, knowingly or unknowingly, to soothe the hurt of her rejection by Heger. The story tells of a teacher who comes to realise that his young student-teacher loves him; he marries her and they live with their two children in an idyllic country cottage, a little Eden. The schoolmaster while correcting his 'pupil's' verse finally recognises that her work is in fact a love poem addressed to him. This was something that Heger never realised, or if he did he never admitted to it. Clearly the story of *The Professor* is an attempt to offer balm to the aching heart, and equally clearly it fails to convince, for it is false. No such denouement was possible, since there had been no such romance. On the other hand the hurt, the loneliness that Charlotte had felt in Brussels, were real, and whereas these could not shine out in the story of William Crimsworth and Frances Henri, they could in the tale of Lucy Snowe. Between the hero of *The Professor* and the heroine of *Villette*, Charlotte matured, found the passion to tell her *own* story with all the power that her grief commanded. The realisation that she had lost her 'master', Heger, fuelled the imaginative fire that took Charlotte Brontë's imagination beyond anything she had yet created, or perhaps even conceived. Why should she not tell her tale? She would employ all that she had learnt at Heger's side, and let her scalding tears refine her vision. Jane Eyre would prove to be a tough, uncompromising, angry character, a young woman who would challenge where she felt there was injustice, would speak her mind even though it cost her dear. From the very start of the story she answers adults back, is what they call impertinent, to the point at which she distresses her guardian aunt and confirms to the Reverend Brocklehurst his contemptible view of children.

The world had not seen the like of Jane Eyre when she appeared before the public in October 1847. In a matter of a few pages Jane progresses from quietly reading to having to defend herself against a tyrannical fourteen-year-old cousin. Almost the last words of the first chapter are spoken, we assume, by Mrs Reed, Jane's aunt, but this is purposely left ambiguous: 'Did ever anybody see such a picture of passion!' That the little orphan girl is ready to fight her older male cousin who has unjustly attacked her, to defy her aunt and physically resist the servants who are instructed to take her away, is still shocking today. Even as a child Jane was a new kind of woman, one who had suffered enough, who had sat still long enough under adversity. We cannot find her like in *The Professor*, and arguably not in literature before *Jane Eyre*. And that is only the beginning. In Chapter 21, on her deathbed, Mrs Reed recalls that her niece Jane 'was born to be her torment' and wonders how she could for nine years have been 'patient and quiescent under any treatment, and in the tenth break out all fire and violence . . . ' In the same way, Charlotte's sadness and anger run their full term; she had been passive enough. The balanced tale of *The Professor* did not satisfy publishers, nor, perhaps, its author. *Jane Eyre* rose from the ashes of disappointment, as full of passion as its predecessor had been reasonable. In truth, it is a blessing that *The Professor* failed to find a publisher, for had that novel succeeded, *Jane Eyre* might never have been written. We may also be quietly glad that Heger did not respond to Charlotte's letters, for had he maintained any kind of sedate correspondence with her, she might never have been spurred on to create the uncompromising and vengeful Jane Eyre. This is no idle conjecture. Some six years later, at the height of her powers as a writer, she turned once more to the hurt Heger had done her ten years before, recast the story of *The Professor* with a female narrator, and produced her acknowledged masterpiece, *Villette*.

There can be little doubt that the scene in the penultimate chapter of *Villette*, in which Paul Emmanuel declares his love for Lucy, is anything other than the scene that Heger and Charlotte never played out, with Madame Heger intervening in the character of Emmanuel's cousin, Madame Beck. The anguish, recreated with great truth, is still fresh:

> *He took my hand in one of his, with the other he put back my bonnet; he looked into my face, his luminous smile went out, his lips expressed something almost like the wordless language of a mother who finds a child greatly and unexpectedly changed, broken with illness, or worn out with want. A check supervened.*
>
> *'Paul, Paul!' said a woman's hurried voice behind . . . 'Come, Paul, come to your friends.'*

> *Madame Beck, brought to the spot by vigilance or an inscrutable
> instinct, pressed so near she almost thrust herself between me and M.
> Emmanuel. 'Come, Paul!', she reiterated, her eye grazing me with its
> hard ray like a steel stylet. She pushed against her kinsman. I thought
> he receded; I thought he would go. Pierced deeper than I could endure,
> made now to feel what defied suppression, I cried –*
>
> *'My heart will break!'*
>
> *What I felt seemed literal heart-break; but the seal of another
> fountain yielded under the strain: one breath from M. Paul, the whisper,
> 'Trust me!' lifted a load, opened an outlet. With many a deep sob, with
> thrilling, with icy shiver, with strong trembling, and yet with relief
> – I wept.*
>
> (*Villette*, Chapter 41)

While developing the theme of love's passion within the story of Jane
Eyre, Charlotte also presented all the options open to a young woman
of her day who was plain, had few accomplishments and no important
family connections. They can be listed. Jane, being poor but educated,
could become a teacher or a governess – she does both; she could
become a wife and rear children – this she sees others doing, but
eventually does herself; she could become a nun – this her cousin does,
and is immured in a convent cell; she could be housed as one of
Rochester's conquests, that is, become a kept woman, adulterous and
unmarried, and indeed Rochester tells her he has such a property ready
in Europe – this she declines; she could be a missionary's wife – to this
end she learns some Hindustani but declines the perfunctory and
condescending offer of marriage from her cousin, the Reverend St John
Rivers; she could remain a spinster and become an old maid – this she
fears. Her dream of marriage above her station but with her spiritual
and intellectual equal is realised when she finally marries Rochester, a
consummation only possible after both have suffered almost to the
point of death and after a legacy from a long-lost relative has provided
her with an income of her own. While *Jane Eyre* is fiction, it nevertheless embodies Charlotte's preoccupations as she found herself 'caged
up' in Haworth Parsonage, caring for her blind father while her
brother set about drinking himself to death. She must have come to feel
that love meant sacrifice, for there was no Rochester, and it was more
than unlikely that there was a rich relative in foreign parts who would
suddenly and miraculously provide for her. This was the woman to
whom Arthur Nicholls proposed, a woman who had nervously faced
what her future might be, who had set out as many possibilities as she

could and found those that beckoned unattractive, while the wished-for love, the true relationship, remained ever elusive.

When Arthur Nicholls proposed, Charlotte had only recently sent the completed manuscript of *Villette* to her publisher, George Smith of Smith, Elder & Co. One of that novel's early chapters contains what is among the most powerful evocations of patient loyalty and constancy in literature, a story worthy of D.H. Lawrence in its power. Lucy Snowe has become the companion to a Miss Marchmont, a rich, bad-tempered old woman, crippled with rheumatism. One night after a terrible storm she tells Lucy a story, a tale that speaks clearly of Charlotte's ideal of love's faithfulness and of a woman's vulnerability:

'. . . *one happy Christmas Eve I dressed and decorated myself, expecting my lover, very soon to be my husband, would come that night to visit me. I sat down to wait. Once more I see that moment – I see the snow-twilight stealing through the window over which the curtain was not dropped, for I designed to watch him ride up the white walk; I see and feel the soft firelight warming me, playing on my silk dress, and fitfully showing me my own young figure in a glass. I see the moon of a calm winter night float full, clear, and cold, over the inky mass of shrubbery, and the silvered turf of my grounds. I wait, with some impatience in my pulse, but no doubt in my breast. The flames had died in the fire, but it was a bright mass yet; the moon was mounting high, but she was still visible from the lattice; the clock neared ten; he rarely tarried later than this, but once or twice he had been delayed so long.*

'*Would he for once fail me? No – not even for once; and now he was coming – and coming fast – to atone for lost time. "Frank! you furious rider," I said inwardly, listening gladly, yet anxiously, to his approaching gallop, "you shall be rebuked for this: I will tell you it is* my *neck you are putting under peril; for whatever is yours is, in a dearer and tenderer sense, mine." There he was: I saw him; but I think tears were in my eyes, my sight was so confused. I saw the horse; I heard it stamp – I saw at least a mass; I heard a clamour. Was it a horse? Or what heavy, dragging thing was it, crossing, strangely dark, the lawn? How could I name that thing in the moonlight before me? or how could I utter the feeling that rose in my soul?*

'*I could only run out. A great animal – truly, Frank's black horse – stood trembling, panting, snorting before the door; a man held it: Frank, as I thought.*

'"*What is the matter?" I demanded. Thomas, my own servant answered by saying sharply, "Go into the house, madam." And then calling to another servant . . . "Ruth, take missis into the house directly." But I was kneeling down in the snow, beside something that lay there – something that I had seen dragged along the ground – something that sighed, that groaned on my breast, as I lifted and drew it to me. He was not dead; he was not quite unconscious. I had him carried in; I refused to be ordered about and thrust from him . . . I gave place to none except the surgeon; and when he had done what he could, I took my dying Frank to myself. He had strength to fold me in his arms; he had power to speak my name; he heard me as I prayed over him very softly; he felt me as I tenderly and fondly comforted him.*

"'Maria," he said, "I am dying in Paradise." He spent his last breath in faithful words for me. When the dawn of Christmas morning broke, my Frank was with God.

'And that,' she went on 'happened thirty years ago.'

(*Villette*, Chapter 4)

It was in such dramatic and passionate terms that Charlotte Brontë now chose to depict love's loss and woman's fidelity, a far cry from the gentle romance of *The Professor*. Her storytelling was consummate, but the depiction of love's tenderness, as well as its vulnerability and violence, was also within her scope.

Against the male pomposity and cruelty, the condescension and chauvinism shown to women in *Jane Eyre*, she sets the embracing kindness of women to each other. Helen Burns dies in Jane's arms; Bessie the nurse-cook at Gateshead, the home of Jane's aunt, can soothe as well as scold, sing to her young charge, and offer food, warmth and reassurance. It is not for nothing that she names one of her own children after Jane. It is Bessie who waves Jane off to boarding school, and who welcomes her back on her visit to her aunt's deathbed. Bessie is a type of decent wife and mother set in a world where there is much that is harsh and troubling. The conversation between them on the night before Jane is sent away to school at Lowood is serenely tender:

'And so you're glad to leave me?'

'Not at all, Bessie; indeed, just now I am rather sorry.'

'Just now! and rather! How coolly my little lady says it! I dare say now if I were to ask you for a kiss you wouldn't give it me: you'd say you'd rather not.'

'I'll kiss you and welcome: bend your head down.' Bessie stooped; we mutually embraced, and I followed her into the house quite comforted. That afternoon lapsed in peace and harmony; and in the evening Bessie

told me some of her most enchanting stories, and sang me some of her sweetest songs. Even for me life had its gleams of sunshine.'

(*Jane Eyre*, Chapter 4)

Bessie is the source of comfort, of caresses, kisses and embraces. Indeed, in the whole novel hers is the most wholesome and secure marriage, her husband one of the few truly good men.

A further seemingly sentimental, but in reality psychologically important, touch in the novel relates to the orphan Jane's little wooden doll:

[Jane prepares for bed:] . . . I undressed hastily, tugging at knots and strings as I best might, and sought shelter from cold and darkness in my crib. To this crib I always took my doll; human beings must love something, and, in the dearth of worthier objects of affection, I contrived to find a pleasure in loving and cherishing a faded graven image, shabby as a miniature scarecrow. It puzzles me now to remember with what absurd sincerity I doted on this little toy, half fancying it alive and capable of sensation. I could not sleep unless it was folded in my nightgown; and when it lay there safe and warm, I was comparatively happy, believing it to be happy likewise.

(*Jane Eyre*, Chapter 4)

Here Charlotte Brontë displays a remarkable insight into play as therapy, noting the importance of the human tendency to invest objects with meaning. Thus, for Jane, make-believe works its magic as a created comfort against the uncontrollable and fickle turns of fate. This is not the only instance in her writing where Charlotte, long before Freud, prefigures modern psychological theory. More important, however, is her understanding that human beings need to love. Significantly, in the story of *Jane Eyre* the scarecrow doll is soon replaced by the real, live Helen Burns, who finds similar comfort in Jane's arms.

Charlotte Brontë was to claim to Harriet Martineau that she 'knew about love', and this seems just. Later in *Jane Eyre*, Charlotte's heroine tells her friend Helen what she believes about human love, in a passage that has an echo in the later description of the death of Miss Marchmont's Frank in *Villette*:

' . . . if others don't love me, I would rather die than live – I cannot bear to be solitary and hated, Helen. Look here; to gain some real affection from you, or Miss Temple, or any other whom I truly love, I would

willingly submit to have the bone of my arm broken, or to let a bull toss me, or to stand behind a kicking horse, and let it dash its hoof at my chest . . . '

(Jane Eyre, Chapter 8)

Arthur Nicholls had read this description of love before he proposed to Charlotte, although he had yet to read of Frank's fatal last ride to meet his lover. On the one hand we can only wonder as to how much he understood of the complex woman he loved; on the other hand, however, he may have known just what it was that attracted him to her. Few of us have such an opportunity to read in print what our partners believe human love to be. For the curate, *Jane Eyre* held out an invitation, if only he could win the love of its creator.

Arthur Nicholls: Curate and Would-be Husband

Real life can sometimes be a disappointment. In Charlotte Brontë's stories lovers braved storms and tempests to be together, offered their chests to horses' hooves or were dragged almost dead by the stirrups of galloping horses to die in their lovers' arms. Her would-be lover, however, Arthur Nicholls, dare not even face her father to ask permission to seek her hand in marriage. Thus reality mocked art. Charlotte must have had to make a considerable adjustment when faced with the opportunity of a partnership over which her pen on the page could not have absolute control. Perhaps she thought of Tennyson's *Lady of Shalott* as she turned from her novels to the everyday world. And yet the pen was to play its part, although, surprisingly, it was not hers, but Arthur's, that was to prove most effective. After Charlotte had rejected his proposal, by letter, as she had hastily promised her father she would, the tormented and distressed curate eventually turned to writing to her. Charlotte replied to these love letters, perhaps unsurprisingly, given her bitter experience with Heger. If this was a clever calculation on Arthur's part, it succeeded brilliantly. While he did not know how much Charlotte had pined for letters from Heger, he still could not have thought of anything better designed to win Miss Brontë over than by plying her with love letters. Moreover, he must certainly have known how greatly Charlotte welcomed the postman's knock at the parsonage door, how eagerly she greeted parcels of books, letters from her publisher and from the ever corresponding Ellen. Arthur, as an exile from his own country and a loving family, may well have understood the importance of letters in the loneliness of Haworth.

After their marriage he made it clear that he considered letters to be important, even if at times dangerous – and this from a man noted for his reticence and for the brevity (mostly) of those of his letters that have survived. It is a great pity that Charlotte, unlike her father, never tied her partner's letters in a bundle with ribbon and hid them for posterity to poke its nose into.

Apart from official letters about church school matters, Arthur's to Charlotte may have been the only long letters he ever wrote. Whatever the case, however, written words worked where the spoken had failed him. His letters slowly worked their way into Charlotte Brontë's approval. Once again, and not from a member of the Brontë family this time, words on the page were having their magical effect in Haworth Parsonage. Few people, now or today, would care to put pen to paper in an attempt to impress as formidable a writer as the author of *Jane Eyre*. Yet Arthur did not lack courage, and in the long run his writing proved to have no little power. The modest clergyman, in winning Charlotte round to accepting him as husband through his *writing*, effectively had the celebrated novelist hoist with her own petard. Her published words had moved him, now his private words moved her, perhaps confounding Charlotte's anxiety about inequality of intellectual interests and other such reservations.

So who was this impertinent, love-sick Irish curate ? Would we ever have known anything about him if he hadn't pursued and eventually married Charlotte Brontë? He wrote no novels, published no sermons, was canon of no cathedral, bishop of no diocese. In his day, however, there were young people, especially from among the poor, who would remember him with gratitude. One such was a teenaged girl from Haworth on whose behalf Arthur Nicholls wrote to the National Society in London in November 1847:

> *Haworth. Bradford Yks*
> *Nov 17th 1847*

Reverend + Dear Sir,

I have to thank for your kindness in forwarding to me the regulations for admission at Westminster + Whitelands. The girl on whose behalf I made application is only fifteen *years of age, but possesses all the qualifications requisite for making a good [school] mistress. It is my intention to put her in charge of an infant school, which we are about to establish, if the National Society will admit her into Westminster to be trained. As her parents are poor and therefore cannot afford to keep her at school I trust that the committee will comply with our request.*

It has ever seemed to me of the greatest importance to keep up (and as far as possible) the connection between our schools and those who have been educated in them. With a view to this object I am most anxious to commence a good Evening *school for adults, but from the badness of trade and other causes I find it impossible raise the funds necessary to complete our arrangements . . .*

(ABN to the National Society, November 1847)

There is no way of knowing whether the girl received her grant and completed her training, but we do know that adult evening classes were conducted at Haworth, and that Patrick Brontë wrote similar letters on behalf of young weavers who wished to train as teachers. These are but a few examples of the nature of the clerics' work in the parish and its schools. Patrick and his curate were pioneering adult education with zeal and intelligence, providing unique opportunities for poor men and women to better themselves by entering a life of teaching. On being appointed to teach at her old school, Miss Wooller's establishment at Roe Head (she taught there from 1835–8, and there met her two close friends, Ellen Nussey and Mary Taylor), Charlotte Brontë proudly announced that she was to teach where she had herself been taught. By the same token, a village girl of fifteen from a poor family must have felt as proud, or prouder. In at least one letter, therefore, the all but invisible Arthur Nicholls becomes a little more visible, and interestingly so. His was an enlightened view of the purposes of educating the poor. Whereas in October 1847 Charlotte Brontë, alias Mr Currer Bell, was enjoying seeing *Jane Eyre* published, in the following month a similar tale of a poor young girl setting out to be a teacher was beginning in real life. The author of the novel might, after all, have had something in common with the author of the letter.

Arthur Nicholls's concern for education, for providing the poor with opportunity, was not, in fact, something he acquired in Haworth. His early adoption into the family of Dr Alan Bell, the master of the Royal School at Cuba House, Banagher, meant that he was steeped in schools and schooling. As has been said, the particular conditions of that small town also provided lessons in poverty and distress that would serve as a good apprenticeship for his curacy at Haworth. There are records of his being hired at the Royal School as classics master, at a salary of £50 a year, and of his later being transferred to another school for a higher fee. His years at Banagher were marred by a cholera epidemic followed by another of typhus, and in the autumn of 1845, as he arrived in Yorkshire, blight struck the Irish potato crop, a time when many cottagers, unable to meet their rents, were being evicted from their homes, some of them owing rent to Dr Bell and the School Commissioners. It was, too, a time when many of the Irish poor found they had no other recourse than to take their families to workhouses, where 'famine fever' killed thousands of them off. Other families, more fortunate, emigrated to America. The population of Banagher, never larger than 2,000, dwindled rapidly. Arthur Nicholls would have become well versed in compassion and understanding for the plight of the poor in Haworth after his experiences in Banagher. His studies in Greek, Latin and Hebrew must have formed a striking contrast to his everyday experience in the world outside the classroom, although there was little better preparation for a life of caring and ministering than studies in the classics and the New Testament. He would have been well prepared to support his parson, who loudly and publicly condemned the New Poor Law, and sought to provide accommodation in cottages in Haworth for the township's poor rather than have them sent, as he was meant to, to the workhouse in nearby Keighley.

The Royal School at Banagher suffered many vicissitudes in its time, some of them while Arthur was living and teaching there. The story is told of a great storm in 1839 (Arthur was twenty-one and enrolled at Trinity College, Dublin, at that time, from which he graduated in 1844) after which scarcely a room in Cuba House was left habitable. Both more alarming, and more interesting in the light of Charlotte Brontë's honeymoon visit to Cuba House in 1854, is the highly damning report of an inspection of the school in April 1856:

> ... *the dilapidation of the schoolhouse must be in my opinion highly injurious to the tone of feeling that ought to prevail amongst the pupils. They cannot in after life fail to look with contempt and aversion upon the dirty and ruinous place in which they followed their early studies. It would surely be desirable, in a country like Ireland, that the children of the middle order, from whom the classes beneath them are expected to learn decency and regularity, should themselves be habituated to something of the kind, while most capable of forming enduring tastes and habits.*
>
> *The schoolhouse is in perfect keeping with the town of Banagher, although it would surely seem to be the duty of those who are charged with the oversight of the school to keep it in as absolute contrast as possible with the squalor and decay in its neighbourhood. According to the explanation offered by Mr Bell [Dr Bell's son, James, who had taken over the school], the Commissioners of Education have directed him to*

make no further repairs than may be necessary to keep out wind and rain . . .
(Report of the Endowed Schools [Ireland] Commission, 1855–8)

Can the Royal School have been so very different in 1854 when Charlotte visited? She made no mention of dilapidation in her letters home. After Dr Bell's death in 1839 and before his son James was appointed in 1848, the school had been completely run down. In 1839 the appointed master refused to take up his post because the buildings were in such bad repair; his successor, James Fahie, received a considerable shock when he arrived:

> *I repaired to Banagher and beg to state that I was never more astonished in my life. Having been assured that the board were spending 'a considerable sum in repairs', I naturally concluded that repairs were in progress . . . but instead I found only one day's work done by two carpenters and the place a complete ruin. It was undoubtedly a fine house but it has been. So far from introducing into it the sons of the most respectable men in Ireland who will accompany me when the place is fit to receive me, I could not think of putting a servant to sleep in it. It is dismal, gloomy and the basement storey not fit to lodge felons in. Surely had the Board any idea of its ruinous and unwholesome state they would not, fathers themselves, expect that any man, accustomed to anything like decency or comfort could or would sacrifice his family by thrusting them into such a dungeon. When the gaols of the country in these days of improvement are kept in such decent order for the reception of criminals, what should be expected from a royal Endowment . . . The house should be newly roofed and the basement requires an Augean cleaning . . .*
> (James Fahie, c. 1841, letter quoted in M. Quane, *North Munster Antiquarian Journal*, Volume X, No. 2, 1967)

This background was at least an appropriate preparation for Arthur Nicholls in taking up his post in Haworth, described by a public health inspector as one of the unhealthiest, most overcrowded and most insanitary townships outside London. Whatever else he might have been, Arthur Nicholls's background and early experiences would have ensured that he was no wilting faintheart or fastidious shirker. The crammed slum township of Haworth would hold no fears for him on that score.

The Curate's Lodgings

The parsonage at Haworth overlooks the house where Arthur Nicholls lodged with the sexton John Brown for all the years he spent in the parish. The house, adjoining the National School a stone's throw from the parsonage windows, had been built at Patrick Brontë's suggestion for the schoolmaster. A delightful letter has survived setting out the manner in which, Brontë felt, he might provide a mistress for the infants and girls of the school, something which, naturally enough, highlighted the need for a decent house to be built:

> ... *our school has commenced, under more favourable circumstances, than ever anticipated. We have now, between one hundred and two hundred children, and the church people seem to be highly pleased with the whole concern ... Now I very much want a Mistress, here, for the girls. But how she might be supported is the question. On talking with our Master, I find that he thinks 'it is not good for man to be alone' – and that he would have no objection, to have a fit conjugal partner in his labours, his joys and sorrows – I must say that I encouraged the idea, only on the grounds, that he might be enabled to support such a connexion with advantage to our establishment ...*

(PB to the Secretary of the National Society, 9 January 1844)

It is interesting to note, in passing, that marriage was not always objectionable in Brontë's eyes. Later letters tell how Mr Ebenezer Rand, the schoolmaster in question, had 'someone in mind' who proved to be quite suitable, but naturally, wrote the Reverend Brontë, having a wife meant more expense; he therefore promptly requested an increased grant to augment the schoolmaster's salary!

By the time Arthur Nicholls arrived in Haworth, Rand, who had indeed married the lady in question, had found other accommodation. John Brown, who now lived in the schoolmaster's house, was the parish sexton, and a stonemason by trade. As sexton he was excused from signing any temperance pledge during campaigns against the consumption of alcohol which, as now, was a prime cause of much criminal activity and misery in the township, it being deemed necessary that a grave-digger needed something to fortify him in his sombre task! Since Brown was a great friend – indeed, an intimate – of Branwell Brontë, it follows that the paths of Arthur Nicholls and Branwell would often have crossed, so that it is inconceivable that the curate would not have known all too well what the parson's son was doing. A note has survived dating from Branwell's late and darkest days, when he was pleading for gin, and it is unlikely that this was the only such message delivered to the sexton's house:

Sunday.
Noon

Dear John,

I shall feel very much obliged to you if can [sic] contrive to get me Five pence worths of Gin in a proper measure. Should it be speedily got I could perhaps take it from you or Billy at the lane top, or what would be quite as well sent out for to you. I anxiously ask the favour because I know the good it will do me. Punctually *at Half past Nine in the morning you will be paid the 5d out of a shilling given me then. Yours, P.B.B.*

(Branwell Brontë to John Brown, c. 1848)

Whatever was going on in the parsonage – at times the village joiner was kept busy mending smashed doors and locks – little would have escaped the notice of the sexton, his family and their lodger. From the windows of either house the comings and goings in the other were clearly visible (it is interesting to note that from his lodgings the rejected Arthur would have been able to see the light in Charlotte's window). John Brown's daughter, Martha, had from the age of ten run errands for the Brontës and since 1841, when she was thirteen, had lived in as a servant to help the ageing Tabby, as Tabitha Aykroyd was known. Little could have happened in the parsonage that the Brown family would not have known about.

Rejected

We know very little of Arthur Nicholls's state of mind at the time when he asked Charlotte Brontë to marry him. Charlotte was well used to telling Ellen Nussey that she had recently turned down an offer of marriage, for she had already done so three times. Each time she rather gleefully recounted her reasons without any hint of emotion or embarrassment. Her reply to Henry Nussey's proposal survives, and is enlightening in showing us Charlotte's character and her views on the subject of matrimony. (Intriguingly, the letter reads, particularly if read aloud, somewhat like vintage Jane Austen, whose work Charlotte ostensibly did not admire.)

. . . do not . . . accuse me of wrong motives when I say that my answer to your proposal must be a decided negative. *In forming this decision – I trust I have listened to the dictates of conscience more than to those of inclination; I have no personal repugnance to the idea of a union with you – but I feel convinced that mine is not the sort of disposition calculated to form the happiness of a man like you. It has always been my habit to study the characters of those amongst whom I chance to be thrown, and I think I know yours and can imagine what description of woman would suit you for a wife . . . as for me you do not know me, I am not the serious, grave, cool-headed individual you suppose – you would think me romantic and eccentric – you would say I was satirical and severe – however I scorn deceit and I will never for the sake of attaining the distinction of matrimony and escaping the stigma of an old maid take a worthy man whom I am conscious I cannot render happy . . .*

. . . Farewell - ! I shall always be glad to hear from you as a friend.

(CB to Henry Nussey, 5 March 1839)

Henry Nussey must have cringed as he found himself so neatly impaled on the pin of Charlotte's perceptions. He was not to be the last suitor to suffer her dismissal, however.

In August the same year a young Irish curate, a Mr Bryce, met Charlotte but once, and then only briefly, at the parsonage, and a few days later sent an offer of marriage in a letter. Charlotte gleefully dispatched another finely composed letter to Ellen reporting this 'rather odd circumstance':

Well thought I, I have heard of love at first sight, but this beats all. I leave you to guess what my answer would be, convinced that you will not do me the injustice of guessing wrong. When we meet I'll show you the letter. I hope you are laughing heartily, this is not like one of my adventures, is it? . . . I am certainly doomed to be an old maid – I can't expect another chance. Never mind, I made up my mind to that fate ever since twelve years old.

(CB to Ellen Nussey, 4 August 1839)

It is hard not to be aware of a certain polish to the confident style of this letter, again so like Jane Austen's prose. It is an exquisite piece of writing – and would make a wonderful speech for a play. Clearly Charlotte was enjoying herself immensely.

In fact, she was to have 'another chance', although it was to be almost twelve years before she received another proposal, this time from James Taylor, an employee of Smith, Elder, her publisher, after she had become established as a successful novelist. Taylor had for some time urgently courted her, but try as she would she could not like him enough. He visited Haworth in April 1851, leaving Charlotte in a turmoil:

> . . . *each moment he came near me, and that I could see his eyes fastened on me my veins ran ice. Now that he is away I feel far more gently towards him, it is only close by that I grow rigid – stiffening with a strange mixture of apprehension and anger – which nothing softens but his retreat and a perfect subduing of his manner . . .*
>
> (CB to Ellen Nussey, 4 April 1851)

In a further letter, she expanded on her feelings:

> *Would Mr Taylor and I ever suit ? Could I ever feel for him enough love to accept him as a husband? . . . As he stood near me, as he looked at me in his keen way, it was all I could do to stand my ground tranquilly and steadily, and not recoil as before . . . no, if Mr Taylor be the only husband fate offers to me, single must I always remain.*
>
> (CB to Ellen Nussey, 23 April 1851)

On this occasion, Patrick Brontë was all for his daughter accepting, especially as Taylor was immediately going to go to India for five years (Smith, Elder were also East India Company agents). Perhaps unkindly, arguably mischievously, probably selfishly, the old man suggested that a five-year engagement was a splendid idea.

Charlotte Brontë was undoubtedly well rehearsed in refusing offers of marriage, and in the catechism of questions she asked herself on such occasions. She knew that she wanted to marry a man whom she could love, not one who made her veins run ice. It is tempting to think that she might have turned down Arthur Nicholls with a letter couched in the same terms as those she used to Henry Nussey, in order to keep the promise she had given her father that Nicholls would have ' a distinct refusal', for such rejections were filed in her memory. True to form and without delay, Ellen had the whole story laid out before her, and was even sent 'this note' – that is, Arthur Nicholls's reply – as witness. It may be, however, that this was an all too sudden reflex action. Just as her father had been dumbfounded by the insolence of Nicholls's proposal, Charlotte had been startled to realise the 'degree or strength of his feelings'. New worlds need assimilating, and gradually Charlotte's protestations, with the benefit of sober reflection and further evidence of the depth of Nicholls's feelings, found her in unknown territory where her map of poised and confident rejection could be of little use. Words can be treacherous, and it may be that Charlotte's superb mastery of language, or her beguilement with it, had tripped her into telling her tale too hastily to Ellen, for good *stories* can often take precedence over true facts and true feelings. Consider for a moment the case of the journalist whose enthusiasm to tell a good story may not be so far removed from that of the novelist. Charlotte's swift rejection proved to be too sudden a response to something that had taken her unawares. Her father's apparently unreasonable outburst had sprung in her a well of concern for Nicholls, perhaps even of curiosity, that she had not realised existed. Sending this fourth suitor packing was not going to be so easy. Besides, it was one thing for her to boast, aged twenty-two, that she had known from the age of twelve that she would be an old maid, but quite another when she was thirty-six: the joke was not so lightly told.

When Arthur Nicholls proposed to Charlotte, the occasion might just conceivably have been the first time that she had ever been close enough to 'see' him for the man he was. In literal terms, too, we know she was very short-sighted, that, in her own words, it was when Taylor 'came near me, and . . . I could see his eyes fastened on me' that her 'veins ran ice'. She could not bear to be close to him. Yet when Arthur came near her that night in December, she saw how moved he was. Her veins, it seems, did not run ice on that occasion.

Charlotte, in common with the heroines of her novels, was vulnerable to sudden shocks, sudden realisations of what was really happening as opposed to what she thought was happening. This is one of the defining characteristics of her art. We have only to consider for a moment any of the plots of her novels to see that her heroines are slow to see what is transpiring. *Jane Eyre* is in part the story of a young woman unable to understand what is taking place around her; bewildered by events she is, significantly, convinced that she is unimportant to any one but herself, and that Rochester her employer must be in love with the pretty, wealthy Blanche Ingram. She quite fails to see that *she* is the object of his love. If suspense is the staple of Charlotte Brontë's storytelling, it is also indicative of the way that she lived her life. The challenge, indeed difficulties, of keeping abreast of events were problems she knew well. During the period of her brother's decline, for example, she seems to have had no idea that his alcoholism and other excesses had put his life in jeopardy; she was to write that Branwell's death had come as a profound shock to her. Again, she had not known that Emily had written so many impressive poems until she 'discovered' them, although there is no evidence to suggest that Anne had not known of Emily's poetry. It is possible that Charlotte's inquisitiveness was one way in which she coped with her feeling that she was always being left out of things, constantly having to catch up with others around her and with the world in general. There may be some truth in her own claim that she was the least promising of her father's children, that she was not as clever as the others. Her short-sightedness brought with it a form of isolation, a life in the shadows to which she frequently referred, and as frequently condemned her heroines. In *Jane Eyre*, Rochester, in love with Jane, pretends that as he intends to marry he is going to have to dismiss her from her post as governess, telling her, in an outrageous joke, that he has already found her a new job, to be governess to the 'five daughters of Mrs Dionysius O'Gall of Bitternutt Lodge, Connaught, Ireland' (*Jane Eyre*, Chapter 23). Jane takes all this dreadful punning seriously and, still believing that when Rochester talks of his bride he means Blanche, agrees that when her employer marries she will spend the evening before the marriage talking to him. She does not see through the ridiculous name and address her prospective employer is given: Dionysius, perhaps a reference to the 'Tyrant of Syracuse'; O'Gall, the bitter cup; Bitternutt, another unwelcome taste, the hard nut to crack; Con-naught, those who will learn or understand nothing . . . (What jokes Charlotte could think up!) In *The Professor* it takes William Crimsworth a very long time to realise that his pupil Frances loves him. In *Villette* it is not until Chapter 41, the penultimate chapter of what is a long novel, that Lucy Snowe realises Paul Emmanuel means *her* when he talks of his love. Women find love in Charlotte Brontë's novels, but only after they have suffered agonies of self-effacement, disbelief and lonely self-doubt.

Charlotte's instinctive understanding of Arthur Nicholls's proposal seems to have been 'It cannot mean me,' 'This is not happening to me,' or even 'What a surprise!' She was to express that surprise to the last. On her deathbed, and hearing her husband praying at her bedside that God might spare her, she said: 'Oh! I am not going to die, am I? He will not separate us. We have been so happy.' Her reaction to Nicholls's proposal might, therefore, be paraphrased as 'Oh, you are not proposing to me, are you? I am going to be an old maid!'

It is clear from both her fiction and her life that Charlotte was by nature intensely reserved, even to the point of living her own reality at a remove from what was really going on around her. We know that she was so introspective as to appear to be socially maladroit, as witness her visit to Thackeray in 1851 when, as a celebrated author and the guest of honour, she vanished, only to be found in a corner talking to the governess. Hiding behind curtains in window-seats was not exclusively reserved for the orphan Jane Eyre, for there is ample evidence that it was also her creator's practice.

Two eminent writers of her day were quick to link her novel *Villette* with her own situation. From different standpoints, Harriet Martineau and William Thackeray, each of whom she had met, fixed upon Charlotte's loneliness as the central preoccupation of this novel. Harriet Martineau publicly declared that

> . . . *all the female characters, in all their thoughts and lives, are full of one thing, or are regarded by the reader in the light of that one thought – love begins . . . at the opening . . . and it closes with it at the last page – so incessant is the writer's tendency to describe the need of being loved . . . [yet] it is not thus in real life. There are substantial, heartfelt interests for women of all ages, and under ordinary circumstances, quite apart from love.*
>
> (Review of *Villette* in the *Daily News*, 3 February 1853)

Charlotte, never forgave Harriet Martineau and broke off the friendship. It is at least arguable, however, that the critic had touched a nerve.

Thackeray was more blunderingly male in his view of *Villette*, simply lampooning the whole idea of love as Charlotte had portrayed it in what can only be seen as a personal and heartless attack:

> *The poor little woman of genius! The fiery little eager brave tremulous homely-faced creature! I can read a great deal of her life as I fancy in her book, and see that rather than have fame, rather than any other earthly good or mayhap heavenly one she wants some Tomkins or another to love her and be in love with. But she is a little bit of a creature without a penny worth of good looks, thirty years old I should think, buried in the country, and eating up her heart there, and no Tomkins will come. You girls with pretty faces and red boots (and what not) will get dozens of young fellows fluttering about you – whereas here is one genius, a noble*

heart longing to mate itself and destined to wither away into old
maidenhood with no chance to fulfil the burning desire.
(W.M. Thackeray, letter to L. Baxter, 11 March 1853)

How right Thackeray was and yet how wrong. Three 'Tomkins' had
been and gone, and even while Thackeray was writing, a fourth, Arthur
Nicholls, was plucking up the courage to ask for the 'little genius's'
hand. But how skilfully Thackeray diagnosed Charlotte Brontë's plight.
He sensed rightly that the author of *Villette* would risk all for love, that
more than anything in the world she sought affection. This Arthur
Nicholls offered to give her, after a false start, his offer was accepted,
proving Thackeray's insight to be correct and giving Charlotte
something that she thought would ever be denied her: happiness in a
relationship with a husband.

There were, however, many obstacles to be overcome before that
happiness would be found, not the least of which was Charlotte's
conviction, bred from bitter experience and loneliness, that she was
destined to live out her days as a single woman. Both Harriet Martineau
and Thackeray had heard the cry that haunted *Villette*.

One of the sources of Charlotte Brontë's loneliness derived from her
belief that she would always be overlooked, or would live outside
normal society. This belief was deep-seated in her character, but to
some extent she was set apart. She also saw to it, however, that she set
herself apart. Perhaps her diminutive stature (four foot ten inches),
slight build, poor health, shortsightedness and acute shyness always set
her apart. Equally, she was perhaps instinctively an isolated figure,
believing herself to be unattractive, and existing, because of her poor
vision, in a dim and hazy landscape.

Yet there is a sense in which all the Brontë family were 'set apart',
as the children of an exiled Irishman, as being intellectual and educated
in a rough poverty-stricken moorland slum township, as the 't'Parson's
childer'; they were a family of outsiders. We have only to think of the
over-excitable, Greek-and-Latin-spouting, little red-haired brother,
Branwell, and his bizarre behaviour for the point to be proven. Perhaps
this is the burden of creative genius, to be to the side of mainstream
social give and take. Intriguingly, the only one of the Brontë sisters to
possess any measure of social grace or ease was Anne, the youngest.
Only she managed to work away from home and to earn the lasting
respect of those she was with. The so-called 'gentle' Anne, who we
are asked to believe would not have said 'boo' to a goose, had more
about her than her two sisters or her brother. Charlotte, in an

uncharacteristic letter – or perhaps one that is more truthful than the bulk of other surviving sources – tells that she, Charlotte, wished she had the poise and capabilities of her sister Anne. But that is a different story.

Chapter Three

❧

'I Wish That Every Woman May Avoid Him For Ever'

The disappointed Arthur wasted no time after receiving Charlotte's firm rejection. He resigned his curacy – and then, it seems, panicked, unable to decide what to do. He clearly had no plan in mind. He was living in a house a stone's throw from the parsonage, from which he could see the light in Charlotte's window. There is no record as to how Nicholls heard of Patrick Brontë's reaction to his proposal to Charlotte. History has assumed that he knew all about it, forgetting or ignoring the fact that we only have Charlotte's version of the old man's response. We do know that Nicholls came to hear of Brontë's objections, and that in old age he stated that he quite understood those objections. It hardly seems likely that he learnt of them from Charlotte, and it is improbable that at her age she would refuse an offer of marriage citing her father's objections as her reasons. The whole narrative of the incident, from start to finish, is in Charlotte's words, through her surviving letters and reported conversations with friends. In her *Life of Charlotte Brontë* Mrs Gaskell was to embalm this version for posterity as the truth. While it may well be a true account, it is inevitably one-sided; moreover, Charlotte was no beginner when it came to writing colourfully about such events.

Although we shall never know all of Nicholls's side of things, some facts are available to us. He did resign from his curacy, did offer himself as a missionary to Australia, and then withdrew that offer. In due course he left Haworth to take up a post at Kirk Smeaton, still in Yorkshire, but some thirty miles away to the south-east. According to Charlotte (there is no other source for this) he then wrote to her, met her secretly, won her over, and agreed a basis for marriage that would ensure Patrick Brontë's continuance in the parsonage. There is no reason to doubt Charlotte's account of Nicholls's behaviour after the failed proposal. As we have seen, it was her custom to tell Ellen Nussey, with some relish, all the details of the proposals she had turned down. It is, however, worth reflecting on the circumstances in which Arthur found himself after Charlotte had rejected him.

It seems likely that, though he was still ignorant of Patrick Brontë's objections, Arthur's excellent working relationship with the old man would, at the very least, have become strained. Charlotte's life had been suddenly thrown into confusion, and by the same token her father now found himself in a difficult position. He depended on the younger man to carry out much of the work of the parish that he himself clearly could not undertake. History tells us more or less what was to happen in the end, but Charlotte, Patrick and Arthur had to live out the implications of the new situation without the benefit of knowing what its resolution would be. Charlotte told Ellen Nussey that Nicholls's behaviour before he proposed had made her suspect that he felt more than a usual regard for her; in short, Arthur may well have been troubled by his feelings towards her for some time. Declaring those feelings seems to have cost him dear, for it made his job untenable, and signalled the end of nine years of effective work in an excellent relationship with his parson.

As has been said, when or how Nicholls learnt of his parson's objections to him as a son-in-law is a mystery. From Patrick Brontë's letter to Charlotte after the event, already quoted, we can see that he was not at all pleased with his curate. Again, however, we must see the letter in its context. He had much to lose in any such marriage, and therefore did not hesitate to blacken Nicholls's character in the strongest terms, telling his daughter that he would not wish *any* woman to marry him. These are harsh words, but it is interesting to note that this bad-tempered exaggeration (for that is what it was), ironically enough, was to rebound on their author when he had finally to accede to the marriage going forward. He made sure, however, that he was not there in person to witness it.

Arthur Nicholls's application to go as a missionary to Australia is interesting. Had he, one wonders, read *Jane Eyre* so carefully that he recalled St John Rivers's rejection by Jane? If so, he would have known that there was little hope that Charlotte would accompany him. That aside, however, Australia was an understandable choice. It was just about as far as it was possible to go away from Haworth and Mr Brontë, and there were plenty of Irishmen and women there in need of clergy. There are, however, doubts about how serious Nicholls was in his intention. Was it perhaps a calculated ploy, something to attract Charlotte's attention? He may have been playing the 'St John Rivers' card, hoping that Charlotte would realise how full of warmth his proposal was, and thus perhaps reconsider her refusal. Whatever the case was, Nicholls withdrew his application, giving poor health as the reason for his withdrawal. A number of commentators have scorned this as a feeble excuse. Knowing a little more about his anxieties about his health, justified or otherwise, we can perhaps be more under-standing; in later years his niece believed that the only reason he eventually gave up preaching and conducting services was because of an illness that affected his throat.

Be this as it may, Nicholls's disappointment at the rejection of his proposal was neither brief nor discreet. However well or badly Charlotte Brontë's other spurned suitors might have behaved, Arthur – at least in the version we have from Charlotte – was dramatically, if not melodramatically, affected. Her letters comprise a kind of episodic narrative. From them we learn how she did not love Arthur, but that soon she came to pity him. She tells us that he was refusing meals in his lodgings and that he stumbled over his words when administering communion to her during his last Sunday in the parish; she even tells us that her father found him to be 'an unmannerly driveller'. As she reports it to Ellen Nussey the whole matter becomes a splendid drama played out in Nicholls's lodgings, in the aisles of St Michael's Church and in the streets of Haworth. Not since Branwell's scandalous decline had such juicy gossip flown round the kitchen doors and looms of the little township. Nicholls, we are told, either because he could not help himself or by design, did not hide his feelings. There must have been plenty for the curious to observe as the weeks during which he worked out his notice unfolded. Moreover, it had been some time since the parsonage had been the source of scandal. The reserved, even aloof, authoress, the sole occupant of the family pew, was as interesting to the congregation now as any of her heroines, and more so to many.

The comparison of these events with those surrounding Branwell's death is not altogether fanciful. Considered from Patrick Brontë's point of view, the situation was possibly too familiar. Here was a young man, born only a year after his tragic only son, in whom he had absolute trust. For nearly ten years they had worked together with confidence and enthusiasm, and there had been times when the parson could not have carried on at all without this curate's unswerving devotion and professional competence.

But if he had always been well pleased with his spiritual and perhaps surrogate son (and fellow Irishman), now Patrick felt once more disappointed, if not betrayed; indeed, the burden of his letters about the matter is that his trust had been betrayed. However unreasonable the old man may seem to us, he did have some cause to feel disappointed. What the curate was proposing was not only inconvenient, it threatened Patrick Brontë's security and wellbeing as he neared the end of his life and work. He would have to find and train up another curate, with who knew what consequences. (His fears were well founded – in the event it meant an incompetent who irritated Brontë so much that even Arthur Nicholls began to appear to him in a more favourable light.)

As Nicholls played the rejected lover, so the Reverend Brontë played the distraught, if not pathetic and mistreated, old father. He complained of deafness, and laughably suggested that were Charlotte to marry he would leave the parsonage and find suitable lodgings with someone in the parish. The threats proved both puny and futile in the face of Arthur's persistent protestations and manifest suffering, however. The rejection of his proposal proved to be but the dramatic, indeed explosive, first scene in a play that progressed through encounters, letter writing, secret meetings and reconciliations, to a denouement worthy of any theatre. Charlotte herself could not have invented such a plot. Once, in a note about the writing of fiction, she had warned against excessive exaggeration. Now she was to be in the thick of it.

So how did the courtship proceed ? Before we can follow its troubled path we need to know more about Arthur. Inevitably we know plenty about Charlotte. Her success as a writer has ensured that the world has scrutinised the tiniest details of her life with her sisters. The balance needs redressing.

Arthur Nicholls is embalmed in one of the hagiographies of the Brontë family thus:

> *A big, tall man, with a strong square face, framed by dark hair and formidably long side whiskers, Arthur Nicholls had something of the Rochester physique. Like Rochester, too, he was a man of hidden depths, as his emotional outburst proved. Though frequently portrayed as something of a bigot in religious matters and stern and unbending in person, there are glimpses of him that show him in a much more favourable light.*

> (Juliet Barker, *The Brontës*, Chapter 24)

Unlike Rochester, Arthur Nicholls *existed* – he is not a fictional character, and there is little point in comparing him with one. More to the point, Arthur's 'formidably long side whiskers' must be a comment about a particular photograph, other photographs show him with a full beard. Heger also sported a beard or what looked like impressive side whiskers, which might, like writing and answering letters, have been one of the elements that were, in time, to endear Arthur to Charlotte. For good measure we should not overlook Leyland's medallion portrait of Branwell, where whiskers are again in evidence, clearly a fashion of the day.

Arthur Nicholls is only a shadowy figure because, like many of his contemporaries, little is documented about him, and, sadly, those who had plenty to say in praise of Charlotte were for a variety of reasons not altogether disposed to think well of him.

Arthur, the Fit Companion?

Thomas Carlyle's suspicion of biography has already been mentioned; he was always quick to warn that it was a suspect, indeed an impossible, art. Silence, he thought – the silence of the dead subjects of biographies – was as deep as eternity and equally as impenetrable, while people 'whose annals are blank in history-books' were blessed. That silence certainly enshrouds Arthur Nicholls, although whether he is blessed as a result is arguable. Throughout his courtship of Charlotte, his rejection, his dealings with Patrick Brontë, his leaving of Haworth and subsequent return, there is, on his part at least, silence. We have no record of his intentions, his feelings, his plans or his worries, except, that is, as they are told in pseudo-narrative by Charlotte in her letters to Ellen Nussey, in what one might call 'the mischief of narrative'. Indeed, we know little of Arthur Nicholls beyond what she recorded in her letters. It is, however, simply too facile to accept these sometimes quite brief mentions as portraying the whole man, and entirely foolish to take Charlotte's account of the courtship and its sequel as the only possible version of what took place. Her biographers, lacking any different view, understandably tread the path along which she leads them, not least because Carlyle's 'silence' means there is little evidence from which to build up an alternative picture.

In Charlotte Brontë's epistolary narrative, Arthur Nicholls has few mentions. It is not until his startling proposal of marriage, eight years after his arrival in Haworth, that he appears as anything but a very minor character. He is the new curate who 'reads well' and who, it is hoped, 'will give satisfaction'. He goes on holiday back home to Ireland, which is seen as an inconvenience, Papa having to preach more than once and to conduct services on Sundays. He is portrayed as bigoted, dour, as silly as any other curate, and scarcely worth noticing. It is commonly held that he provided the model for the curate Mr Macarthey in *Shirley*, a novel that gave him considerable pleasure and thereby earnt him a much fuller mention than usual in a letter to Ellen:

> *Mr Nicholls has finished reading* Shirley *he is delighted with it – John Brown's wife seriously thought he had gone wrong in the head as she heard him giving vent to roars of laughter as he sat alone – clapping his hands and stamping on the floor. He would read all the scenes about the curates aloud to papa – he triumphed in his own character . . .*
>
> (CB to Ellen Nussey, 28 January 1850)

Macarthey's character, which, as can be seen above, Charlotte confessed was based on Nicholls, is given in this thumbnail sketch :

> *Being human, of course he had his faults; these, however, were proper, steady-going clerical faults; what many would call virtues: the circumstance of finding himself invited to tea with a dissenter would unhinge him for a week; the spectacle of a Quaker wearing his hat in the church, the thought of an unbaptized fellow-creature being interred with Christian rites – these things could make strange havoc in Mr Macarthey's physical and mental economy; otherwise he was sane and rational, diligent and charitable.*
>
> (*Shirley*, Chapter 37)

Since, however, Macarthey is a 'native of dreamland', like the novel's eponymous heroine, we should hesitate before accepting the character in the composition as a 'character' of the man in life (the created character being always much tidier and more manageable than the actual). We can confirm that Nicholls read aloud to Patrick Brontë, for we know that after Charlotte's death he read the unpublished manuscript of her novel *The Professor* to him with a view to editing it prior to a posthumous publishing.

There is something heart-warming about a young cleric reading aloud to his elderly and poorly sighted parson. It suggests that the two ministers of parish and the church schools enjoyed an affectionate as well as a professional relationship. That Nicholls enjoyed Charlotte's published writing should not come as a surprise. He was a well-educated man, and also a widely read one. Evidence for this can be found in a commonplace book of his that has survived. This affords us a rare insight into the kind of clergyman he was and, though we cannot put too much weight upon this one collection, some idea of his taste in literature. Here we have evidence, through his choice of passages and the trouble he went to in carefully copying them into the book, of what appealed to him and of what he thought worth remembering or keeping to hand.

From Charlotte's satirical description of Nicholls as Macarthey, it might be expected that this small anthology would comprise rather worthy, biased (if not bigoted) quotations from theological tracts concerning the advantages of baptism and the correct procedure for Christian burial. It does nothing of the sort. Instead, it is a compilation of provocative ideas, and a select anthology of excellent poetry from authors whose works are still regularly anthologised and are recognised as being of the first order. From the first entry to the last the selection shows a true intellectual grasp, and also provides some indication of what a Nicholls sermon might have been like. Surprisingly, there is little that has dated because of its dealing with what were then topical doctrinal matters. The whole is evidence of an inquiring mind, one that shunned sentimental verse in favour of good poetry, and avoided the triviality of religious tracts for the challenge of good prose. The first entry in the book, a quotation from St Bernard of Clairvaux, sets a high standard: 'If a man think that he knoweth anything, he knoweth nothing yet, as he ought to know.'

With such a precept as preface the anthology continues with prose from Jeremy Taylor, the seventeenth-century Divine; Sir Walter Ralegh; George Herbert; John Milton; George Crabbe; Robert Southey; and Edward Young. Clearly this is not the collection of a shallow reader or a literary magpie. The book also signifies rather more than its single volume suggests. Here are the fruits of a wide, intelligent reading, indicative of an educated good taste; furthermore, for every item included others will have been discarded, or perhaps copied into other books which have not survived. The entries, which, sadly, are not dated, are written in ink in a light hand, suggesting that they are from early years rather than late. It is not hard to see that the collection would be useful as part of a preacher's necessary stock in trade. The quotations there set out represent material for thought, or quotes for sermons; indeed, many of them remain relevant to this day, and often startlingly so.

Clearly it is wrong to patronise Nicholls as inferior in intelligence and intellect to Charlotte Brontë. The proof in the selection of prose and poetry of value to him confirms that he appreciated and could distinguish between the first and the second rate. There is no more justification for seeing this book as untypical as there is for imagining Nicholls to be another Palgrave. The prolific early writings of Charlotte and Branwell, and Charlotte's letter writing, make us impatient of any in their circle who did not leave bundles of papers for posterity. Their case, however, is the more unusual, for the paucity of surviving writing from Arthur Nicholls is far more the common run of things. At all events we should remember that it is the Brontë family who, so profligate with words, pen and ink, are so unusual, not those lesser-known people who happened to live alongside them. We do wrong when we judge others by their standards, for they were in all ways an extraordinary group of individuals.

Charlotte: A Compulsive Storyteller

In writing *Shirley*, Charlotte Brontë invented 109 characters (if we include dogs), and 37 different places for them to inhabit. At the completion of her last novel, *Villette*, which coincided with Arthur Nicholls's proposal, she had created and set marching through the pages of literature 351 characters. That is invention of a high order, indicative of a fecund, if not perhaps a fevered, imagination. If the total population of her juvenile writings is added to this sum, we see at once what an extraordinary mind we are dealing with. Her sisters in their three published novels restricted themselves to between forty and forty-six characters in eight or ten settings in each of their novels. Of the three sisters, Charlotte was the most inventive, the most prolific, indeed compulsive, storyteller. Her novel *Jane Eyre* is in large measure composed of many short, episodic stories, tales that interweave, which are repeated at different moments in the overall narrative from different points of view. Thus we find Jane is twice told the story of her life, once by her cousin, St John Rivers, and again at the end of the novel by the innkeeper of the Rochester Arms. It is clear that Charlotte had an intuitive gift for invention, for fictionalising reality – in short, a genius for creative reporting. Equally, from the age of fifteen, she had become practised in describing her feelings, hopes and fears, as well as events in her life, in letters to her intimate friend Ellen Nussey. These letters alone show the whole range and scope of her ability with words. She could make words do whatever she wanted; plead, chide, rebuke, soothe, passionately or dispassionately protest. Above all, words beguile, not only the reader but also the writer.

The impulse to write is the impulse to shape experience, to utter the unutterable feeling, to record the fleeting senses. Above all, writing offers a comforting order to life, a syntactical refuge when unstructured experience presses upon us. Charlotte Brontë was well practised in deploying words in this way, to the point where, for her, writing became instinctive, and compulsive. All her experiences, it would seem, were swiftly converted into words. This continuous narrative impulse is beguiling, for her accounts of events, of people, even of her feelings, have an authenticity that can dazzle. A simple example suffices to show this ability. An incident during a train journey when a young girl is suddenly ill becomes, when placed in one of Charlotte's letters an elegant and complete piece of writing. It is a miniature and a gem:

About half-way between Hull and Hornsea, a respectable-looking woman and her little girl were admitted into the coach. The child took her place opposite me; she had not sat long before, without any warning, or the slightest complaint of nausea, sickness seized her, and the contents of her little stomach, consisting apparently of a milk breakfast, were unceremoniously deposited in my lap! Of course, I alighted from the coach in a pretty mess, but succeeded in procuring water and a towel at the station, with which I managed to make my dress and cloak once more presentable.

(CB to Miss Wooler, 8 October 1853)

The incident is elevated by artistry, captured and ordered as it would not be in life. The rhythms of this little piece echo perfectly the movement of the railway carriage, that 'gave rise' to the young person's problem and the shared events. There is in this paragraph a relishing and sheer enjoyment of the way writing can shape the recounting of an experience, the discursive acting as a palliative to our non-discursive experience of life. Read aloud, it works as a miniature story, it is complete from opening phrase to its pleasing final cadence as the clothes are made 'once more presentable'. Nothing needs adding, nothing could be taken away. Such a transformation of life into art was instinctive to Charlotte Brontë, beguiled (if not seduced) as she was by the magic of words. Clearly she had a finely developed ear and an intuitive ability to make words weave their magic spell, events in life undergoing a metamorphosis to be recast with an irresistible authority and presence. This gift Charlotte shared in some measure with Mrs Elizabeth Gaskell, her friend and biographer. Both women were prolific letter writers, both wrote successful novels, both were somehow compelled to relate every detail of their lives in words. It is, however, sometimes necessary to resist being swept along by their narratives to the extent of taking them to be the definitive – indeed, the only – possible records of the events they describe. This is not easy, especially where theirs are the only accounts to have survived.

As an example, recent researches have established the unreliability of Charlotte Brontë's published remarks about her sisters' novels and poetry. Some of her claims about Emily's poems are wrong and misleading; her strictures about Anne's choice of subject for *The Tenant of Wildfell Hall* are clearly prejudiced. In short, Charlotte was an unreliable editor of her sisters' work, nor was she above destroying letters and papers as she felt fit.

So it is with the story of Arthur Nicholls's courtship. Almost without exception, every detail of that courtship, including the wedding and honeymoon tour, has been handed down to us from Charlotte's letters. Thus the narrative is of her composing, and written from her point of view. All her novelist's skills lend power to the account, making it doubly convincing, yet we should not expect her to be a dispassionate reporter of a sequence of events that involved her deepest hopes and fears. Even so, the tale of the courting of Charlotte Brontë by the Reverend Arthur Nicholls has been confidently handed down through biography after biography from a single source, that source being Charlotte herself.

Charlotte's Tale of Courtship

Arthur Nicholls's proposal posed several problems for Charlotte Brontë. She was not in love with him, nor had she ever considered him as a potential suitor. Over the years he had received scant mention in her letters. Early in his time at Haworth he had suffered a little teasing, as had William Weightman, one of the previous curates. Ellen Nussey had later suggested that there were rumours that Charlotte was going to marry Nicholls; this, however, was mere fooling, mischievous banter among young women, to which Charlotte had tartly replied that the curate was of no interest to her. There was truth in this, for however much the family depended on him, they ignored him almost completely in the accounts of their lives. In December 1852, however, having disturbed Charlotte's universe – and her father's – with his proposal, Arthur Nicholls became for the first time someone to be reckoned with.

Other events conspired to keep his proposal in the forefront of Charlotte's mind. We cannot be sure whether Arthur timed the bomb-shell of his proposal to coincide with Charlotte's completion of the final pages of *Villette*, or even whether he knew of Charlotte's preoccupation. It is, however, telling that, fresh from the management of fictional phrases of love, she now had to contend with words spoken in reality, the dream world of the novel replaced with a personal problem in her own life that would affect her own future. Earlier that December, while Arthur was summoning his courage to make his offer, Charlotte was writing to her publisher claiming that her concern in *Villette* had been to make the heroine true to life, that she did not want her story to be 'at variance with probability'. Now, suddenly, composing the last pages of her love story had been overtaken by the opening moments of her own, real, love story. It is as though Charlotte, bent over her manuscript, had not noticed what was happening around her, and had looked up from her writing to discover that the preoccupation and dilemma of her heroine had somehow left the page to become her own. She now had to face herself all the anguish, uncertainty and bewilderment that she so skilfully depicted in her fiction.

Characteristically, and true to her habit, the eighteen-month journey that would lead to her marriage was chronicled in letters to Ellen:

You may well ask, How is it? for I am sure I don't know. This business would seem to me like a dream, did not my reason tell me it has been long brewing. It puzzles me to comprehend how and whence comes this turbulence of feeling.

You ask how Papa demeans himself to Mr Nicholls. I only wish you were here to see Papa in his present mood: you would know something of him. He just treats him with a hardness not to be bent, and a contempt not to be propitiated. The two have had no interview as yet: Papa wrote, I must say, a most cruel note to Mr Nicholls on Wednesday. In his state of mind and health (for the poor man is horrifying his landlady, Martha's mother, by entirely rejecting his meals) I felt that the blow must be parried, and I thought it right to accompany the pitiless despatch by a line to the effect that, while Mr Nicholls must never expect me to reciprocate the feeling he had expressed, yet at the same time I wished to disclaim participation in sentiments calculated to give him pain; and I exhorted him to maintain his courage and spirits. On receiving the two letters, he set off from home. Yesterday came the enclosed brief epistle. You must understand that a good share of Papa's anger arises from the idea, not altogether groundless, that Mr Nicholls has behaved with disingenuousness in so long concealing his aim . . . I am afraid also that Papa thinks a little too much about his [Nicholls's] want of money; he says that the match would be a degradation, that I should be throwing myself away, that he expects me, if I marry at all, to do very differently; in short, his manner in viewing the subject is, on the whole, far from being one in which I can sympathise. My own objections arise from a sense of incongruity and uncongeniality in feelings, tastes, principles.

(CB to Ellen Nussey, 18 December 1852)

The extent to which 'Papa' features in this letter is significant. How did Charlotte know what her father had written to Nicholls? Given his poor sight, had Patrick Brontë dictatd the letter to her (there were times when she wrote all his letters), or did he write it himself and show it to her? Yet whatever he intended by letting her know the harsh terms in which he had written to Nicholls, the result was far from what he hoped. Rather than settling the matter once and for all, his unjust letter provoked her there and then to write a kinder one as a mediating companion.

From all accounts, Charlotte's father was a force to be reckoned with. As an aspiring writer himself he was understandably and inordinately proud of his daughter's success, and he, more than anyone, welcomed the attention that her fame brought to the parsonage. Just when he was looking forward to the excitement that would attend the publication of her new novel, and anticipating weighing up the subsequent reviews, he was faced with his curate's impertinent and, to him, underhand proposal. As has already been said, that proposal threatened the old man at every turn. Marriage would shift Charlotte's attention and energies away from her writing, and away, too, from caring for 'Papa' – she was, after all, his only surviving child. Who knew what such a change in her life would bring? Besides, he would have to find and train up another curate. Would a new man be as amenable as Arthur Nicholls? Would he be content to run the whole parish, for it was clearly too much for Patrick Brontë himself? Nor would a new curate be likely to stay as long as Nicholls; indeed, perhaps only now did it become clear why Arthur had been so content not to seek a parish of his own.

All this was clearly too much for Patrick Brontë to contemplate. Always a fighter, he set about doing all he could to make such a shake-up impossible. But he was too late. His campaign – as can be seen from Charlotte's letter to Ellen – merely summoned up a counter-offensive. The more he railed, the more unjust he became towards Nicholls, the more a sense of fairness and justice grew in his daughter. Where the father could be satisfied to enjoy his daughter's fame and the attention of the literary world, she could not. Loneliness, the silences after she had seen her father safely off to bed and closed the door of the room where she and her sisters had for years talked and written together, conspired to make her restless. Her heroines' yearnings for affection derived from a loneliness that also troubled their creator, at times driving her into deep depression. Was it this that she began to recognise in Arthur Nicholls? Did she see something all too familiar in his reported behaviour? Was his misery somehow a reflection of her own ? Be that as it may, it is worth noting how well informed Charlotte was about what was happening to the object of her father's calumny. This should, perhaps, come as no surprise. After all, Nicholls lodged in the house of the parents of the Brontës' servant, Martha, a house Charlotte could see from her bedroom window. How else would she have known that he was 'entirely rejecting his meals', that as soon as he received any letter or note from Charlotte 'he set off from home'? The rest of Charlotte's letters about the courtship show her to have been equally well informed; perhaps curiosity, prompted by desire, encouraged her to find out all she could about the man who had so disturbed life in the parsonage. Perhaps the real world was going to be as interesting as the world of her creative imagination after all! From being the rather shadowy figure who reliably ran the church school and took Sunday services for Papa, he was now worth watching. How unpredictable would this taken-for-granted man prove to be? Might he have hidden depths ? He was refusing to eat and shunning company in the tradition of many a lover – how could any woman put such a troubled and responsive admirer out of her mind ? Whatever else Arthur Nicholls had achieved, he was now the chief topic of many of Charlotte's letters, and was to remain so for some time.

Charlotte must have had informants everywhere. Not only did she know what her father wrote to Nicholls and what the latter wrote in reply, she also knew whether or not the curate was eating his meals; knew what he said in answer to parishioners' enquiries about his future; knew that he did not blame her father for his attitude; knew that he had offered his resignation of his own accord. All this she learnt without exchanging a word with her lovelorn suitor. Despite the many protestations to the contrary in her letters, she was clearly drawn to, if not intrigued by, the turn in events. Indifference was withheld, she claimed, by her sense of justice. This seed was nourished either by curiosity or simply by the warmth that attends any recipient of affection and admiration however unlooked for. Everything she heard about her rejected suitor told her he was abject, devastated by having his hopes dashed. Who would be able to resist so flattering a compliment, especially when it came with that most beguiling of endorsements, the strongest parental disapproval? By January of 1853 she reports to Ellen on the state of things:

> *I am sorry for one other person whom nobody pities but me. Martha is bitter against him. John Brown says, he should like to shoot him. They don't understand the nature of his feelings – but I see now what they are. Mr N. is one of those who attach themselves to very few, whose sensations are close and deep – like an underground stream, running strong but in a narrow channel. He continues restless and ill – he carefully performs the occasional duty – but does not come near the church, procuring a substitute every Sunday.*
>
> *A few days since he wrote to Papa requesting permission to withdraw his resignation. Papa answered that he should only do so on condition of giving his written promise never again to broach the obnoxious subject either to him or to me. This he has evaded doing, so the matter remains unsettled.*

(CB to Ellen Nussey, 2 January 1853)

What a 'card game' was now in progress. Patrick Brontë was now playing his cards with imperious authority, confident that he held the winning hand. Charlotte clearly looked on while the men played out the game. Nicholls persisted, his cards being his loss of appetite through love and a very public inability to attend church. St Michael's Church it must be remembered, stands just across the narrow lane from the house where he lodged. What did he do on Sunday ? Did he hide in his room with his hands over his ears as first the bells then the organ and the hymn-singing would ring out ? Haworth is still too small a parish in which to hide without drawing attention to oneself, particularly if you were part of the clerical team.

If only we had surviving letters from Arthur Nicholls to augment Charlotte's version of the story. Did Martha relay to him how Miss Brontë was coping – or eating – as readily as she clearly conveyed the details of his appetite to the parsonage? As for Charlotte, she concluded her letter to Ellen with a significant protest: 'without loving him – I don't like to think of him, suffering in solitude, and wish him anywhere so that he were happier. He and Papa have never met or spoken yet.'

What suspense there is here. Much as she knew what was happening she really was guessing. Perhaps she rather wished Papa and Nicholls had met? Was Arthur Nicholls playing a subtle waiting game? After all he had waited some years before declaring himself. Perhaps the lady protested too much, for compassion and pity are often the forerunners of love. Besides, Charlotte's writer's reflexes were at work, seeing Arthur as being 'like an underground stream, running strong but in a narrow channel', such hidden power is seldom commonplace. The author of *Jane Eyre* knew well how surfaces deceive. The simile she used to describe Arthur fits her overlooked heroine Jane Eyre like a glove.

At this point in the story Charlotte fled to London, ostensibly, and truthfully, to be available while the proofs of *Villette* were being read and the book going through the presses. She could forget all about the problems of Haworth, of elderly fathers and would-be suitors, of whether or not she loved Arthur. But then, perhaps she could not. The imagined experience of Lucy Snowe, the heroine of *Villette*, based as it unquestionably was upon Charlotte's own real experiences in Belgium, centred upon love and loneliness. To read the proofs of that text was to rehearse once more the pros and cons of love, the need for affection, the bitter loneliness of the single life. Even the ambiguous ending of the novel, from which the reader is left to decide whether the lovers meet again or whether Paul Emmanuel is drowned at sea, paraded before Charlotte her own choices. Was she to be alone for ever, caring for her father until he too, through his death, left her? What were her prospects then? To be turned out of the parsonage to make way for the new incumbent? To leave the house where she had grown up with her brother and sisters, to leave all those memories? Her conjectures and anxieties would have accompanied her to London, where she stayed with her publisher, George Smith. Having left Haworth on 5 January, she wrote ten days later to Ellen Nussey: 'No news yet from home – and I feel a little uneasy to hear how Papa is – I left him well – but at his age one specially feels the uncertainty of health.'

It was while Charlotte was in London that Patrick Brontë launched his out-and-out attack on Nicholls using the device – already quoted – of a letter from the dog Flossy, and concluding that he could not wish any woman to have the misfortune to marry the curate, let alone his daughter, the celebrated novelist. These letters sped their way from Charlotte to Ellen with instructions that when read, they should be burnt . This was not, however, to be the only time that Ellen Nussey, dear friend as she might be, felt able to ignore Charlotte's request. The letters were not burnt, and survive to allow us to read for ourselves the depth of Patrick Brontë's feelings about what he termed 'the obnoxious subject'. For this we must be grateful for Ellen's guile.

Villette was published while Charlotte was in London. If she thought she had escaped having to fret about whether or not she loved Arthur Nicholls and whether or not he loved her, Harriet Martineau, first in a private letter and then in a public review of the book (again, already quoted), flung the subject before her with some force. Charlotte's fellow novelist was blunt and to the point, and innocently touched what must have been a very tender nerve: 'I do not like the love, either the kind or the degree of it; and its prevalence in the book, and effect on the action of it.' (Harriet Martineau to CB, February 1853)

Charlotte retorted:

> *'I know what love is as I understand it; and if man or woman should be ashamed of feeling such love, there is there nothing right, noble, faithful, truthful, unselfish, as I comprehend rectitude, nobleness, fidelity, truth, and disinterestedness.'*
>
> (CB to Harriet Martineau, February 1853)

Yet such criticisms must have forced her to survey her own situation. It was all very well for Harriet Martineau to claim that Lucy Snowe's predicament in *Villette* did not reflect real life. Charlotte knew that it did, and certainly of the 'real life' of her present circumstances. *Villette* drew attention to the problems of the single woman, and, as we have seen from Thackeray's letter about the novel, Martineau was not the only one to connect the novel with its author. In March another writer, Catherine Winkworth, who had met Charlotte at Mrs Gaskell's house in Manchester, asked some pertinent questions in a letter to a friend:

> *'Villette' makes one feel an extreme reverence for anyone capable of such deep feeling and brave endurance and truth, but it makes one feel 'eerie', too, to be brought face to face with a life so wanting in* Versöhnung *[reconciliation] as Germans would say. I wonder if Miss B. is so, and I wonder too, whether she ever was in love, surely she could never herself have made love to anyone, as all her heroines, even Lucy Snowe, do . . .*
>
> (Catherine Winkworth to Emma Shean, 23 April 1853)

However loudly she might protest that her works were pure fiction, Charlotte Brontë does seem to have revealed a good deal about herself in this novel, and at least to have set people wondering about the circumstances of her life.

Apart from Harriet Martineau's critical review, *Villette* was well received, George Eliot recording her delight in finding it better even than *Jane Eyre*. Charlotte was relieved at the book's reception, not least because she knew that reading the favourable notices would give her father great pleasure – and, it might be added, take his mind off other things. He promptly wrote to Charlotte's publisher suggesting that a review copy ought to go to the *Leeds Mercury* for he wanted his daughter's work to attract as much local notice as possible. Perhaps he thought thereby to spike Nicholls's guns by giving Charlotte as much publicity in the locality as possible and thereby emphasising the gulf which he believed should exist between a very successful author and an impoverished curate: in short, broadcasting what he saw as the unsuitable nature of any such match between Charlotte and Arthur.

It was while Charlotte was in London that Nicholls applied to be a missionary in Australia, an application which, as we have seen, he withdrew two months later. There must have been some communication between him and Charlotte's father, for we find the latter supporting his application, perhaps glad to have the chance to be rid of this troublesome curate:

> *[Nicholls] behaved himself, wisely, soberly, and piously – He has greatly promoted the interest of the National and Sunday Schools; he is a man of good abilities and strong constitution – he is very discreet etc . . .*
>
> (PB to the Society for the Propagation of the Gospel,
> 31 January 1853)

Others were to comment that Patrick Brontë had often remarked that 'should he [Nicholls] leave him he should not know how to supply his place'. He was soon to discover the truth of this remark.

Charlotte returned to Haworth with reinforcements, having arranged for Ellen Nussey to meet her at Keighley railway station and come back with her to stay at the parsonage for a few days. Now there would be no need for letters between them; they could gossip about suitors to their hearts' content. What did they do as they passed the door of Nicholls's lodgings in the narrow lane leading to the parsonage? Did they hurry past, or did they linger in case they caught a glimpse of him as he went into the school next door or set off with Flossy out to the moor ? They could hardly pretend he didn't exist.

Papa's Dilemma

Patrick Brontë in his seventy-sixth year, once more losing his sight and in poor general health, found himself in a state of confusion and uncertainty. The younger generation, yet again, were letting him down. He had lost his wife after only eight years together, the health of five of his children had failed – one of them significantly contributing to his own destruction – and now there was, it seemed, a threat that the stay and support of his last years, Charlotte, might leave him. He could not have foreseen that Arthur Nicholls would prove both trustworthy and honourable, and would look after the older man until his death; nor could he have known in February 1853 that Arthur would agree, on marrying Charlotte, to stay in Haworth and to live in the parsonage. While Charlotte was busy convincing herself by repeatedly telling Ellen that she *did not* and *could not* love Arthur Nicholls, Patrick Brontë must have been equally busy fretting about what his last years might bring. Just when he could bathe in the reflected glory of his daughter's literary fame, of which he was exceptionally proud, the wretched Nicholls had undermined the foundation of that pleasure and security. Moreover, Charlotte's success, great though it was, was not the sole source of Patrick Brontë's pride and comfort. Beside her books on his study shelves were those of her sisters, in first and subsequent editions, placed next to his own early writings in prose and verse. As he savoured the reviews of *Villette* he could also take pride in the body of work that his daughters had produced. He must have known that the family had found a place in history. Was not his daughter Charlotte a guest at William Thackeray's dinner table? Was she not sought after by the leading educationist of his day (and writer and doctor to boot), Sir James Kay-Shuttleworth, and was she not the friend of another leading novelist, Elizabeth Gaskell? This surviving child had achieved all that he, as a heroically aspiring undergraduate of peasant stock and background, had reached for at the start of the century. He had plenty to lose as his life drew to a close. If only his curate had not raised the 'obnoxious matter'. Just as Branwell had let his father down, now this other young man, upon whom he had long depended, had destroyed his peace of mind. All the old man had left was words, and these he deployed at every opportunity to hold on to his daughter and to the comforts, mental as well as physical, of his last years. Did he really have to face losing his only surviving child ? He knew the answer, no wonder he lost his temper!

While Patrick Brontë worried, Charlotte seems to have played hide-and-seek with Arthur some two months after she had rejected him:

We had the parsons to supper as well as to tea. Mr Nicholls demeaned himself not quite pleasantly. I thought he made no effort to struggle with his dejection, but gave way to it in a manner to draw notice; the Bishop was obviously puzzled by it. Mr Nicholls also showed temper once or twice in speaking to Papa. Martha was beginning to tell me of certain 'flaysome' looks also, but I desired not to hear of them. The fact is I shall be most thankful when he is well away; I pity him, but I don't like that dark gloom of his. He dogged me up the lane after the evening service in no pleasant manner; he stopped also in the passage after the Bishop and the other clergy were gone into the room, and it was because I drew away and went upstairs that he gave that look which filled Martha's soul with horror. She, it seems, meantime, was making it her business to watch him from the kitchen door. If Mr Nicholls be a good man at bottom, it is a sad thing that nature has not given him the faculty to put goodness into a more attractive form. Into the bargain of all the rest he managed to get up a most pertinacious and needless dispute with the Inspector [of Schools], in listening to which all my old unfavourable impressions revived so strongly, I fear my countenance could not but show them.

(CB to Ellen Nussey, 4 March 1853)

How exciting it must have been. Servants watching from kitchen doors and telling what they could see; a lady having to rush upstairs to avoid a man's protestations; or having to hurry up the lane from church because he was 'dogging' her steps. Beatrice in Shakespeare's *Much Ado About Nothing* could have written such a letter. If we take a kindlier view of Nicholls's behaviour than did Charlotte, we might see a clergyman so desperately in love that he dares to misbehave before his bishop – not a common aberration in clergy; a frustrated suitor who desperately seeks a look of reassurance, or a word of comfort. All of which is denied to him by the loved one's alacrity in excusing herself, scuttling off, one suspects, to put pen to paper and recount the latest development to her confidante, Ellen Nussey. This was not the breathless behaviour of teenaged young-sters, Charlotte was approaching her thirty-seventh birthday when she was fleeing from 'flaysome' looks. Indeed, it might have seemed more likely for Charlotte to have watched the behaviour of the young servant, Martha, with a curate, rather than the servant her mistress.

Arthur Nicholls was not going to be put off, however, either by Charlotte's behaviour or her father's. His resignation stood, and although he abandoned his dramatic plan to flee to Australia (possibly a ploy that failed, for no one seems to have rushed forward urging him not to go), he found a post as curate at Kirk Smeaton. Although this might have seemed a victory for Patrick Brontë, Arthur's new parish was still in Yorkshire, and not *too* far from Haworth:

You ask about Mr Nicholls. I hear he has got a curacy, but do not yet know where. I trust the news is true. He and papa never speak. He seems to pass a desolate life. He has allowed late circumstances so to act upon him as to freeze up his manner and overcast his countenance not only to those immediately concerned but to everyone. He sits drearily in his rooms. If Mr Croxton, or Mr Grant, fellow curates in the area, or any other clergyman calls to see, and as they think, to cheer him, he scarcely speaks. I find he tells them nothing, seeks no confidant, rebuffs all attempts to penetrate his mind. I own I respect him for this. He still lets Flossy go to his rooms and takes him to walk. He still goes over to see Mr Sowden [a local clerical colleague and friend of Arthur Nicholls. It was he who eventually conducted their marriage service] sometimes, and, poor fellow, that is all. He looks ill and miserable. I think and trust in heaven that he will be better as soon as he gets away from Haworth. I pity him inexpressibly, we never meet nor speak, nor dare I look at him, silent pity is all I can give him, and as he knows nothing about that, it does not comfort. He has now grown so gloomy and reserved, that nobody seems to like him, his fellow curates shun trouble in that shape, the lower orders dislike it. Papa has a perfect antipathy to him, and he, I fear, to papa. Martha hates him. I think he might almost be dying and they would not speak a friendly word to or of him. How much of all this he deserves I can't tell, certainly he never was agreeable or amiable, and is less so now than ever, and alas! I do not know him well enough to be sure there is truth and true affection, or only rancour and corroding disappointment at the bottom of his chagrin. In this state of things I must be and I am, entirely passive. *I may be losing the purest gem, and to me far the most precious life can give – genuine attachment – or I may be escaping the yoke of a morose temper. In this doubt conscience will not suffer me to take one step in opposition to papa's will blended as that will is with the most bitter and unreasonable prejudices. So I must leave the matter where we leave all important matters. [by which Charlotte meant God's hands]*

(CB to Ellen Nussey, 6 April 1853)

How did Charlotte know all this? It is a report worthy of a private detective! Did Flossy report back? How did she know how Nicholls responded to his fellow curates' visits? Had she asked them ? Clearly she went to some lengths to find out what was going on and precisely what Nicholls's state was. If it had been his intention that she should go to such trouble, then his plan was clearly effective, for it is almost impossible to believe that Charlotte could have known so much without a considerable amount of questioning as well as the inevitable gossip. The account is too detailed to be the sole product of the latter; we have a complete picture of the man, and incidentally of 'love in idleness', of the melancholic spurned lover.

There are, too, other more serious implications here. While her father, Martha and others railed against the man and were indifferent to his fate, Charlotte could not be. She had once before been indifferent to a man's suffering, and that ostensibly from the same cause. She had watched her brother Branwell pine to the point of death for the love of a woman he could not have. She had been scornful of his weakness and unmoved by his suffering. It is not too fanciful to see this note of concern in her letter to Ellen. Charlotte had been greatly troubled, when Branwell had died, by the part she had played in trivialising the tragic importance to the young man of his bitter loneliness. Remorse over that failing in her sisterly compassion might have been a spur to her in wanting to know what was happening to Nicholls, and in caring, as the letter shows she clearly did, about him as a fellow human being. Furthermore, if the letter tells us nothing else, it shows her impatience with her father's unreasonable attitude and the struggle she had to balance her sense of duty towards him with her own feelings.

There is no other record of what Nicholls was feeling, thinking, or indeed doing, during these months. It is not, perhaps, too unrealistic to imagine that the informants who kept Charlotte so well supplied with news might have conveyed back to him news of the effect his presence and behaviour were having in the parsonage. After all, the curates had been present when Nicholls 'puzzled' the Bishop by his conduct, and must have had some little curiosity about the way things were developing. Nor is it only servants who gossip.

Information about the entire situation now becomes scarcer, as Charlotte soon left Haworth once more, only too pleased to accept an invitation to stay with Elizabeth Gaskell in Manchester. Both novelists had books newly in print, Mrs Gaskell's *Ruth*, like *Villette*, also receiving favourable reviews. There is, however, a nice irony in Charlotte having to think of 'Ruth' and her loneliness amid the alien corn, while she was away from Haworth, a resonance that with her knowledge of the Bible she could not have overlooked. Charlotte seems to have had an almost reckless disregard for her father's health during this time. Normally her fears for Papa provided her with her best reason for staying at home. Papa, however, equally anxious that she be out of Nicholls's sight, encouraged her to be with her literary peers as much as possible.

In May she was back home and relating to Ellen her latest encounter with Arthur:

'The east winds about which you inquire have spared me wonderfully till to-day, when I feel somewhat sick physically, and not very blithe mentally. I am not sure that the east winds are entirely to blame for this ailment. Yesterday was a strange sort of day at church. It seems as if I were to be punished for my doubts about the nature and truth of poor Mr Nicholls's regard . Having ventured on Whit-Sunday to stop for the sacrament, I got a lesson not to be repeated. He struggled, faltered, then took command over himself, stood before my eyes and in the sight of all the communicants, white, shaking, voiceless. Papa was not there, thank God! Joseph Redman [the parish clerk] spoke some words to him. He made a great effort, but could only with difficulty whisper and falter through the service. I suppose he thought this would be the last time; he goes either this week or the next. I heard the women sobbing round and I could not quite check my own tears. What had happened was reported to Papa either by Joseph Redman or John Brown; it excited only anger, and such expressions as 'unmanly driveller'. Compassion or relenting is no more to be looked for from Papa than sap from firewood.

I never saw a battle more sternly fought with the feelings than Mr Nicholls fights with his, and when he yields momentarily, you are almost sickened by the sense of strain upon him. However he is to go, and I cannot speak to him or look at him or comfort him a whit, and I must submit. Providence is over all, that is the only consolation.

(CB to Ellen Nussey, 16 May 1853)

There can be only one reason why Charlotte was unable to 'speak to him or look at him or comfort him,' and that was Patrick Brontë's adamant opposition to Nicholls and her complete subjugation to her father's wishes. The letter does show, however, her increasing frustration at feeling pity for a suffering person and being denied the opportunity to help. One can only wonder what the tears of the 'women sobbing round' were for. Could they have been prompted by the touching story of frustrated love being played out before them? And what was the reason, if she did not love Nicholls, for the tears that Charlotte had to choke back? Were they, perhaps, the tears of a daughter who dare not gainsay her father? In the event, Patrick Brontë showed a poor understanding of the compassionate impulse in his daughter's novels if he thought that his rule of word – and indeed his contempt for Nicholls – would totally control her. We shall see just how much longer Charlotte was to be content to 'submit' to her father's will. In each letter to Ellen, her sympathy for Nicholls seems to grow, while her references to 'Papa' increasingly dwell on his prejudice and his unreasonable outbursts.

Two more letters complete the tale of Nicholls's last days as the unwelcome and 'unmanly driveller'. The first shows Charlotte as well informed as ever:

I cannot help feeling a certain satisfaction in finding that the people here are getting up a subscription to offer a testimonial of respect to Mr Nicholls on his leaving the place. Many are expressing both their commiseration and esteem for him. The churchwardens recently put a question to him plainly. Why was he going? Was it Mr Brontë's fault or his own? 'His own,' he answered. Did he blame Mr Brontë? 'No he did not: if anybody was wrong it was himself.' Was he willing to go? 'No! it gave him great pain.' Yet he was not always right. I must be just. He shows a curious mixture of honour and obstinacy; feeling and sullenness. Papa addressed him at the school-tea drinking, with constrained civility, but still with civility. He did not reply civilly; he cut short further words. This sort of treatment offered in public is what Papa never will forget or forgive; it inspires him with a silent bitterness not to be expressed. I am afraid both are unchristian in their mutual feelings. Nor do I know which of them is less accessible to reason or least likely to forgive.

It is a dismal state of things.

(CB to Ellen Nussey, 19 May 1853)

While Charlotte herself had witnessed Nicholls snub her father, it seems clear that she would not have known, verbatim, the exchange between the curate and the churchwardens if she had not had a clear interest in knowing.

A week or so later, Nicholls's departure from Haworth gave Charlotte a remarkable episode to relate:

You will want to know about the leave taking; the whole matter is but a painful subject, but I must treat it briefly. The testimonial was presented in a public meeting. Mr T. and Mr Grant [fellow curates] were there. Papa was not very well and I advised him to stay away, which he did. As to the last Sunday, it was a cruel struggle. Mr Nicholls ought not to have taken any duty. He left Haworth this morning at six-o'clock. Yesterday evening he called to render into Papa's hands the deeds of the National

Sunday School, and to say good-bye. They [servants] were busy cleaning, washing the paint etc. in the dining room, so he didn't find me there. I would not go into the parlour to speak to him in Papa's presence. He went out thinking he was not to see me, and indeed, till the very last moment, I thought it best not. But perceiving that he stayed long before going out at the gate, and remembering his long grief, I took courage and went out trembling and miserable. I found him leaning against the garden door in a paroxysm of anguish, sobbing as women never sob. Of course I went straight to him. Very few words were interchanged, those few barely articulate. Several things I should have liked to ask him were swept entirely from my memory. Poor fellow. But he wanted such hope and such encouragement as I could not give him. Still I trust he must know that I am not cruelly blind and indifferent to his constancy and grief. For a few weeks he goes to the South of England – afterwards he takes a curacy somewhere in Yorkshire, but I don't know where.

Papa has been far from strong lately. I dare not mention Mr Nicholls name to him. He speaks of him quietly and without opprobrium to others, but to me he is implacable on the matter. However, he is gone – gone – and that's an end of it. I see no chance of hearing a word of him in future, unless some stray intelligence comes through Mr Sowden or some other second hand source. In all this it is not I who am to be pitied at all, and of course nobody pities me. They all think, in Haworth that I have disdainfully refused him, etc. If pity would do Mr Nicholls any good, he ought to have and I believe has it. They may abuse me if they will; whether they do or not I can't tell.

(CB to Ellen Nussey 27 May, 1853)

As a piece of writing, this letter embodies all the characteristics of Charlotte's mature style, and is a fine example of her storytelling. For the rest, however, it is a heartbreaking piece of description. There can be little doubt that it was her father's attitude to Nicholls that so troubled her; this, however, was only one element in the circumstances she had come to find so trying. Patrick Brontë, for a variety of reasons, allowed his daughter little freedom. Mrs Gaskell, in her biography of Charlotte, observed how she deferred to him in every way :

Mr Brontë was a most courteous host . . . he never seemed to have lost the feeling that Charlotte was a child to be guided and ruled, when she was present; and she herself submitted to this with a quiet docility that half amused, half astonished me.

(Elizabeth Gaskell, *Life of Charlotte Brontë*, Chapter 13)

Clearly Charlotte was afraid to cross her father, and this had skewed her response to Arthur Nicholls from the first. Elizabeth Gaskell, however, and unlike so many other contemporary commentators, showed a liking for Nicholls, something which is most evident in the careful way in which she described the whole courtship episode when she came to record her dead friend's life:

> *One of the deepest interests of her life centres naturally round her marriage, and the preceding circumstances; but more than all other events . . . it requires delicate handling on my part, lest I intrude too roughly on what is most sacred to memory. Yet I have two reasons, which seem to me to be good and valid ones, for giving some particulars of the course of events which led to her few months of wedded life – that short spell of exceeding happiness. The first is my desire to call attention to the fact that Mr Nicholls was one who had seen her almost daily for years; seen her as daughter, a sister, a mistress and a friend. He was not a man to be attracted by any kind of literary fame. I imagine that this by itself might repel him when he saw it in the possession of a woman. He was a grave, reserved, conscientious man, with a deep sense of religion, and of his duties as one of its ministers.*
>
> (Elizabeth Gaskell, *Life of Charlotte Brontë*, Chapter 12)

No one is quite sure where Arthur Nicholls went after he left Haworth in May 1853, for he did not take up his duties at Kirk Smeaton until the following August. Away from Haworth for a time, he no longer appears in Charlotte's correspondence. The dutiful daughter had bent to her father's will, though at what cost to herself can only be conjecture. Shortly after Nicholls's departure things took a turn for the worse at the parsonage. Charlotte was confined to her bed for some ten days after succumbing to influenza, a remarkable parallel with what happened after her brother's death, when she was also ill. Her father suffered a stroke which left him for a time completely blind, and which must have focused Charlotte Brontë's mind on her plight. She may once have joked with Ellen that 'marriage might be defined as the state of two-fold selfishness'; perhaps she now thought otherwise. She must have realised how vulnerable and lonely she and her father were, and must also, if only momentarily, have wondered whether things might have been different.

Chapter Four

The Men in Charlotte Brontë's Life Before Arthur Nicholls

With Arthur Nicholls out of sight, it became a good deal easier for Charlotte to concentrate upon other aspects of her life. While Nicholls's life had centred without question upon the church at Haworth, the parsonage, and the church school, hers did not. She was, after all, a very successful novelist and something of a celebrity, however coyly she fled from recognition or lionisation. In the spring of 1853, Nicholls was not the only man in whom she showed more than a passing interest. While her father protested that she could do far better than marry a poor curate in Haworth – a comment which has come down to us *only* because Charlotte wrote it in a letter to Ellen Nussey – it is not too improbable that the well-established author might *herself* have had higher hopes. Correspondence with her publisher at this time gives credibility to such conjecturing. George Smith, the sole head of the firm of Smith, Elder & Co., publishers, of Cornhill, London, the man who had recognised at once the commercial, as well as the literary, potential of *Jane Eyre*, was a significant figure in Charlotte Brontë's life. And yet it is in 1853 that Smith features for the last time in Charlotte's story. It is possible, therefore, that his removal from her life was a key element in the way the last months of that year were to work out for her.

Together with her father, her brother Branwell and Constantin Heger, George Smith completes a quartet of influences that were of considerable, if not crucial, importance in her development. Charlotte had known Smith almost as long as she had known Arthur Nicholls. He must take his place in the imaginary gallery of men who influenced her, whom she admired, and upon whom she drew for the male characters in her novels.

Charlotte knew few people well, and fewer still intimately; those she did she clung to with an almost pathetic emotional tenacity. When a person became important to her, she built great hopes upon their affection and expected them to reciprocate her devotion in equal measure – hence her deep hurt when her 'master', Heger, abandoned her once she left Brussels. Charlotte needed people to look up to and whom she could trust, seeking passionate commitment and high integrity in those of whom she approved. William Thackeray failed in these respects, being far too frivolous in his attitude to writing for Charlotte's taste; indeed, almost as soon as she met him she berated him for his lack of serious purpose, the tiny woman holding the tall man spellbound.

The man who exerted the chief and perhaps the most enduring influence upon Charlotte Brontë was her father, Patrick. His wife's influence over Charlotte's early years – she was five when her mother died – was superseded by that of her father as sole parent. Her Aunt Elizabeth – 'Aunt Branwell' – who came to run the household after the death of the children's mother, was a mature forty-five at the time, and would always be seen as an aunt rather than a parent by all the Brontë children except the youngest, Anne, who was a mere eighteen months when her mother died. Throughout Charlotte's life her father provided something of a role model in matters intellectual, political and educational. The story of his setting out to find himself an education, his early teaching and his success as a sizar at Cambridge, his ordination in the chapel of a royal palace, all impressed his daughter. His achievements were absorbed into family legend, and she kept them in mind throughout her life, taking pride in what her father had managed to do with his life, and acquiring a sense that through the struggle with formidable and seemingly insurmountable difficulties or disadvantages great things could be achieved, rich prizes won. She did not hesitate, when seeking her father's support for her plan to go to school in Brussels, to remind him of the example he had set:

> *Papa will perhaps think it a wild and ambitious scheme; but who ever rose in the world without ambition? When he left Ireland to go to Cambridge University, he was as ambitious as I am now. I want us all to go on. I know we have talents, and I want them to be turned to account.*
> (CB to Elizabeth Branwell, 29 September 1841)

The 'talents' to which this letter refers were inherited from Patrick Brontë: the gift of being able to play with words, to use them effectively; of having the concentration to persevere with composition and creative, imaginative writing both in prose and verse. Along with these talents Charlotte, perhaps even more than her sisters, inherited the need for an audience and thus the desire to publish. Where the Reverend Brontë, in his writing, was stiff and scholarly, however, always free with biblical quotations or Latin quips deployed with a classical scholar's wit, she was both more natural and less affected, more the storyteller than the pedant, a style she perfected in her prolific letter writing to friends. Given her debilitatingly low opinion of herself and her profound sense of her 'ugliness', writing would seem to have been her only hope. Here, behind the pen-name, that masculine disguise, she could overcome her plainness and her crippling lack of self-confidence and be received as she would have wished. This need to speak through another voice, to be seen in a different image, seems to have been among the impulses that drove her, almost compelled her, to write. Writing offered her control, as well as comfort.

It is easy to underestimate the influence that her father's career as a clergyman had upon Charlotte Brontë's life and writing. This influence is evident in the pages of all his children's writing, not least in the simple and obvious instance of their knowledge of church services, their familiarity with the Bible and their understanding of the day-to-day routine life of the clergy. There was, however, a more subtle and more important influence which tends to be overlooked.

However evangelical or 'low church' a parson might be, he is nevertheless a priest. As such he is a go-between, standing as intercessor between his earthly flock of parishioners and God; he connects the spiritual with the physical. When there was a landslide on 2 September 1824 on Crow Hill on the moors above Haworth, Patrick Brontë felt it incumbent upon himself to preach on the event, and to publish prose and verse accounts of the 'Act of God', to show the true meaning of this 'natural' phenomenon. He saw himself as the translator and explainer of God's laws, the preacher of the Word of God. When administering the Sacrament during Holy Communion, conducting a baptism, performing a marriage service, or presiding over a funeral, the priest is administering the sacraments of the Church; he acts as mediator between heaven and earth, between this world and the next. It is not an exaggeration to see this as standing between knowledge and faith, or between science and superstition. Thus stood Patrick Brontë for over forty years at Haworth. The topography of the township and the countryside in which it is set reinforced this singularity or 'betweenness'. The parsonage was the first house after the moor and before the village. It stood between the elements and society, a feature that did not escape Emily Brontë when she created the setting for *Wuthering*

Heights, that sustained and symbolic exploration of the meeting between elemental forces and those of civilisation. Isolated by his cloth, Patrick Brontë was also separated from his parish by the fact that he was without doubt the most highly educated person in Haworth, as well as being the most experienced in committee work and the best versed in law. It is easy to see that his whole family were therefore set apart in the parish, and that for want of social equals in the neighbourhood its members were to a large extent isolated and thrown back upon their own company and resources, a preoccupation that can be found in all the writings that his children ever published.

Patrick Brontë was a stern and outspoken clergyman, very much his own man, who possessed a high moral sense based upon what he saw as a biblical authority. He could be an exacting father, his own achievement in rising from poverty and ignorance to graduation and ordination tending to make him a difficult man to live up to. He was proud of what he had accomplished by his own efforts, and looked for similar energetic industry in his children. Never a man to suffer fools gladly, he took perhaps too great a pride in himself and in his judgement. His only son found him impossible to please. The father's confidence and Protestant zeal seem to have been matched by the son's inability to hold his life together in any circumstances. Patrick Brontë's proper sense of his own value in his ministry bore with it an equal shadow in Branwell's reckless ineptitude and self-indulgence. Finding his father impossible to keep up with, he tended to give up in everything, descending into a mire of self-pity.

Conceivably the only boy was at a disadvantage in the family, being challenged by his father's masculinity in a way that his sisters were not. Any challenge he made to his father's will would be direct, while the girls' waywardness could easily, given attitudes towards women in the early nineteenth century, be excused. Branwell's collision with his father was to be head-on. He would find his father's success a hard act to follow.

Charlotte Brontë greatly admired her father, inheriting his stoical resilience and his obstinacy of purpose. After the deaths of her brother and sisters, she found a way of living with him that suited them both and which seems to have worked admirably, she accepting the role of devoted, dutiful and caring daughter, while he fully exploited that of the elderly and often infirm parent. If, to modern eyes, this seems a demeaning life for a woman, let alone one as intelligent and strong-spirited as Charlotte, in the mid-1800s it was neither unusual nor thought to be in any way degrading.

Haworth Parsonage today, as seen from the front door of Arthur Nicholls's lodgings in the lane leading past the schoolroom.

ABOVE: A very early photograph of Haworth Parsonage at the time of the Brontës.

LEFT: View of Haworth Parsonage today, as seen from the graveyard. There were no trees to relieve the starkness of the burial ground during the Brontë family's lifetime.

RIGHT: The main street in Haworth as it is today.

A photograph of Reverend Arthur Bell Nicholls believed to have been taken
at the time of his marriage to Charlotte Brontë in 1854.

LEFT: Drawing from the foot of a letter that Charlotte sent to her friend Ellen Nussey in which she parodies herself as an 'ugly duckling' in contrast to her elegant friend.

ABOVE: The walls of the town of Conway, North Wales, whe Charlotte and Arthur Nicholls spent the first night of their honeymoon in a comfortable i

LEFT: View from Mr Brontë's bedroom showing the schoolro and Arthur Nicholls's lodgings

RIGHT: The main entrance to Gawthorpe Hall, Padiham, home of Sir James Kay and Lady Janet Shuttleworth. It is believed that Charlotte, now Mrs Nicholls, caught a chill by walking in the wet in thin shoes while staying her

RIGHT: Reverend Patrick Brontë
in old age, *circa* 1854. The high
silk scarf was worn to ward
off bronchitis.

LEFT: A view of the pulpit that
Patrick Brontë and Arthur Nicholls
shared, and from which the old man,
sole survivor of the Brontë family,
preached his last sermon.

She knew her father well, and while acknowledging his authority was not afraid to exert her independence; indeed, if anyone was able to set a course to disobey him, it was Charlotte. She always managed her life against his prejudices and with her own interests at heart. She bowed to him when it suited her, and never more so than when it was convenient for her purposes, when she would use him as a shield against anything she did not wish to confront or to do. That she used Patrick Brontë as a defence is clear from the way that her deep concern for his health, indisputably sincere, could be conveniently set aside when she wished to be away from Haworth. Dutiful as she was as his sole surviving child in his late years, she felt able to leave the parsonage to stay elsewhere as she wished, and if her own health permitted. After that evening of the 'obnoxious' proposal she had no difficulty in being away from Haworth for weeks rather than days.

From her father Charlotte understood the habitual dominance of the male, the husband, the parson, an authority deriving from St Paul and the traditions of the Church of England as well as from society's teaching at that time. Obedience was the order of the day at Haworth Parsonage. Patrick Brontë's authority derived from his unswerving faith and from biblical sanction; there could be no equivocation. Yet all his children challenged this, and none more so than his youngest child in her portrayal in *The Tenant of Wildfell Hall* of the spirited refusal of Helen Huntingdon to let either convention or the law prevent her from taking her child away from her decadent husband. Patrick Brontë's own beliefs about the natural authority of men over women are clearly set out in the closing paragraphs of one of his early published stories, 'The Maid of Killarney', where through the character of a clergyman he sets out advice to those about to marry. As this tale was meant to be educative we can be confident that it is indeed Patrick Brontë's beliefs that are represented.

> *... do not look forward to an uninterrupted flow of happiness. This is not the portion of mortals on this side eternity. Make up your minds for some difficulties ... let each look upon the other as the best earthly friend. And be not blind to faults on either side but cover them with a mantle of charity. Either never let your minds be ruffled at all, or be not angry at the same instant; let not the sun go down upon your wrath. Differ but seldom in your opinions; but if at any times you cannot agree, the law of God and nature requires, that the husband should bear the rule.*

(PB 'The Maid of Killarney', 1818)

Liberal and kindly though some of this advice might be, Patrick Brontë is nevertheless unequivocal about who is to be in charge: to him, the law of nature and of the Christian God clearly state that the *man* should hold sway, compelling his wife and children to bow before his judgement, his wisdom and his wishes. There were times, however, when the Reverend Brontë's sense of compassion led him to flout or overturn convention. At least once, he advised the wife of a drunken clergyman that her best course would be to leave him – to desert him, in fact. The wife did so, and returned some time later to express her thanks for this excellent, if unorthodox, advice. The ambiguity and complexity of life's problems was one of Patrick Brontë's favourite topics. (He once gave a lecture at the Mechanics' Institute at nearby Keighley with the beguiling title 'On the Influences of Circumstances'; sadly, the text is lost to us.) Elsewhere he spoke of the need to withhold judgement until 'all the circumstances of a case' had been taken into consideration. In this respect he was more liberal than most clergy of the day, and certainly more liberal than perhaps all the clerics in the novels his children wrote, whose uncharitable and hypocritical lack of kindness and tolerance combine to depict a judgemental and punitive Church.

Finally, it was from her father that Charlotte derived her own high moral sense, her unfailing belief that duty, once recognised, must be done. From him also, as we have seen, came her great love of literature and her fascination with the magic of words. In common with her brother and sisters, she also inherited his pride in learning, that sense of dignity derived from an intellectual curiosity and the habit of avid and eclectic reading.

The next most important male influence upon Charlotte must be that of her brother Patrick Branwell, the 'Branny' of the family nickname. Here we are dealing with a passionate relationship between congenial quick intelligences and wild reckless imaginations. The spoilt boy, always considered to be the one true genius of the family and destined for great things, was her closest and most constant playmate through the whole of her childhood. Like him, she drew and painted, like him she scribbled prose and verse, brought increasingly elaborate fantasy kingdoms into being and planned their elaborate political, social, military and romantic histories. Emily and Anne seem to have followed suit, with the 'Chief Genius Branni' and his co-genius, Charlotte, setting the pace. Either by chance or because they were so prolific, more of the juvenilia of Branwell and Charlotte has survived, comprising a veritable library of articles, histories and romances (indeed, nothing in prose survives of the kingdom of Gondal invented by Emily and Anne).

From their earliest childhood, it was Branwell who was dearest to Charlotte; when she was away at boarding school it was him she missed most pitifully, and yet as they grew up he was to betray her faith in him and her trust, and thereby cause her the deepest distress. His lack of self-discipline, his inability to keep any job or position that he undertook, his reckless and eventually dissolute decline, all grieved her to the point at which she renounced him, showing, in greater measure than her two sisters, a bitterness towards his idleness, and a complete absence of sympathy at all for his self-destruction by alcohol and opium. While, through her father's example, she knew a straight-backed, sober propriety and discipline, in her brother in his last years she saw weakness, self-indulgence and waste brought upon by a heedless disregard for convention or personal constraint. Branwell gave all his sister novelists an insight into 'the terrible effects of talents misused and faculties abused', as Charlotte put it in her 'Biographical Notice' of Anne. Much of the drunken and violent Arthur Huntingdon's appalling behaviour in *The Tenant of Wildfell Hall* must derive from Anne's observation of her sad brother.

Monsieur Heger's influence upon Charlotte, and to some degree upon Emily, was of a different order. In Constantin Heger Charlotte perceived all the virtues of her father in a younger man. Heger was thirty-two when she first met him, and she twenty-five. He, the scholar that Branwell would never be, the revolutionary educated in Paris, seemed, with his authority and learning, to be like her father and Branwell combined in one person. It is little wonder that Charlotte idolised him, was ready to set him upon a pedestal and then to fall completely under his spell. Nor should the atmosphere of fertility in Heger's household be overlooked. Madame Heger gave birth to her third child only six weeks after Charlotte and Emily arrived to live in her household; by the time Charlotte left in 1844 another child had been born. In Heger, Charlotte found a fit subject for her fantasies, with or without any encouragement from him. After her father and Branwell, Heger was without doubt the man who influenced her most; indeed, he obsessed her to such a degree that she was able, or was compelled, to write two complete novels exploring and embodying – if not exorcising – the influence that he had upon her.

By any account Patrick Brontë must be seen as the most dominant man in Charlotte Brontë's life, demanding unswerving love and obedience from his daughter. Whereas her brother had offered, and received, congenial companionship in imaginative play until his post-adolescent collapse, while Heger had offered the romantic and intense ideal beyond her reach, and Arthur Nicholls, at least until December 1852, had been the overlooked and taken-for-granted curate, her father's influence never diminished.

There was, however, a fourth man of more than a little influence in Charlotte Brontë's life. George Smith was her publisher, which by December 1853 meant that he was the publisher of a very successful female writer (though she still used the pen name, there was no longer any secret about 'Currer Bell's' identity) whose books had made his firm considerable sums of money. The professional relationship between author and publisher had blossomed since publication of *Jane Eyre* in 1847 into a genuine friendship. Parallel with Charlotte's letters to Ellen Nussey was an equally sustained correspondence with the Cornhill offices of Smith, Elder and with George Smith himself.

Charlotte's first meeting with Smith is well documented. He himself left a clear and amusing account of the unexpected appearance one day in the summer of 1848 of two 'ladies' in Smith, Elder's front office. When they entered his room, the bemused man saw

> *Two rather quaintly dressed little ladies, pale-faced and anxious-looking . . . one of them came forward and presented me with a letter addressed, in my own handwriting, to 'Currer Bell Esq.' I noticed that the letter had been opened, and said, with some sharpness, 'Where did you get this from?' 'From the post-office,' was the reply; 'it was addressed to me. We have both come that you might have ocular proof that there are at least two of us.'*
>
> (George Smith, *Cornhill Magazine*, New Series, ix, December 1900)

Thomas Newby, the disreputable publisher of *Agnes Grey* and *Wuthering Heights*, had been circulating the idea that all three 'Bell' authors were but one person, and that he was about to publish the next work by Currer Bell; in fact, Smith, Elder had agreed to publish that novel. Deciding that Newby had impugned their honour, Charlotte and Anne hurried to London to see Smith and prove their identity. In the event, George Smith and Charlotte both saw the comical side of this abrupt encounter. He was twenty-four and she thirty-two, and from the first, after the shock Smith had sustained on first meeting had subsided, their relationship was warm. The publisher must have realised at once that he not only had a bestselling author on his list, but was party to an intriguing and most unusual phenomenon – three women writers masquerading as men. He had only to learn that there was yet another secret 'Bell', who wished to remain anonymous in Haworth, to understand fully the unique nature of the Brontë sister-writers, two of whom had stood, trembling with nervous determination, before him. Enterprising young publisher that he was, he set about whirling the two quaint ladies about London, first to meet his mother and sisters, then to Covent Garden for the opera, until their heads spun and they were glad to scurry back to Haworth. They might at that moment have envied Emily her elected anonymity; on the other hand, they might have inwardly glowed at the fuss made of them, and at tasting for the first time what it was to be introduced to the London literary scene. It is, after all, one thing to dislike being lionised, it is quite another never to have experienced it. Relating the visit to the opera to her old schoolfriend Mary Taylor, Charlotte displayed her brilliance at creating a whole scene in a single paragraph. In contrast to the two Brontës, George Smith and his sisters were in full evening dress:

> *They must have thought us queer quizzical-looking beings, especially me in my spectacles. I smiled inwardly at the contrast which must have been apparent, between me and Mr Smith, as I walked with him up the crimson carpeted staircase of the Opera House and stood amongst a brilliant throng at the box door, which was not yet open, with a slight graceful superciliousness, quite warranted by the circumstances. Still I felt pleasurably excited, in spite of headache, sickness, and conscious clownishness; and I saw Anne was calm and gentle, which she always is.*
>
> (CB to Mary Taylor, 4 September 1848)

The scene might have been taken from an episode in one the imaginary kingdoms of Charlotte's childhood writings. Many of the special qualities of the author of *Jane Eyre* are here at work, including the juxtaposition of the humble with the extravagant, the meek with the self-assured, the narrator's sense of being an outsider, the balancing of all points of view. It is typical of Charlotte that she complained that the opera, Rossini's *The Barber of Seville*, was 'very brilliant', but that she fancied there were things she 'should like better'. Charlotte Brontë, on her first visit to London, her first performance at Covent Garden, her first meeting with her publisher, remains critical, anything but overwhelmed, the superficially timid, shy, parson's daughter in fact possessed of considerable confidence and self-assurance. Like Arthur Nicholls, she had hidden depths.

She must have intrigued George Smith. This tiny, bespectacled, plainly dressed woman had created Jane Eyre and Bertha Mason, had written of adultery and madness with such passion and power that her book had taken literary London by storm. He must have reflected on the incongruity of the contrast between the retiring writer and the strong, emotional narrative of the novel, and wondered about that other mysterious Bell who had created Heathcliff and Cathy. How often would such people come to his office in Cornhill?

While in London, Charlotte and Anne also visited William Smith Williams, an older member of George Smith's firm, the reader who had first recommended *Jane Eyre* for publication. It was the gracious and constructive letter that Williams had written when he rejected Charlotte's manuscript of *The Professor* that had encouraged her to complete *Jane Eyre* without delay. From that first letter Charlotte had sustained a warm and friendly correspondence with Williams, a correspondence that was to serve her well in the desperate months that were to follow their meeting. Williams, a retiring, sensitive man, and father to eight children, acted as a guide to London to the two sisters, inviting them to meet his wife and family in his 'humble but neat residence'. He was something of a favourite with Charlotte, possibly because she did not in her deeper being feel as overwhelmed by him socially as she did by George Smith. She found Williams's letters highly intelligent, his advice continually helpful; indeed, she came to trust him to such an extent that it is in letters to Williams that we have the clearest and most detailed accounts of the tragedies at Haworth during the next few months:

My Dear Sir,

. . . 'We have buried our dead out of our sight.' A lull begins to succeed the gloomy tumult of last week. It is not permitted us to grieve for him that has gone as others grieve for those they lose. The removal of our only brother must necessarily be in the light of a mercy rather than a chastisement. Branwell was his father's and his sisters's pride and hope in boyhood, but since manhood the case has been otherwise. It has been our lot to see him take a wrong bent; to hope, expect, wait his return to the right path; to know the sickness of hope deferred, the dismay of prayer baffled; to experience despair at last – and now to behold the sudden early obscure close of what might have been a noble career.

I do not weep for a sense of bereavement – there is no prop withdrawn, no consolation torn away, no dear companion lost – but for the wreck of talent, the ruin of promise, the untimely dreary extinction of what might have been a burning and a shining light. My brother was a year my junior. I had aspirations and ambitions for him once long ago – they have perished mournfully. Nothing remains of him but a memory of errors and sufferings. There is such a bitterness of pity for his life and death, such a yearning for the emptiness of his whole existence as I cannot describe. I trust time will allay these feelings . . . my unhappy brother never knew what his sisters had done in literature – he was not aware that they had ever published a line. We could not tell him of our efforts for fear of causing him too deep a pang of remorse for his own time misspent, and talents misapplied. Now, he will never *know. I cannot dwell longer on the subject at present – it is too painful.*

I thank you for your kind sympathy, and pray earnestly that your sons may do well, and that you may be spared the sufferings my father has gone through.

(CB to W.S.Williams, 2 October 1848)

Four days later she sent Williams another letter, again pondering over the meaning of her brother's death. Clearly this correspondence meant a great deal to Charlotte, for in it she was able to write of things that touched and troubled her most:

When I looked on the noble face and forehead of my dead brother (Nature had favoured him with a fairer outside, as well as a finer constitution than his sisters) and asked myself what had made him ever go wrong, tend ever downwards, when he had so many gifts to induce to, and aid in an upward course – I seemed to receive an oppressive revelation of the feebleness of humanity; of the inadequacy of even genius to lead greatness if unaided by religion and principle. In the value, or even the reality of these two things he would never believe till within a few days of his end, and then all at once he seemed to open his heart to a conviction of their existence and worth . . .

When the struggle was over – and a marble calm began to succeed the last dread agony – I felt as I had never felt before that there was peace and forgiveness for him in heaven. All his errors – to speak plainly – all his vices seemed nothing to me in that moment; every wrong he had done, every pain he had caused, vanished; his sufferings only were remembered; the wrench to the natural affections only was felt.

(CB to W.S.Williams, 6 October 1848)

Williams's role here would seem to be that of confessor, and Charlotte accordingly unburdens herself to him with great candour. Almost all her formal dealings with her publisher had been through this diffident, kindly man, with whom she had established a comforting relationship. The accumulated letters to him show a Charlotte altogether different from the woman who tittle-tattled so archly and mischievously with Ellen Nussey. Indeed, so great was her trust in William Williams that she was to write giving him the most frank descriptions of Emily's final illness, of Anne's decline, and of her own misery and desolation at their deaths.

The contrast between her implicit trust in this man with Charlotte's bitter disappointment in her brother could not be more eloquent. More perhaps than her father, whose personal tragedy and pain she had no wish to increase, she could confide in this sympathetic man, the first, after Heger, to appreciate fully her potential as a writer. Since Branwell, like the heroine's cousin John Reed in *Jane Eyre*, had proved to be set upon a course of self-indulgent excess, Charlotte sorely needed to be able to confide in a man whom she could trust; for her, there was no better way of doing this than through letters, which were both her life-line and rehearsals for the business of creative writing. The comparative isolation of Haworth increased the importance of letter writing for Charlotte. The hilltop township must have daily encouraged a withdrawal into an almost hermit-like seclusion, something exacerbated by the family's detachment from the community under the rigid social codes of the day, and while Emily welcomed this isolation, both Charlotte and Branwell had at times found it stifling. The youngest Brontë, Anne, however, found stability and purpose in work as a governess, even with all its drawbacks. She, unlike any other member of the family, managed to break free of the spell of their home, earning her living for some six years away from the place. Each member of the family had to deal with the thraldom of the parsonage and the beguiling companionship that their shared intelligence and gift for words encouraged. Charlotte reached out through her letters, and never more eloquently or frankly than in those she wrote to William Williams. He clearly had a place in the gallery of males she stored in her memory. Once more it was to an older, married man that Charlotte warmed.

To her father's authoritarian and old-fashioned stance (there was something archaic, even 'antique', about both his manners and his prose style); to Heger's heady intellectual and romantic appeal and ultimate neglect; to her brother's flawed erratic maturity; to all these may be added Williams's letters as examples of steady and compassionate understanding and a considerable intellectual grasp. For while her father would brook no disobedience, Heger would hear no pitying plea, and Branwell was unable to look beyond his own concerns, Williams offered a sustaining sympathy, a sympathy sorely needed by Charlotte.

One of her most poignant letters to Williams acknowledges the high regard in which she held him, and the importance of her correspondence with him:

My dear Sir,

In sitting down to write to you I feel as if I were doing a wrong and a selfish thing; I believe I ought to discontinue my correspondence with you till times change and the tide of calamity which of late days has set so strongly against us, takes a turn. But the fact is, sometimes I feel it absolutely necessary to unburden my mind. To Papa I must only speak cheeringly, to Anne only encouragingly, to you I may give some hint of the dreary truth.

Anne and I sit alone and in seclusion as you fancy us, but we do not study; Anne cannot study now, she can scarcely read; she occupies Emily's chair – she does not get well . . .

When we lost Emily I thought we had drained the very dregs of our cup of trial, but now when I hear Anne cough as Emily coughed [Anne was to die of the consumption that carried off every one of her siblings, including, in the end, Charlotte herself]. I tremble lest there should be exquisite bitterness yet to taste. However, I must not look forwards, nor must I look backwards. Too often I feel like one crossing an abyss on a narrow plank – a glance round might quite unnerve. So, circumstanced, my dear Sir, what claim have I on your friendship – what right to the comfort of your letters? My literary character is effaced for the time – and it is by that only that you know me – care of Papa and Anne is necessarily my chief present object in life to the exclusion of all that could give me interest with my Publishers or their connections – should Anne get better, I think I could rally and become Currer Bell once more – but if otherwise – I look no further – sufficient for the day is the evil thereof . . .

If you answer this write to me as you would to a person in an average state of tranquillity and happiness – I want to keep myself as firm and calm as I can . . .

(CB to W.S. Williams, 18 January 1849)

The theme of these letters written at this time is crucial to any understanding of Charlotte Brontë's state of mind when she came to weigh up the advantages and disadvantages of marrying Arthur Nicholls in 1853. Charlotte never fully recovered from the sudden loss of her sisters, which so abruptly removed the congenial companionship upon which she depended as if for breath itself. The three women had been inseparable, never truly happy out of each other's sight. Side by side they had sat and mended their brother's and father's shirts; together they had teased and giggled at the curates. At the very moment when they had realised their lifelong ambition, had all seen their manuscripts published, had held their own books in their hands and seen them reviewed, taken seriously as literature, tragedy had struck, destroying the loving company of women who had lived and worked so happily together. The well-matched companionship of equal talents and inventiveness was suddenly shattered. The fact that Charlotte had lost not only sisters, but sister-novelists, should never be underestimated. In the death of Emily it was the creator of Heathcliff and Cathy that she missed – we can only guess at the kind of company such an inventive, uncompromising artist would have been. In Anne she lost a sister-writer who had two novels in print while she only had the one. The call for reprints of *Wuthering Heights*, *Agnes Grey* and *The Tenant of Wildfell Hall* would be a reminder of her sisters' abilities and her own sad, sudden loss of companions, confidantes, competitors even. For Charlotte it must have suddenly been like thinking in a void, she must have known the bitter loneliness of a Robinson Crusoe yearning for the sound of voices. She was now alone at the table where she and her sisters had sewed their samplers, made their little books, toiled over intricate pencil drawings and delicate watercolours, and around which they walked for hours at a time, talking about their plots and the plans for the characters in their stories. To have lost all this so suddenly, within so few months, must have been unbearable. The bereaved and grieving father still had his parishioners, still had the work of the schools he oversaw, still had his daily offices to read. Charlotte had no such sustaining rituals, no institutional regime [other than a faith in a merciful Christian God] to follow. Her life had been a shared one, both in her organising of her sisters and in her mothering of them since the deaths of their mother and older sisters all those years earlier. At Branwell's death the girls would have had each other to cling to. To whom could Charlotte now turn? The pining dogs, her dead sisters' perplexed pets, would look to her, and in doing so would break her heart:

My dear Sir,

I am now again at home where I returned last Thursday. I call it home still – much as London would be called London if an earthquake should shake its streets to ruins . . . Papa is there – and two most affectionate and faithful servants [Tabitha Ayckroyd and Martha Brown] and two old dogs, in their way as faithful and affectionate – Emily's large house dog which lay at the side of her dying-bed, and followed her funeral to the vault, lying in the pew couched at our feet while the burial service was being read – and Anne's little spaniel. The ecstasy of these poor animals when I came in was something singular – at former returns from brief absence they always welcomed me, warmly – but not in that strange heart-touching way – I am certain they thought that, as I was returned, my sisters were not far behind – but here my sisters will come no more, Keeper may visit Emily's little bed-room as he stills does by day – and Flossy may look wistfully round for Anne – they will never see them again – nor shall I – at least the human part of me . . .

When evening darkens something within my heart revolts against the burden of solitude – the sense of loss and want grows almost too much for me. I am not good or amiable in such moments – I am rebellious . . . as to the night – could I do without bed – I would never seek it – waking I think of them – sleeping I dream of them . . .

(CB to W.S. Williams, 25 June 1849)

Charlotte Brontë never stopped dreaming of her dead sisters, nor did she ever stop thinking about them. The abruptness of their deaths, so close together, left her bereft of all companionship and support. Above all, she had lost the forum for discussion that the three of them had comprised, and with it the opportunity to try out her ideas. After Anne died her life became a flight from the reality of her bitter loneliness. It is easy to underestimate the shock she felt at finding herself the sole surviving child of the family. There was no aspect of her life that was not affected by loss. Faced with this, she took the only course open to a woman of such gallant and independent spirit. Her sanity depended on her writing. Since she was no longer a sister to anyone, she would revive Mr Currer Bell. Her literary alter ego now became more important to her than ever. Having endured the deepest grief and faced despair she took refuge in writing.

Soon after Anne's funeral in June 1849, Charlotte forced herself to set about completing the last novel that she had discussed with Emily, and which she had been working on since early in 1848. The story became increasingly haunted by her sisters, turning into a celebration of them. In what might be termed the alternative reality of the plot Charlotte acted out the return of a lost mother and the recovery of a very sick sister, two joys life had denied her. Through heroic application the novel *Shirley* was completed and sent off to London. The grieving woman could be the industrious man of her pen-name. The *author* could correspond with the *publisher*, the sister-no-more could find an identity in the world away from the parsonage. No longer could Charlotte say we 'are three sisters', the lone child and the only living writer of her generation in the house, she was now bitterly and finally alone.

All that was familiar now served to remind her of her great loss. The rooms of the parsonage were settings for scenes which could no longer take place, at every turn she would miss her sisters and brother. Her father's remoteness, habitually alone in his study or involved with parish affairs, left her further by herself . Where could she go in that house to avoid the empty chairs and the closed writing desks. How sour at times her success must have seemed; her sisters' books alongside hers on the shelf must have cried out in protest. Currer Bell now voyaged alone in the sea of the sisters' imaginations, there was no one to share, to laugh with or to compete against. Claiming Ellen Nussey as a surrogate sister was all right as far as it went, but it did not go far enough. Ellen had neither the intellect nor the love of literature that the Brontë children had developed from their earliest days; there were limits to the comfort she could bring Charlotte.

Flight, in the form of periodic absences from the parsonage, was one comfort, another was to have people to stay. Currer Bell's writing and correspondence with 'his' publishers offered Charlotte an escape, lifted her horizon beyond the parsonage and the parish.

The Need for Heroes

George Smith was a young man when Charlotte Brontë first met him. To her, however, he was an almost godlike figure. He was a publisher – moreover, he was the publisher who had approved the manuscript of *Jane Eyre* and published it. Charlotte, with her brother and sisters, had been brought up by her father to have heroes. The Duke of Wellington was the household's supreme hero (and inspired much of Charlotte's juvenilia); William Makepeace Thackeray was another (although Charlotte found him less satisfactory in real life), as was Sir Walter

Scott. There were to be connections with all three in George Smith's friendship with Charlotte: he presented her with a picture of Wellington, as he did another of Thackeray, to whom he also introduced her; he accompanied her on a trip to Scott's home at Abbotsford, in the Borders; and took her to the chapel of St James's Palace so that she could catch sight of the Duke of Wellington, who regularly worshipped there.

Clearly this was no ordinary relationship from any point of view. The device of the male pen-name, which had released Charlotte in no small measure from her loneliness, became even more important to her now that her 'brother' writers were dead, now that she was the only remaining Mr Bell. As that writer, she maintained a close contact with her publishers. George Smith even found himself given the role of a surrogate brother when, disguised as Mr and Miss Fraser, he and Charlotte visited a Dr J.P. Browne, a London phrenologist who provided them both with a 'character' based upon a phrenological examination of their heads. More important than the pseudo-scientific analysis Dr Browne provided was the significance of the mutual conspiracy. George Smith was joining in a Brontë game; whether or not it was at his suggestion or Charlotte's, he was now her conspirator in the make-believe, playing a reality into being as Ellen Nussey never could, but as Charlotte and her brother and sisters had done all the time. It is little wonder, therefore, that Charlotte's letters to Smith show a warm humour and a flirtatious frivolity that is found nowhere else in her correspondence. By playing brother and sister, however momentarily, Smith inevitably touched Charlotte's heart, gave her a comfort beyond that offered by any other man.

Her friendship with George Smith was slow to develop, however. At first her warmest letters were to Williams, and it was only after she had stayed with Smith's mother and sisters at their house in London that the relationship began to develop, a growing intimacy that can be traced in her letters step by step. Charlotte, as ever, could not maintain a cool relationship. As Harriet Martineau – and Constantin Heger – had discovered, she was apt to adore where she admired:

> *I thought her the smallest creature I had ever seen (except at a fair) and her eyes blazed as it seemed to me. She glanced quickly round . . . she held out her hand frankly and pleasantly. I introduced her, of course, to the family; and then came a moment which I had not anticipated. When she was seated by me on the sofa, she cast me up such a look – so loving,*

so appealing – that in connection with her deep mourning dress, and the knowledge that she was the sole survivor of her family, I could with utmost difficulty return her smile, or keep my composure. I should have been heartily glad to cry . . .

(Harriet Martineau, *An Autobiographical Memoir*, Chapter 12)

Vulnerable and guileless, Charlotte clearly needed protecting; indeed, it seemed impossible that so timorous a person from so enclosed a background could be the creator of the fire and passion of *Jane Eyre*. For her part, Charlotte tended to keep people in clearly defined roles. Ellen Nussey was her close intimate female friend; Papa was simply Papa; Branwell a ne'er-do-well, a dissolute drunkard; Williams someone whom she respected and in whom, to a degree, she could confide; George Smith was her publisher; Arthur Nicholls just her father's curate. It was only when she drew close to people, over time and in shared situations, that their role and their importance to her became defined. Again, it is conceivable that this might have been, at least to a certain extent, a product of her myopia, that tendency to generalise about things (and thus perhaps about people) that she could not clearly see until she drew close and saw fully what was before her. Only close scrutiny would lead her to understanding, yet her shyness meant that there would be few in her life to whom she drew close, and to those few she clung with the tenacity of a limpet. It was this that had frightened Madame Heger who, possessed of a watchful nature, had seen clearly how infatuated Charlotte had become with her husband Constantin. Jane Eyre is just such a person, someone passionately seeking love; seeking special friend-ships – never passing aquaintanceships with those she meets; someone who yearns for and pursues release from the lonely imprisonment of solitary living.

Charlotte Brontë first stayed with the Smith family in November of 1849, less than a year after Emily's death, and only a few months after Anne's. She was moved to find herself once more in the midst of a family and to see her publisher as the brother to his sisters, irresistibly confronting her own isolation. As was her custom, she reported her progress with the Smiths to Ellen Nussey:

Mrs Smith received me at first like one who had received the strictest orders to be scrupulously attentive. I had fires in my bedroom evening and morning, two wax candles, etc., and Mrs Smith and her daughters seemed to look upon me with a mixture of respect and alarm. But all this is changed . . . the alarm and the estrangement are quite gone. She treats me as if she liked me, and I begin to like her much; kindness is a potent heartwinner.

(CB to Ellen Nussey, 4 December 1849)

Clearly many who met Charlotte Brontë saw her as someone needing care. George Smith, who had met Anne when she and Charlotte had impetuously arrived in his office, seemed particularly sensitive to her sadness. Charlotte warmed to him as she saw him in his home with his sisters, as she made clear in her letter to Ellen: 'I had not judged too favourably of her son on first impression; he pleases me much. I like him better as a son and brother than a man of business.'

Here Charlotte was acknowledging her own habit of mind. She first saw people in their role or station, as entities in the world. A publisher was such an entity, a man of business; the man amongst his sisters she warmed to. All things connected with family living, with homes, appealed to her. In her grieving over the loss of her sisters she was susceptible to the comforts of sibling companionship. She clearly revelled in the warmth of Mrs Smith's welcome and the attentions of the 'publisher's' sisters. Her letter of thanks to the former after her return to Yorkshire speaks of sisterly if not motherly kindnesses:

> . . . *Tell Miss Smith that her little boots are a perfect treasure of comfort; they kept my feet quite warm the whole way.*
>
> *It made me sad to leave you; regretful partings are the inevitable penalty of pleasant visits . . .*

(CB to Mrs Smith, 17 December 1849)

Included with this letter was a special note for George, a note that already displays the tone of light and humorous badinage that was to grow over the next few years:

> *My dear Sir,*
>
> *I should not feel content if I omitted writing to you as well as to your mother, for I must tell you as well as her how much the pleasure of my late visit was enhanced by her most considerate attention and goodness. As to yourself, what can I say ? Nothing. And it is as well; words are not at all needed . . .*
>
> *Currer Bell bids you farewell for the present.*

(CB to George Smith, 17 December 1849)

The young man, wittingly or unwittingly was being cast in a playful role by his successful author. In him Charlotte had perhaps found a surrogate brother, and one who, moreover, was making a success of his life, while caring for his sisters in a way that Branwell had never done. George Smith was a man whom she could admire and respect. The whole of London's literary scene was open to him; to be part of his household, however briefly, would be heady stuff for the shy Northern writer.

It was during this first stay with the Smiths that Charlotte seems to have decided to acknowledge that she was indeed 'Currer Bell'. This was unavoidable when she met Thackeray at dinner in the Smiths' house, but she herself initiated a meeting with Harriet Martineau that showed a willingness for her identity to be known at least in London literary circles. In a letter to William Williams, Charlotte showed how hard she found the return to her lonely state in Haworth, and at the same time demonstrated the almost fantastical way in which she enhanced events to make them more enthralling in her memory:

> *My dear Sir,*
>
> *I am again at home; and after the first sensation consequent on returning to a place more dumb and vacant than it once was, I am beginning to feel settled . . .*
>
> *Brief as my visit to London was, it must for me be memorable. I sometimes fancied myself in a dream – I could scarcely credit the reality of what passed. For instance, when I walked into the room and put my hand into Miss Martineau's, the action of saluting her and the fact of her presence seemed visionary. Again when Mr Thackeray was announced, and I saw him enter, looked up at his tall figure, heard his voice, the whole incident was truly dreamlike, I was only certain it was true because I became miserably destitute of self-possession.'*
>
> (CB to W.S.Williams, 19 December 1849)

Clearly this dreamland was Charlotte's refuge, her escape from the heavy reality of her loss. The manner in which she heroically completed *Shirley* so soon after Anne's death, and the vigour with which she first corresponded with Smith, Elder and then visited the Smiths, indicate a desperate drive for some kind of normality, even sanity. Life as the only daughter in the lonely house just would not do, it was not bearable. Only through Currer Bell could Charlotte Brontë go on. Whatever the original reason for assuming the Bell persona, whether it was solely to disguise the fact that they were female, the device now helped its author in a particular and sustaining way. Charlotte's 'playing' nature, seen in that imaginative and creative play that she and Branwell had originated and shared with Emily and Anne, was now a necessity. Meetings with such renowned authors as Martineau and Thackeray were at once translated into more than ordinary events; for Charlotte they were epiphany-like moments as magical and wonderful as they were actual. In the same spirit did the playful correspondence with George Smith develop. Not since her happy childhood days with Branwell had she indulged in such teasing compositions. The Smith family became uniquely important to Charlotte, Mrs Smith even provoking Mr Currer Bell to knit a pair of baby socks. Both George Smith and his mother were metamorphosed into the Bretton family, important characters in *Villette*, where their significance to Charlotte is eloquently displayed. The Brettons celebrate all the virtues of the 'good' family, a sustaining refuge without which the heroine, Lucy Snowe, could not manage. Just as Haworth Parsonage, tragically empty, was for Charlotte peopled only by memories and the creations of her imagination, so in *Villette* she interwove her real experiences with her imagined characters and their dreamt-up world.

It is easy to forget just who it was that Charlotte had lost. Her sister Emily was one of history's most remarkable writers, her novel *Wuthering Heights* being generally considered a work of genius. It was the fine poet, the author of *Wuthering Heights*, that Charlotte missed, and the degree of that loss should not be underrated. When Charlotte claimed that she, the sole survivor, was the least promising of the Reverend Brontë's children, she truly meant just that. She was not being falsely modest when she described her talent as second to Emily's, perhaps even to Anne's (certainly the latter's ability to make her way in the world, to live among people, was greater than her brother's or either of her sister's). Discussing the plot and plans for a novel with Emily Brontë must have been quite an exercise, one not lightly to be undertaken, for as a critic she was a truly daunting concept. This is the centre of the Brontë uniqueness. By no stretch of the imagination can that family be termed ordinary, their talents and creative energy are without parallel in literature. It is impossible to imagine two novelist sisters for Jane Austen, only the Mozart or Bach families offer any comparison and that in music.

In the light of the Brontës' uniqueness, their extraordinary talents and creative energy, it becomes possible to see why Charlotte hesitated when Arthur Nicholls proposed to her. He was a reader of her work, not a fellow writer. As she kept Ellen Nussey firmly within her role of lifelong intimate, but would 'put her hands over her ears' if her friend ever read out loud to her, so she saw the curate as just another tedious assistant to her father. She reached out in her loss to those who understood literature, to those who shared the writer's gifts and torments. She needed recognition in the world of artistic creation, compelled to go on along the path that the three young women had travelled together. It was now up to her and her alone to carry on the creative processes that the four children had perfected in their play from their nursery days until – for the three sisters, at least – the days of publication and (albeit anonymous) recognition.

Turning her back on Haworth, Charlotte Brontë eagerly sought new friends. She found them in Mrs Gaskell, Harriet Martineau, W.S. Williams, George Smith and his family, and even, although with great reluctance, Sir James Kay-Shuttleworth, MD, a Lancashire baronet who had been the first secretary to the National Education Committee, was an aspiring novelist as well as a social reformer, and who sought her out in Haworth and pursued her as an author with whom he wished to be closely acquainted. At this time it counted against Arthur Nicholls that he was so closely connected with Haworth. While trips to London were available and Mrs Gaskell was happy to receive her in Manchester, Charlotte willingly fled, finding new friends, and increasingly friends who knew her as Currer Bell, the novelist, not as Charlotte Brontë the bereaved sister. Pursued by loneliness, she was nourished by the idea that her life as a writer, as Currer Bell, might be more bearable than life as Charlotte Brontë, only surviving child of the Reverend Patrick Brontë. And so at times it was, though not without a great struggle with periods of ill health, with the haunted emptiness of the parsonage rooms, and with the pining of her dead sisters' dogs. As late as three and a half years after Anne's death, Charlotte was still writing of her loss; manifestly, hers was not a pain that time could diminish. Writing to George Smith about the difficulty she was experiencing in trying to complete *Villette*, she is eloquent on the subject of her creative isolation:

> *You must notify honestly what you think of 'Villette' when you have read it. I can hardly tell you how I hunger to hear some opinion beside my own, and how I have sometimes desponded, and almost despaired, because there was no one to whom I could read a line, or of whom to ask counsel. 'Jane Eyre' was not written under such circumstances, nor*

were two thirds of 'Shirley'. I got so miserable about it, I could bear
no allusion to the book. It is not finished yet, but now I hope.'
(CB to George Smith, 30 October 1852)

There were people to read to, of course. What Charlotte meant,
however, was no Branwell, no Anne, and particularly no Emily. She
had lost those who had habitually provoked her and, as it were, fired
her with the energy to write, that extraordinary group of exacting yet
congenial imaginations which are the essential element in the mystery
that is the Brontës' creativity. Of the three sisters, only Charlotte had
to work on her own. However secretive Emily and Anne might have
been, the stimulus of other minds was always present for them. Their
books were written alongside Charlotte's, driven by the enlivening
provocation of competition and 'egging on' that the children of the
family had perfected. It is little wonder that Charlotte so eagerly
sought George Smith's opinion, needed his friendship, and seemed
to welcome the idea of pretending that he was her brother. Since her
sisters' deaths she had written in an empty room, as if in a vacuum,
lacking all encouragement or resonance. Recognition of this isolation
may help us to understand her reservations about marrying Arthur
Nicholls. He was fixed in her mind as one of the preposterous curates
of *Shirley*, one of those whom, with Emily and Anne, she had
habitually giggled at and ridiculed. If she missed her sisters' advice
about writing, how much more must she have felt its absence over
whether or not she should marry a curate. It is scarcely any wonder
that she left the end of *Villette* provocatively inconclusive. In that novel
she defers the idea of marriage for the heroine beyond the ending;
indeed, she only allows Lucy Snowe the luxury of knowing she is
loved at the very end of the long story. Lucy's loneliness and regrets
dominate the book; any happiness has to be provided by the reader's
imagination.

In her letters from 1849 through to 1852, Charlotte rehearses again
and again the difficulty she faced living in the parsonage without her
sisters. We can be pleased that she had Miss Wooler and Ellen Nussey
beside her at the altar rail for her own wedding, how much more she
would have liked it to have been her sisters, and for her brother to have
given her away when her father had felt unable! But that, as Charlotte
would remind us, could only be an event 'in dreamland', where so
many things would be different. The house had become a confining
cell filled with memories. Her duty towards her father, her loyalty
to him, meant that she was inexorably fixed. She was as inseparable

from the parsonage as her father, but whereas once the companionship of her sisters sustained her, now the silences of solitude would torment her.

Success as a writer gave her a measure of financial independence, which in turn enabled her to get away from Haworth, to buy train tickets and hire gigs to take her from the station to wherever she was staying. Otherwise the walls of the dining room were like those of the cells of the nuns she described in her writing with such dread.

In the September immediately after Anne's death, Charlotte set out her situation in a letter to Williams:

> *The two human beings who understood me, and whom I understood, are gone. I have some that love me yet, and whom I love without expecting, or having a right to expect, that they shall perfectly understand me. I am satisfied; but I must have my own way in the matter of writing. The loss of what we possess nearest and dearest to us in this world produces an effect upon the character: we search out what we have left that can support and, when found, we cling to it with a hold of new-strung tenacity. The faculty of imagination lifted me when I was sinking, three months ago; its active exercise has kept my head above waters since; its results cheer me now, for I feel they have enabled me to give pleasure to others. I am thankful to God who gave me the faculty; and it is for me a part of my religion to defend this gift and profit by its possession.*
>
> (CB to W.S.Williams, 28 September 1849)

In this most revealing passage, Charlotte sets out the central tenets that she sought to uphold. One is a genuine sense that God would direct her path, that her inadequate mortal understanding was, fortunately, not all that guided her through life. Above all, however, she writes of the sustaining help of her 'faculty of imagination'. This was her true centre. Charlotte was always able to metamorphose life, with its complexities and harsh realities, into the more manageable metaphors of art, the dream world of her stories offering an alternative existence where justice might be found and tragedy overcome, where life's harshest experiences could be redeemed – the transient reality being given a kind of immortality that would long outlive its author.

Her purpose in her writing was not didactic, although critics have often levelled that charge at her. She rebuked Ellen Nussey for labelling her a 'teacher'. In a letter where she tells of *Shirley* being reviewed in French in a cosmopolitan Parisian magazine, she is emphatic:

I am no teacher – to look on me in that light is to mistake me – to teach is not my vocation – what I am it is useless to say – those whom it concerns feel and find it out. To all others I wish to be only an obscure, steady-going, private character.

(CB to Ellen Nussey, 22 November 1849)

The following spring Charlotte offered a further revelation about her beliefs in a letter consoling a friend at the death of her mother:

We should never shrink with cowardice from the contemplation of Death but after a near view, and actual contact with that King of terrors it is not good to be left unoccupied and solitary to brood over his awful lineaments. Often when I am alone, I try with all my might to look beyond the grave, to follow my dear sisters and my poor brother to that better world where – I trust – they are all now happy, but still, dear Amelia, I cannot help recalling all the details of the weeks of sickness, of the mortal conflict, of the last difficult agony, there are moments when I know not whither to turn or what to do, so sharp, so dark and distressing are these remembrances, so afflicted am I that beings so loved should have had to pass out of Time into Eternity – by a track so rough and painful. I ought not to write this but you have a kind heart and will forgive me. Mention not a word of it to Ellen; it is a relief to write it down, but it would be great pain to talk it over.

(CB to Amelia Ringrose, 31 March 1850)

It is often so much easier to write what we cannot speak. Here Charlotte dared to write down what she could not bear to talk about with Ellen. In the same letter, she sets out her belief in the inscrutability of other people:

. . . it is not given to man or woman to read the heart of others: they can but conjecture – they can but infer – and whether the conjecture or inference be just God alone knows. Even after an acquaintance of years – of a whole life – we may still be uncertain about the bearings of a character – we find in human nature such anomalies, such contradictions, such enigmas. The carefully formulated opinion of today may at once be over-turned by the opposing evidence of tomorrow.

What sound advice, and how apt a warning for biographers. Some two years later, when trying to understand the implications of Arthur

Nicholls's proposal of marriage, and later still her Protean change from knowing she could never marry him to finally agreeing to be his wife, she might well have quoted this advice to herself. Today's carefully formulated 'No' can indeed become tomorrow's 'Yes'.

Chapter Five

The 'most industrious of modern authors' and 'the most spirited and vigilant of modern publishers': Charlotte Brontë and George Smith

From the first time she stayed with the Smith family in London in November 1849, Charlotte's friendship with them flourished. After her second visit in July 1850 she told Mrs Smith that she had never enjoyed herself more; moreover, she admitted that she was 'deeply sad' to be back in Haworth, for she missed, and could never have again, 'the gentle spur of family discussion'. During this time her letters both to and about George Smith take on an increasingly friendly tone. When a tour of the Rhine was proposed – one that never happened, in fact – and again when Ellen 'raised her eyebrows' at Charlotte's readiness to go unaccompanied to meet George Smith in Edinburgh, Charlotte pertly replied that :

> *George and I understand each other very well, and respect each other very sincerely. We both know the wide breach time has made between us; we do not embarrass each other, or very rarely, my six or eight years of seniority, to say nothing of lack of all pretension to beauty, etc., are a perfect safeguard. I should not in the least fear to go with him to China.*
> (CB to Ellen Nussey, 21 June 1850)

Ellen was not convinced, however, and it was not long after this that she was asked by Charlotte to stop tormenting her father with tales of an impending match. It appears that what had perhaps begun as teasing between the two young women was now getting out of hand. Whatever alarm bells were ringing for Charlotte's friend, herself still a spinster, Charlotte heard none. Her familiarity in her letters to Smith steadily increased. When he suggested that many fine upper-class people would be pleased to meet his successful author in London, she replied, with deep but jocular sarcasm:

You touch upon invitations from baronets etc. As you are well aware, a fondness for such invitations and an anxious desire to obtain them is my weak point. Aristocratic notice is what I especially covet, cultivate and cling to. It does me so much good, it gives me such large, free and congenial enjoyment. How happy I am when counselled or commended by a baronet or noticed by a lord!

(CB to George Smith, 5 February 1851)

In March that year Smith suggested, perhaps humorously, that she might like to write a novel about his publishing house. Charlotte wrote a flighty and frivolous reply, couched in the most suggestive symbolic, even Freudian, imagery:

Do you know that the first part of your note is most dangerously suggestive? What a rich field of subject you point out in your allusion to Cornhill etc. – a field at which I myself should only have ventured to glance like the serpent at Paradise; but when Adam himself opens the gates and shows the way in, what can the honest snake do but bend its crest in token of gratitude and glide rejoicingly through the aperture?

But no! Don't be alarmed. You are all safe from Currer Bell – safe from his satire.

(CB to George Smith, 11 March 1851)

This is a very different Charlotte Brontë from the unwordly provincial novelist of literary history. The playfulness of these letters, not too dissimilar from some to Ellen Nussey, is eloquent testimony to the very special friendship that Charlotte had developed, or even, perhaps, had allowed to grow, with George Smith; indeed, the light-heartedness is reminiscent of her letters to Branwell, her real brother. It is unusual to see Charlotte in so light a mood, for it is generally only in her novels that such mischievousness appears from time to time. There is, too, a hint of happiness here that is so often missing in the details of her life. Such hints should warn us not to cast her in too dark a light. Her potential for laughter, for iconoclastic teasing, should alert us to a more cheerful figure than that which the biographies of the suffering and 'dark' Charlotte have tended to create.

Letters from London, sometimes accompanying boxes of books that the thoughtful publishers occasionally sent to their lonely author, were as rays of sunshine to Charlotte. She repeatedly told Ellen and others of the depression that closed in upon her whenever she returned home after however short a time away. After her trip to London and her visit to Edinburgh, she complained in a letter to Ellen, sent on 23 October 1850, that she felt 'a reaction that sank me to the earth – the deadly silence, solitude, desolation were awful – the craving for companionship – the hopelessness of relief – were what I should dread to feel again'.

Somehow Charlotte kept going, always seeking to lose herself in her writing. It had not helped that George planned to reissue *Wuthering Heights* and *Agnes Grey* and that she had undertaken to provide an introduction to the new edition. Writing about her sisters and going through their papers brought on a deep depression. She had to do her work in the mornings, for in the evening she found it too upsetting. Even then, she told Ellen, she had several unbearable sleepless nights. It is not surprising to learn that she spent Christmas away from home, although doubtless her father found the festival somewhat lonely.

It was in the spring of 1851, that Charlotte had been surprised to receive the unwanted proposal of marriage from James Taylor, one of George Smith's employees at Smith, Elder in Cornhill. While she could not entertain the idea for a moment, her father found it a splendid suggestion, especially as Taylor was going almost at once to work in India, so that any marriage would be deferred for some years. It would have suited Patrick Brontë very well to have his daughter engaged but still at home for the next five years. Charlotte's response was to accept an invitation to visit George Smith and his family in London and to stay away for over a month, even visiting Mrs Gaskell in Manchester before reluctantly returning to Haworth. Her father, Ellen Nussey, even Sir James Kay-Shuttleworth, all had to accept alterations to their plans once Charlotte had made up her mind to be in London with the Smith family. Her letter to George Smith upon her eventual return is high-spirited and as light-hearted as one could wish, celebrating her enjoyment of their incognito visit to the phrenologist. She is even confident enough to tease George over his writing to her at all, pretending that she cared nothing for his letters:

> *After a month's voyaging I have cast anchor once more – in a rocky and lonely little cove, no doubt, but still – safe enough. The visit to Mrs Gaskell on my way home let me down easily ... I went to church by myself on Sunday morning [while staying with the Gaskells] ... On my return shortly before the family came home from chapel [Mr Gaskell was a Unitarian minister] the servant said there was a letter for me. I wondered from whom, not expecting my father to write, and not having given the address elsewhere. Of course I was not at all pleased when the*

small problem was solved by the letter being brought; I never care for hearing from you the least in the world. Comment on the purport of your note is unnecessary. I am glad, yet hardly dare permit myself to congratulate till the manuscript [of her new novel, Villette*] is fairly created and found to be worthy of the hand, pen and mind whence it is to emanate. This promise to go down into the country is all very well; yet secretly I cannot but wish that a sort of 'Chamber in the Wall' might be prepared at Cornhill, furnished . . . with a desk, pens, ink, and paper. There the prophet might be received and lodged, subject to a system, kind (perhaps) yet firm; roused each morning at six punctually, by the contrivance of that virtuous self-acting couch which casts from it its too fondly clinging inmate; served, on being duly arrayed, with a slight breakfast of tea and toast; then with the exception of a crust at one, no further gastronomic interruption to be allowed till 7 pm., at which time the greatest and most industrious of modern authors should be summoned by the most spirited and vigilant of modern publishers to a meal, comfortable and comforting – in short – a good dinner – elegant, copious, convivial (in moderation) – of which they should partake together in the finest spirit of geniality and fraternity – part at half-past nine and at that salutary hour withdraw to recreating repose . . .*

In a day or two I expect to be quite settled at home, and think I shall manage to be quite philosophic . . .

(CB to George Smith, 1 July 1850)

Whatever George Smith may have thought of the relationship between him and his diminutive author, she could not have written a more light-hearted or carefree letter. No wonder her father grew increasingly alarmed as his daughter sought to spend more and more time away from home. It is easy to underestimate his growing unease as to what she might do next. Charlotte was secretive. Together with her brother and sisters she had created a secret world, and no outsider, their father included, knew what was going on in their play. As they grew so this secrecy continued. Their father's periods of blindness, their brother's abuse of opium and alcohol, meant that the girls could easily hide their writing, and even their success in publication, from the men of the house. Patrick Brontë was later to put a brave face on this, saying that he had known perfectly well what they were up to. This, however, was wishful thinking. Charlotte told Mrs Gaskell that her father had had no idea that she had written *Jane Eyre* until she placed the printed copy in his hand, and the same must have been true of Emily's *Wuthering Heights* and Anne's *Agnes Grey*. Furthermore, even had he tried, the near-blind old man would have had little hope of keeping up with what his daughters were doing. Wasn't it enough that he was trying to manage his wayward son, and keep the parish running? Nevertheless, the highly principled, autocratic parson must have been bemused when he learned what had gone on under his nose. All the evidence suggests that he had thought he was completely in charge of the daily life, and of the inhabitants, of the parsonage (albeit with Branwell's behaviour apt to be that of a loose cannon). The truth was quite different, however, with things happening apace of which he had no knowledge and over which he had little or no control, while he continued to believe his judgement to be final and his wishes irresistible.

In many ways Charlotte was inscrutable to her father, almost as great an enigma to him as she was to the literary world. Without exception everyone who met her was bemused. Nothing about her – her sex, her plainness, her diminutive stature, her short-sightedness, her shyness, her lack of any social graces, her complete lack of confidence when among strangers – suggested that she could be Currer Bell. Thackeray became exasperated with her solemnity and shyness, as intrigued as any by the disparity between her artistic imagination and her public gaucheness.

Given what his daughters had produced without his knowledge, and his difficulties in understanding the eldest of them, Patrick Brontë's unease about what Charlotte might do next was not without foundation. Not only did he know very little of what she was doing at any given time, he had the evidence of Heathcliff in *Wuthering Heights*, and of his youngest daughter's potent portrayal of male debauchery in *The Tenant of Wildfell Hall*, to remind him that Charlotte's imagination, like Emily's and Anne's, was dry powder in which the merest spark would set off extraordinary creative explosions. Nothing in Patrick Brontë's life since his marriage had encouraged him to expect an ordinary, peaceful, steady, smooth passage. His whole story had been one of unforeseen and extraordinary events. Whatever else he may have been, however, he was not a complacent or overconfident man, however many Latin tags he put in his letters however bombastic his rhetoric. He had good cause to be uneasy when, in his seventy-third year, Charlotte uncharacteristically developed the habit of staying away from home a month at a time. Charlotte complained to Ellen Nussey that her father frequently mentioned marriage in a disparaging way. One legend much repeated in the township of Haworth being that at this time he seldom married people, leaving the performance to his curate. Her father's frequent references to marriage, undoubtedly provoked by Ellen Nussey's mischievous gossip, tell us more about him than about his daughter. In time Charlotte grew impatient with Ellen's interference, and it is significant that she more than once wrote rebuking her friend for starting wild rumours, and indeed stopped writing to her altogether when she began seriously to consider Arthur Nicholls's proposal. Charlotte was no fool where her own life was concerned; she could be tenacious and fearlessly determined on her own behalf. If ever she was forced into a battle of wills she mostly prevailed; her father may have known that to be true, and feared it.

Charlotte's enjoyment of her friendship with the Smith family, and especially with George, seems to have filled her with goodwill towards all. Writing home from London she sends her kind regards to Mr Nicholls. To what extent this was genuine, rather than simply the expression of her canny understanding that without the ever-reliable Nicholls keeping the parish afloat, Currer Bell would not have been so free to stay away from the parsonage, remains conjecture. It would appear that her eyes, and possibly her hopes, were too firmly fixed on London, the 'most industrious of modern authors' looking to please the 'most spirited and vigilant of modern publishers', to notice the hard-working sober cleric. In any case, she had a novel to write.

Her growing closeness to the Smith family had inspired Charlotte. She would resurrect much of *The Professor*, place a family based upon the Smiths in opposition to that based upon the Hegers, and exorcise her loneliness through the effort of creativity. As with her completing of *Shirley* immediately after Anne's death, she would seize upon writing as a 'boon', looking to her work to take her 'out of dark and desolate reality into an unreal but happier region'. She would also, in taking up the theme and Belgian setting from *The Professor*, be putting her life back together again. The frustrations of Jane Eyre could live again in Lucy Snowe, the dramatic stories of the girls' school in the rue d'Isabelle in Brussels were crying out to be retold. She could at last open the drawer where *The Professor* had lain hidden since the last of its many rejections and find employment for those of its episodes that she had always believed to be worthwhile. What is more, she could tell the story of all that she had suffered through her infatuation with M. Heger, a defining experience in her development and her psychological makeup. The burning and maiming and subsequent regeneration of Edward Rochester in *Jane Eyre*, the exploration of imprisonment and madness, had not been a sufficient palliative to her suffering. The hurt was still there. A new novel that reshaped her Belgian experiences with a more mature passion than could ever have been realised in the character of Frances Henri, the demure little lacemaker of *The Professor*, was a beguiling and irresistible challenge. In the event, however, the writing of this story cost Charlotte dear, proving almost as troublesome to her as the events from which its plot derives.

Ill health and the intractable nature of her material – perhaps it was too close to the truth of her own situation – meant that the writing of *Villette* was, for her, more difficult than any other story she wrote. For Lucy Snowe, as once for her creator only 'the Professor' will do, but in keeping with Charlotte's nature and abiding theme, Lucy, like Jane Eyre, is the last to see where her happiness lies, and to believe that she might be the object of anyone's admiration. Charlotte Brontë does seem to have believed that her plainness was sufficient chaperone and impediment to any romantic attachment; her heroines, like her, are all so self-effacing, all creatures of such seething frustration and loneliness. Here at least Charlotte could write in the way that she knew best, 'from the fulness of one's heart spontaneously'.

That her heart was full, or at least filling, with hope is abundantly clear from her letters to George Smith. Indeed, she was now cautious about letting Ellen Nussey see his letters to her:

> *I have heard again from Mr S. and his mother – I would send you the notes, only that I fear your comments – you do not read them by my lights – and would see more in an impetuous expression of quite temporary satisfaction – than strict reality justifies.*
>
> (CB to Ellen Nussey, 26 May 1851)

Her letters to George contain many examples of what she coyly terms 'expressions of quite temporary satisfaction'. As has been said, the whole tone of her correspondence with him had become familiar, open, light-hearted and appealing. Even when she writes to decline his invitation to write a story for publication in serial form, she is unable to resist a warmth and bright-eyed pertness:

> *Oh that serial! It is of no use telling you what a storm in a tea cup the mention of it stirred on Currer Bell's mind, what a fight he had with himself about it. You do not know, you cannot know, how strongly his nature inclines him to adopt suggestions coming from so friendly a quarter; how he would like to take them up, cherish them, give them form, conduct them to successful issue; and how sorrowfully he turns away, feeling in his inmost heart that this work, this pleasure is not for him. But though Currer Bell cannot do this you are still to think him*

your friend, and you are still to be his *friend. You are to keep a fraction of yourself – if it be only the end of your little finger – for* him, *and that fraction he will neither let gentleman or lady, author or artist, not even Miss McCrowdie (the Scotch gentlewoman whose portrait you so graphically depict), take possession of, or so much as meddle with. He reduces his claim to a minute point, and that point he monopolises.*

(CB to George Smith, 22 September 1851)

Miss McCrowdie receives three mentions in the letter, none of them free from irony. In the 'safety' afforded by the persona of Currer Bell, the possessive Charlotte is able to stake her claim, signing the letter: 'Yours sincerely and faithfully, C. Brontë' – a unique double affirmation. Charlotte is here unashamedly holding on to George Smith, she will be faithful to him whatever Miss McCrowdie – who might have 'a rude sort of worth in her' – might mean to him.

The autumn of 1851 saw Charlotte settling down to write over the coming winter. She resisted the temptation to visit London again, lest she be continually 'rambling about', as she put it. She had said that she should have to earn her next visit to London by getting on with her work. The truth was that she found it hard to settle back into the solitude of Haworth after the heady time she had spent in visiting. In early November she wrote to George Smith telling him that she must 'get accustomed to a life of solitude', and later in the month warned him not to expect her novel to be finished until the following autumn:

Winter is a better time for working than summer; less liable to interruption. If I could always work, time would not be long, nor hours sad to me; but blank and heavy intervals still occur, when power and will are at variance.

(CB to George Smith, 20 November 1851)

Charlotte's anxiety about her writing proved to be justified. Illness made the autumn and the turn of the year a great trial. Her depression and suffering lasted until the following spring. Charlotte recorded the seriousness of her illness in a long letter to Mrs Smith and in a shorter account to Mrs Gaskell:

Certainly the past winter has been to me a strange time; had I the prospect before me of living it over again, my prayer must necessarily be 'Let this cup pass from me.' That depression of spirits, which I thought was gone by when I wrote last, came back again with a heavy recoil; internal congestion ensued, and then inflammation. I had severe pain in my right side, frequent burning and aching in my chest; sleep almost forsook me, or would never come except accompanied by ghastly dreams; appetite vanished, and slow fever was my constant companion. It was some time before I could bring myself to have recourse to medical advice. I thought my lungs were affected, and could feel no confidence in the power of medicine. When at last, however, a doctor was consulted, he declared my lungs and chest sound, and ascribed all my sufferings to derangement of the liver, on which organ it seemed the inflammation had fallen. This information was a great relief to my dear father, as well as to myself; but I had subsequently rather sharp medical discipline to undergo, and was much reduced. Though not yet well, it is with deep thankfulness that I can say I am greatly better. *My sleep, appetite, and strength seem all returning.*

(CB to Elizabeth Gaskell, 6 February 1852)

As late as September in the same year Charlotte wrote to Ellen telling her that she was still suffering from trouble with her liver and finding writing heavy going:

> *. . . I really must not trust myself to say how much I wish the time were come when without let or hindrance I could once more welcome you to Haworth.*
>
> *But oh Nell! I don't get on – I feel fettered – incapable – sometimes very low – However – at present the subject must not be dwelt upon – it presses me too hardly – nearly and painfully.*
>
> *Less than ever can I taste or know pleasure till this work [the completion of the last chapters of* Villette*] is wound up. And yet – I often sit up in bed at night – thinking of and wishing for you.*
>
> *. . . Papa's health continues satisfactory thank God! As for me – my wretched liver has been disordered again of late – but I hope it is now going to be on better behaviour – it hinders me in working – depresses both power and tone of feeling. I must expect this derangement from time to time.*

(CB to Ellen Nussey, 24 September 1852)

Somehow she struggled on and was able in October, as she had forecast, to send about three-quarters of the manuscript to London. By the end of November not only had she finished *Villette*, but she had begun proof-reading the first pages.

Yet whatever George Smith meant to Charlotte, her correspondence with him over the previous twelve months (or more precisely those letters which have survived) has a more businesslike tone, with little of the frivolity and imaginative touches of earlier letters. The heady days of visiting the opera, the theatre, art galleries, the Bedlam lunatic asylum, the Zoological Gardens and the Great Exhibition, as well as more literary occasions, had been supplanted by weary months of severe illness and depression at home. Once again writing helped her lift her spirits, but even so she found it a hard task. Many chapters in *Villette* bear witness to the depths to which Charlotte plummeted while struggling to complete it. Now the task was over she could look up, she could enjoy some of the visiting that she now felt she had earnt.

Over the autumn, Mrs Smith had again been plying Charlotte with invitations to visit. She had declined; the intervening eighteen months had not been good to her, she warned Mrs Smith, and people who had not seen her 'for a year and a half, will find some change'. She did, however, suggest that a visit might be possible after Christmas. Little did Charlotte know, as she penned that letter on 10 December, that three days later her world was going to be turned upside-down by Arthur Nicholls's sudden proposal. London would suddenly become very attractive indeed as a haven from the turmoil of her home and her father's parish. It is possible, too, that once she realised she was pursued by Arthur she needed to look closely at George and shake herself out of dreamland to face reality. Her father, she told Ellen, expected her, if she were to marry at all, to do better than a mere curate, and it may be that she thought so too. London was where she had spent her most enjoyable times; Haworth was full of bitter memories. She could see all too clearly what London offered in comparison with her life in the moorland parish.

Whatever her reasons and innermost thoughts, the events of the next few days tipped the author of love stories into a world in which she had to consider the claims and counter-claims of affection and interest. The creator of Jane Eyre was about to face problems similar to those she had invented for her heroine; in short, she would have to make some difficult choices in matters concerning her own heart.

Harriet Martineau was quick to read between the lines of *Villette*, sensing that the book was a cry from the heart. She was not alone in thinking that 'Mr Currer Bell' was much in need of a mate. Thackeray famously summed up the feelings of a good many people in the celebrated passage from his letter to Lucy Baxter, already quoted, in which he expertly anatomised Charlotte's situation: 'The poor little woman of genius! . . . she is a little bit of a creature without a pennyworth of good looks, thirty years old I should think, buried in the country and eating up her own heart there . . . a noble heart longing to mate itself and destined to wither away into old maidenhood with no chance to fulfil the burning desire.'

Thackeray would have been surprised to learn that, even as he wrote, 'the little bit of a creature' was busy hiding from Arthur Nicholls, who was seeking every opportunity to corner the old maid 'without a pennyworth of good looks' and beg her to marry him, or at least to reconsider his proposal of three months earlier.

Chapter Six

❧

The Obstinate Arthur Nicholls and the End of the False Courtship

The departure of Arthur Nicholls from Haworth in May 1853, while appearing to solve the immediate problem for Patrick Brontë, in fact had the effect of raising the stakes for all three players in this courtship game. Nicholls's leaving must have been to some extent a relief for Charlotte. She could now walk down the lane by the parsonage without having to wonder whether she would encounter the suffering curate, she could attend church service without fear that the liturgy would be accompanied by sobs. There would be no more episodes chronicling his behaviour in the sexton's house or about the parish, and perhaps fewer interrogations by her father. And yet Flossy would still be expecting walks over the moors, and would not so easily have understood that there was no longer any point in waiting at the door to the curate's lodgings. Even so, escape from prying eyes and gossip must have brought the greatest relief for both Charlotte Brontë and Arthur Nicholls. No longer would their every move and response be observed, commented upon, and relayed to the Reverend Brontë.

The burden of obedience and the duty of explanation to her father that fell upon Charlotte must have been heavy. Whatever her own feelings – and her probable confusion over the way things were should not be overlooked – the fact that she was accountable to such a domineering father must have been distressing. Now, with Nicholls gone from the parish, she could perhaps move about more freely, even enjoy the success of her latest novel, published in January 1853, with less distraction. Yet the easing of the immediate problem did not mean that the long-term difficulty had been resolved. There was, however, now room for thought and reflection which the unremitting proximity of the two other protagonists had made virtually impossible in such public settings as church, school and small township. But how dull life must suddenly have become!

Her father had, however, evidently won the day; his daughter had been appropriately dutiful, and the impertinent curate had been sent packing. But separation and absence are powerful catalysts in affairs of the heart. Spared the constant and embarrassing – perhaps even guilt-inducing – possibility of encounter that must have pressed upon her with Arthur living so close to her home, was she coming to believe that she had indeed 'lost a gem', and with him the chance of true affection? Were her words coming back to haunt her? Waiting on her ailing father could hardly have been as exciting as daily wondering whether she would bump into a love-sick admirer. She sought escape in writing, beginning a new work, which not surprisingly, considering how preoccupied she was, came to nothing. Writing did not ease her suffering or take her mind off Nicholls's protestations of enduring love.

Flight from Haworth was her best comfort, and next to that the summoning of reinforcements by inviting friends to stay with her in the parsonage. Unhappily for Arthur, Charlotte's invitations to visit had increased considerably since she had owned up to being Currer Bell and had allowed herself to appear in London literary circles. The young aspiring poet who, at twenty-one, had nervously written to Robert Southey, at that time Poet Laureate, now had an impressive list of distinguished correspondents which included men and women of letters and scientists, as well as the general public. By now Charlotte accepted that she had quite a following. While she protested that she found it irksome that 'tourists' toiled their way to Haworth to see what they took to be the home of Jane Eyre, like any writer she must have been inwardly gratified that her books had found readers. For his part, her father was only too delighted to be associated with her success, allowing himself more than a hint of paternal pride. While it pleased him that Charlotte had found fame, he was also quick to encourage Charlotte to look beyond Arthur Nicholls for companion-ship. The old man found himself on the horns of a dilemma, however, for the more he urged her to accept invitations the more she left him on his own to be cared for by the servants, and the greater the possibility that she might meet someone who would sweep her off her feet. Patrick Brontë was not so sure that his successful author daughter was as unattractive in the world's eyes as she herself seemed to believe. No wonder that at least once, when she had stayed away from the house for a long time, he sent a man from the village to find out where she was. This, it should be noted, was no teenager, but a woman in her mid-thirties.

Amongst the new friends who visited the parsonage was Elizabeth Gaskell, whom Charlotte had met in 1850 when visiting Sir James Kay-Shuttleworth who was on holiday in the Lake District. With more than a touch of serendipity Mrs Gaskell's first visit to the parsonage, and her first meeting with Patrick Brontë, came during the aftermath of the impertinent curate's proposal. Almost nine months after the fateful day the house still simmered with tension. Mrs Gaskell, her novelist's instincts aroused, noticed everything, not least the father's angry looks at his daughter and the daughter's need to talk through her problems. Elizabeth Gaskell was in her element, her letters to friends bearing witness to her fascination with all she saw:

He [the Reverend Brontë] was very polite and agreeable to me; paying rather elaborate old-fashioned compliments, but I was sadly afraid of him in my inmost soul; for I caught a glare of his stern eyes over his spectacles at Miss Brontë once or twice which made me know my man; and he looked at her sometimes; he is very fearless; has taken the part of the men against the masters – and vice versa *just as he thought fit and right; and is consequently much respected and to be respected. But he ought never to have married. He did not like children; and they had six in six years, and the consequent pinching and family disorder – (which can't be helped), and noise etc., made him shut himself up and want no companionship – nay be positively annoyed by it. He won't let Miss Brontë accompany him in his walks, although he is so nearly blind; goes out in defiance of her gentle attempts to restrain him, speaking as if she thought him in his second childhood; and comes home moaning and tired: – having lost his way.*

(Elizabeth Gaskell possibly to John Forster, September 1853)

Many facts in Mrs Gaskell's account are wrong. Nevertheless when she came to write her biography of Charlotte Brontë she held to these first impressions, the result being that she produced a parody of Patrick Brontë that readers were only too ready to believe. She was right, however, about his old-fashioned style compliments:

My Dear Madam –

From what my daughter has told me and from my perusal of your able, moral, and interesting literary works, [this was the year Cranford *and* Ruth *were published] I think that you and she are congenial spirits, and that a little intercourse between you might under the strange vicissitudes*

*and frequent trials of this mortal life and under providence be productive
of pleasure and profit to you both. We are gregarious beings and cannot
always be comfortable if alone.*

(PB to Elizabeth Gaskell, 7 September 1853)

In encouraging the friendship between the two women, the
Reverend Brontë set in train a sequence of events that would have far-
reaching effects, not the least being his own pillorying in print as a
cruel, bullying father who, according to Mrs Gaskell, ought to have
been shot. Mrs Gaskell also claimed that Charlotte unburdened her
heart to her at this time, telling her all about Arthur's proposal and her
father's objections to the marriage, which confirmed Charlotte's fellow
novelist in her jaundiced view of Patrick Brontë.

Charlotte's friendship with Mrs Gaskell had been growing since
they had first met in 1850. Like much that happened to Charlotte after
her sisters' deaths it had a special importance for her. Elizabeth
Gaskell was not only a fellow writer, she was also a wife and a mother,
and was, moreover, as adept in society as Charlotte was gauche. Here
was a woman who was not an old maid, who did not see that she had
to choose between writing and marriage. The idea must have charmed
Charlotte as much as it intrigued her, since for a married woman to
have her own career ran strongly against the tenor of the times. Yet
it must also have added to her sense of frustration. She saw Mrs
Gaskell at the centre of a loving happy family, something which
emphasised her own solitude. Nor would it have helped her to be
reconciled with the prospect of a future in the parsonage with her
ageing father.

We know from some of her letters to Ellen Nussey, and from a
reading of the first half of *Jane Eyre*, how much Charlotte longed
for physical comfort, for tenderness, from others. The scene in which
Jane creeps into bed with Helen Burns finds an echo when the ill
Charlotte, writing to Ellen, cries out for her friend's close comforting,
grieves for a 'bed-mate'. More than once in her life Charlotte was
'taken' with babies or made a small child her special favourite.
The scenes depicting the child Polly in the early chapters of *Villette*
are eloquent witness to Charlotte's tenderness, her appreciation of
caresses:

*The child advanced promptly. Relieved of her wrappings she appeared
exceedingly tiny; but was a neat, completely-fashioned little figure, light,
slight and straight. Seated on my godmother's ample lap, she looked a*

mere doll; her neck delicate as wax, her head of silky curls increased, I thought, the resemblance.

Mrs Bretton talked in little fond phrases as she chafed the child's hands, arms and feet; first she was considered with a wistful gaze, but soon a smile answered her. Mrs Bretton was not generally a caressing woman: even with her deeply cherished son, her manner was rarely sentimental, often the reverse; but when this small stranger smiled at her, she kissed it asking – 'What is my little one's name?'

'Missy.'

'But besides Missy?'

'Polly . . . '

(*Villette*, Chapter 1)

One cannot help feeling that Charlotte might have been a 'caressing person' in the right situation, for there is a physical, even a sensual, dimension to her writing. As to other relationships, she found her friendship with Mrs Gaskell comforting. It would prove to be more so as her dealings with Arthur Nicholls progressed.

Yet what of Arthur Nicholls himself, while Mrs Gaskell was being told the story of his proposal – and heaven knows what else in her opportune, though discreet, gossiping with the parsonage servants?

An overlooked outcome of Arthur Nicholl's resignation and leaving of Haworth was the freedom he, like Charlotte, now found he possessed. Once clear of the parish he must surely have realised that the influence of the Reverend Brontë, no longer his immediate superior, was naturally diminished. No landlady, landlord or their daughter would be relaying his moods, his comings and goings, to the parson and his daughter. He was now free of the parsonage and its inhabitants. From afar, Patrick Brontë must have seemed even more unreasonable, domineering and obstinate, and in some ways less relevant to the issue. Arthur now pursued the daughter of a clergyman, rather than his parson's daughter – a significant difference.

An obstinate man, Nicholls was not going to give up his plan; he would not abandon his intention to win Miss Brontë. Nor was he acting upon a sudden impulse. He had long been attracted to Charlotte; he knew the obstacles that would have to be overcome; next to her father he knew her better than anyone. She did not need to tell him of her illness as she did George Smith, for he knew how ill she had been, and knew, too, and completely understood, the demands her father made upon her. He also recognised what a frightened old man the latter was.

Arthur would not have expected Patrick Brontë to approve of his approaches to his daughter – in that respect he knew his man only too well. Indeed, in some ways nothing about the events of the past six months would really have surprised him. All he needed was the chance to explain himself, and to convince Charlotte of the depth and sincerity of his feelings. Clearly this was difficult under Patrick Brontë's roof, neither he nor Charlotte seemed able to function so close to her father's domineering presence. Every time Arthur had tried to catch a brief word with Charlotte, she had fled. Fear of her father, and perhaps fear for her father's health, must have played an important part in this apparent coyness.

Now that Arthur was away from Haworth the natural thing for him to do was to write to Charlotte. This he did – and received no reply. He wrote again, but again there was no answer. He persisted, steadfastly sending letter after letter until he provoked a reply. Whether he knew it or not, such dogged letter writing was quite the best way to appeal to Miss Brontë. Only too well did she know what it was to pine for a reply to a letter, to 'love unloved'. Had she not spent many months waiting for just one letter from Heger, hoping for the merest crumb of comfort? Had she not repeatedly written, desperately, frantically begging for a single line from a man she adored, from 'her master'? Now she was herself to receive letters of the same kind, the identical appeal.

Perhaps unwittingly, Arthur played his hand extremely well. If there was any way that he would advance his cause it was through an appeal for a letter, for words of any kind. Knowing nothing of Charlotte's infatuation with Heger, even so he might well have used her words in his own case: 'To forbid me to write to you, to refuse to answer me would be to tear from me my only joy on earth, to deprive me of my last privilege' (CB to Constantin Heger, 18 November 1845). However it was that Arthur Nicholls worded his pleas, they must have struck a chord and aroused a bitter memory in Charlotte. She knew the cruelty of silence, and we have already seen how much she had pitied Nicholls's suffering when he left Haworth.

Charlotte was to claim that she ignored six letters before she eventually replied. None of them has ever come to light. We can only guess at the terms in which the upright and rather distant Irishman couched his love letters, and indeed what it might have been about the seventh of these that finally provoked a response. Somehow Nicholls's words worked their magic; ironically where Charlotte's had failed with Heger. Catherine Winkworth, who had met Charlotte Brontë during one of the latter's visits to Mrs Gaskell, later relayed Charlotte's version of this episode:

> *. . . he wrote to her miserably, wrote six times then she answered him –*
> *a letter exhorting him to heroic submission to his lot, etc. He sent word it*
> *had comforted him so much that he must have a little more, and so she*
> *came to write to him several times.*
>
> (Catherine Winkworth to Emma Shean, 8 May 1854)

From Kirk Smeaton, Arthur achieved what he had been denied in Haworth; he had evoked sympathy in Charlotte, and now received a response to his requests. Free from Patrick Brontë's scrutiny and no longer indebted to him for his livelihood, the curate could more fervently present his feelings to Charlotte. It could be done discreetly with the added excitement that it was done in secret and without the overbearing father's knowledge. Once again, engaged in a secret correspondence, Charlotte found herself looking out for the postman. Lover's petitions, even if they are to be rebuffed, make not unwelcome reading.

Patrick Brontë had underestimated both Nicholls and his daughter in thinking that the curate's removal would be the end of the whole 'obnoxious' business. In the end, his own unbending condemnation of Arthur served to sharpen an edge of compassion in Charlotte. Banished from the woman he loved, the ardent curate beguiled her with *secret* love letters inviting her to *secret* meetings. Having established a correspondence through the late summer months of 1853, by October he had succeeded in arranging the first of several clandestine meetings. Arthur stayed with one of his former fellow curates, the Reverend Grant, formerly a curate with Patrick Brontë in Oxenhope, a village immediately bordering on Haworth, and a tryst was held in the back lanes of Haworth. The curate and the parson's daughter were meeting like millhands half their age. While this doubtless had its excitement, with the added charm that the meetings were forbidden, it was also surely ridiculous that a grown man and woman, aged thirty-five and thirty-seven and both single, should have to resort to such measures merely in order to have a conversation. If, as Charlotte protested, this was one of the very few occasions on which she had gone against her father's wishes, then it was not before time.

The True and Final Courtship

When Charlotte Brontë finally replied to Arthur Nicholls's letters the true courtship began. Until this time the initiative had always come from Arthur with not the slightest encouragement from Charlotte; indeed, all he seemed to have done was confuse her and test her obedience to her father. Matters in the second half of 1853 were to be different, however, for there was a change in her attitude which may well have been encouraged by her altered circumstances.

Unwittingly, in proposing to Charlotte in the preceding December, Arthur had chosen a most unfortunate time. The delay to the completion of the manuscript of *Villette* because of her ill health had not left its author in the best of spirits; the anxiety of waiting for the publishers' comments, particularly as George Smith and his mother were depicted in the book, would have been a considerable preoccupation; the proof-reading, publication and the anticipation of the book's reception by critics would have been an equally anxious time. She had a considerable literary reputation, and knew full well that critics would not pull their punches should she have failed to live up to the standards her two other novels had set. What is more, during her long period of serious and debilitating illness, Charlotte must have realised just how vulnerable she was, and how her father's age and his poor health (he was now in his seventieth year and almost blind) could only become increasingly heavy burdens upon them both.

The year from December 1852 to December 1853 saw a complete realignment of all Charlotte Brontë's friendships and affairs. Arthur Nicholls was but one player in this game, the others being Ellen Nussey, Elizabeth Gaskell and George Smith. Arthur would have had no idea how his fortune was so bound up with these other shifting relationships. It is unlikely that he knew much of the detail of Charlotte's visits to London, but there can be little doubt that he would have believed that he knew the 'real' Charlotte Brontë, nor would her game of being Currer Bell have fooled him for a moment.

The autumn and winter of 1853 saw Charlotte's health restored and the beginning of the last act of her love story. The months leading up to her engagement and marriage to Arthur Nicholls have something of the quality of one of Shakespeare's comedies. All the players in the game are known, and since the various possibilities have been established the characters are left with the choices confronting them. Some of these choices the players may make for themselves, others are made for them. For Charlotte and Arthur, the next months proceeded in such a way that opinions once so definitely held and decisions so clearly understood became once more fluid and debatable. Only such a change in her views and realignment of her motives could have led to her surprising her friends by disregarding her father's wishes and deciding that she would after all marry the impoverished but sincere curate. Such a reversal is eloquent of the alacrity with which Charlotte realised she needed someone to care for her. With this denouement came a realisation of Arthur's worth, and the end of dreams for better things. How this change came about can be traced through the events of a few months during which Charlotte's circumstances altered and Arthur's persistence proved worthwhile.

The Last Act

To the cast list – Patrick Brontë, elderly, frightened parent; Arthur Nicholls, lovesick, impoverished curate; George Smith, attractive publisher and sometime 'brother'; W.S. Williams, literary adviser and correspondent; Mrs Gaskell, famous fellow author, wife and mother; Ellen Nussey, lifelong intimate friend; and Miss Wooler, respected teacher and mentor – must be added James Taylor, of Smith, Elder, publisher, who in 1851, on the eve of his departure for Bombay, had expressed an interest in marrying Charlotte. While she had recoiled from the idea at the time, Charlotte kept up a faithful correspondence with the man who made her veins 'run ice', until, sadly for whatever plans she had, he repeated Heger's crime of neglecting to reply to her letters and Charlotte's enthusiasm or curiosity in that quarter cooled.

After Arthur's withdrawal from Haworth Charlotte herself spent time away with her three female friends and confidantes, or had them to stay with her. It was during the autumn of 1853 that Mrs Gaskell paid her first visit to Haworth parsonage when, she later claimed, Charlotte told her of Arthur's infatuation and the problems she was facing with her father's opposition to her marriage. Mrs Gaskell's friendship, well established by this time, had shown Charlotte that it was possible to be a wife, a mother *and* an author. Charlotte had taken great pleasure in meeting Mrs Gaskell's children, seeing for herself that motherhood and being a wife did not necessarily preclude being a writer. From the beginning, either out of mischief or compassion, Mrs Gaskell made up her mind to do all she could to further Arthur

Nicholls's cause, enlisting the help of others and freely spreading gossip among her friends about the 'romance'.

Both before and after Mrs Gaskell's visit Charlotte had stayed with her old schoolteacher – and former employer at Roe Head – Miss Margaret Wooler, once in Ilkley and then on the Yorkshire coast at Hornsea. In between these visits she had stayed with Ellen Nussey. All of these trips away from Haworth had taken place after Arthur had left. If Charlotte was seeking to escape, it was no longer from him; indeed, it is far more likely that she was fleeing from the crushing solitude she felt in the parsonage and, as Mrs Gaskell had witnessed, from her father's petulant dominance.

If Elizabeth Gaskell was an ally, a friendly agent promoting what she saw as a possibility of happiness for Charlotte, Ellen Nussey was not. Some biographers believe that there was a breakdown in the close friendship that she and Charlotte had enjoyed for so long. Certainly there is a break in the letters to Ellen – at least in those that have survived – as well as evidence from other sources that the two women who had so quizzed each other over their progress in matters of the heart became more than a little distanced. It could be argued that such a break was necessary, that Charlotte's scoffing at any proposal she received, as was her habit in reporting to Ellen, tended to inhibit her psychologically when it came to disqualifying herself from taking any such proposal seriously. It is more than a coincidence that once Charlotte allowed herself to consider Arthur more favourably, she would have to stop making fun of him to others. Needing peace of mind in order to weigh up her situation, she uncharacteristically withheld from Ellen Nussey all discussion of her progress with Arthur until *after* it had taken place. Conciliatory letters pick up the story as soon as she knew her own mind and was able to report her decision to Ellen as a *fait accompli*. The latter was none to pleased to be cast in a minor role, excluded from a day-by-day account of developments; that this was the first time was possibly because Charlotte was no longer playing games.

Miss Wooler and Mrs Gaskell seemed to have been particularly important and helpful to Charlotte at this time. Both older women, they supported her through what must have been a confusing time when Nicholls plied her with letters and she hesitated to reply. At some time in October Arthur Nicholls came to Oxenhope, at the edge of the township of Haworth, to stay with a fellow curate. Having finally replied to one of his letters Charlotte met him for the first time since his departure in May. There is no record of why she gave in and replied to his letter, or why she met him, or even of what they may have discussed. All she reported was her unease at writing to and meeting him without her father's knowledge.

In November, matters, for Charlotte, took an unexpected turn. For some time letters to and from George Smith had become less frequent, those that were written being more formal and less light-hearted than before. Several times Charlotte had hinted that letters that were a chore to write should perhaps not be written at all, gently chiding Smith, who had by now more than once disappointed his 'devoted author'. In particular, she had been dissatisfied with the payment she received for the manuscript of *Villette*. Since her reputation was now well established, she and her father had expected that she would receive £700; Smith paid her only £500. Was the businessman taking over from the friend, she wondered? She intuited that things with her 'surrogate' brother, 'Mr Fraser', were not as they had been and she was right. She surmised that overwork was the cause of the change in his letters to her, and she was quick to counsel him to take care of his health. That November she became so alarmed by a strangeness in his writing that she wrote to his mother asking what could be wrong. The reply she received did nothing to cheer her. Since April of that year George Smith had been in love with a pretty young woman. He lacked the courage to tell Charlotte, and it was his mother who answered Charlotte's question, 'Was he about to undertake a change in his life?' Indeed he was, Mrs Smith replied, he was engaged to be married.

The effect of this news on Charlotte was electric, and galvanised her into action. The last box of books from the publisher were swiftly repacked and returned to Williams with the request that no more be sent:

> *My dear Sir, – I forwarded last week a box of return books to Cornhill, which I trust arrived safely. Today I received the 'Edinburgh Guardian' for which I thank you.*
> *Do not trouble yourself to select or send any more books. These courtesies must cease some day, and I would rather give them up than wear them out – Believe me, yours sincerely,*
> C. Brontë
> (CB to W.S. Williams, 6 December 1853)

Four days later she sent the curtest of notes to George Smith by way of 'congratulating' him:

My dear Sir,

In great happiness as in great grief – words of sympathy should be few. Accept my meed of congratulations – and believe me

Sincerely yours

C. Brontë

(CB to George Smith, 10 December 1853)

She then promptly set about meeting Arthur Nicholls regularly.

Perhaps Arthur never knew what finally fanned into flame the dull spark of interest Charlotte may have had in him, but just as his early appeals had all been in vain, so in a moment they became valued. From that time all obstacles would be overcome, all objections overruled. It was 'C. Brontë' who had written so tersely to George Smith upon his engagement. 'Currer Bell' was nowhere to be seen. It was as though Charlotte had woken from her dreamland and was now facing reality. Her father's age, his illnesses, his poor sight, her own vulnerability, her disappointment that she could no longer write teasing letters to George or undertake genteel escapades with him in London, all those left her bereft. Arthur's continued courtship from afar, his unswerving protestations of affection, and his persistence may have been all she had left to distract her from her loneliness. However many visitors she had to stay, they all left eventually; however many times she fled the parsonage she had sooner or later to return. Where but to Arthur Nicholls could she look for understanding, and for whatever comfort he could offer? Perhaps after all she had been hasty in so promptly dismissing his proposal. Whatever else she did, however, this time she kept her thoughts to herself. There is no latest bulletin to Ellen, who would only hear of her friend's growing interest in Arthur once it was well established and that Charlotte herself, like her publisher, was engaged to be married.

After the announcement of George Smith's engagement, Charlotte's loneliness once more depressed her. Several times she had started upon a new book but, dissatisfied and low in spirits, each time she had left the work unfinished. A letter to Mrs Gaskell after her stay at Haworth that September eloquently describes Charlotte's situation at the end of the year:

. . . after you left, the house felt very much as if the shutters had been suddenly closed and the blinds let down. One was sensible during the remainder of the day of a depressing silence, shadow, loss, and want . . .

(CB to Elizabeth Gaskell, 25 September 1853)

Now that she had cut herself off from London the silence settled around her, more profound and more unbearable than at almost any time. Two days after her curt letter to Smith she wrote to her friend Margaret Wooler, admiring her ability to live alone without sadness or bitterness:

> *My dear Miss Wooler, – I wonder how you are spending these long winter evenings. Alone – probably – like me. The thought often crosses me, as I sit by myself – how pleasant it would be if you lived within a walking distance, and I could go to you sometimes, or have you come and spend a day or night with me . . .*
>
> *. . . I fear you must be very solitary at Hornsea. How hard to some people of the world it would seem to live your life – how utterly impossible to live it with a serene spirit and an unsoured disposition! It seems wonderful to me – because you are not like Mrs Ruff – phlegmatic, impenetrable – but received from nature feelings of the very finest edge. Such feelings when they are locked up – sometimes damage the mind and temper. They don't with you. It must be partly principle and partly self discipline, which keeps you as you are.*
>
> (CB to Margaret Wooler, 12 December 1853)

Here Charlotte was as much musing upon her own predicament as praising Miss Wooler for her serenity. It is clear that by now she was preoccupied with a fear of remaining single, and of what she termed 'turning sour', this, perhaps, being something she had observed in her Aunt Branwell.

George Smith's falling in love in April of that year had coincided with the publication in the *Christian Remembrancer* of a review of *Villette* which had angered Charlotte. Uncharacteristically, she took seriously its accusation that she had first presented herself to the world in *Jane Eyre* as 'soured, coarse and grumbling; an alien, it might seem from society, and amenable to none of its laws'. The words 'soured' and 'alien' particularly stung her. Without consulting her publishers, she wrote a letter trouncing her reviewer and setting the record straight. As might be expected she proves to be quite the best narrator of her own circumstances:

> *Sir, – To him [the reviewer] I would say that no cause of seclusion such as he would imply has ever come near my thoughts, deeds, or life. It has not entered my experience. It has not crossed my observation.*
>
> *Providence so regulated my destiny that I was born and have been*

reared in the seclusion of a country parsonage. I have never been rich enough to go out in the world as a participator in its gaieties, though it early became my duty to leave home, in order partly to diminish the many calls on a limited income. The income is lightened of claims in another sense now, of a family of six I am the only survivor.

My father is now in his seventy-seventh year; his mind is as clear as it ever was; and he is not infirm, but he suffers from partial privation and threatened loss of sight; and his general health is also delicate – he cannot be left often or long: my place consequently is at home. There are reasons that make retirement [that is, a retiring life] a plain duty; but were no such reasons in existence, were I bound by no such ties, it is very possible that seclusion might still appear to me, on the whole, more congenial than publicity; the brief and rare glimpses I have had of the world do not incline me to think I should seek its circles with very keen zest – nor can I consider such disinclination a just subject for reproach.

This is the truth. The careless, rather than malevolent insinuations of reviewers have, it seems, widely spread another impression. It would be weak to complain, but I feel that it is only right to place the real in opposition to the unreal.

Will you kindly show this note to my reviewer? Perhaps he cannot now find an antidote for the poison into which he dipped that shaft that he shot at 'Currer Bell', but when again tempted to take aim at another prey, let him refrain his hand for a moment till he has considered consequences to the wounded, and recalled 'the golden rule'.

(CB to the Editor, the *Christian Remembrancer*, 18 July 1853)

This letter provides an extraordinary insight into Charlotte's state of mind at the time. It is as if she were taking stock of her situation, and offering a public statement of the life she was living. Clearly she felt it necessary to make such an announcement to the world. Here she made an unequivocal public statement of the duty she owed her father, the nature of her isolated existence and the sense of loss she felt as the only survivor of six children. More significantly, she nailed to the door her obligation to look after her father, and her dislike of publicity and of the lionising she had experienced in London. The most important comment, however, is her statement that she should 'place the real in opposition to the unreal'. Arguably, the failure to do this was Charlotte Brontë's peculiar problem. Had she not all her life played imaginative games that replaced the real with the unreal? Had she not entertained all manner of romantic ideas about love, about being swept off her feet by a reckless, Byronic passion? Coming to terms with the 'real', as opposed to the wished for, or ' unreal', was precisely what the courtship of Arthur Nicholls symbolised. Escape from Haworth was futile, for while her father lived she knew that the reality of life there would always overcome the fantasies associated with being Currer Bell. There is even a message in this statement for Arthur Nicholls. Anyone who would know Charlotte Brontë or would seek to share her life would have to recognise her bond of filial duty to her father, and have to accept some responsibility for her father as well as for her. This, of course, in time, is exactly what Arthur agreed to do.

How cogently Charlotte the author could sum up her situation. The letter may well seem to some as out of character but it was essential for her to write it, to see set out in words, and possibly in print, where she found herself, what she believed and what she wanted the world to know about her. In this respect it is a most unusual letter and a unique exposition of some of Charlotte's deepest feelings and beliefs. It is as if she brought Currer Bell face to face with Charlotte Brontë to see which of them she really was, and with which her future lay. The single underlying reality was solitude. In Haworth when the east wind rattled about the parsonage she missed her 'bed mate'. Estranged from Ellen Nussey she found herself more lonely than ever as the long nights of winter drew on. She could not escape the reality of the lonely fireside, the empty chairs and her sisters' closed writing boxes in the dining room. The dreamt-of companionship so explicit in the scene where the little Jane Eyre creeps into bed with Helen Burns at Lowood School derived as much from its author's natural aching longing as from her imagination. Seeing her life stretching away in such aloneness, therefore, yet always aware of the duty that kept her tied to that life, it is scarcely very surprising that in October she finally answered Arthur Nicholls's letters, and began to take an interest in this persistent man who already knew the truth of her situation, who had no need to read her letter in the *Christian Remembrancer*. Other than Patrick Brontë he was the only person who could have written the letter himself, so well did he know its contents.

In November of that year, 1853, Charlotte's options became suddenly yet more limited, her horizons drawing in. She had cut off her connection with George Smith and London, she no longer enjoyed Ellen Nussey's friendship (although the breach was only temporary), and she regretted the geographical distance between her and Miss Wooler, and equally between herself and Mrs Gaskell. It was in this situation that she turned to Arthur Nicholls, who, whatever else he did, took notice of her and himself refused to be ignored. At least he was offering affection and loyalty, if of a somewhat dogged kind. It is curious to reflect that while Arthur may have thought it was the strength of his affection that finally won Charlotte's attention and brought her company, for her the erosion or ending of other pleasures and possibilities may have had no little influence. As the reality of her situation became more and more apparent and she realised once again how firmly rooted she was in Haworth while her father lived, she may also have realised, however regretfully, that it could only be there that she would have any hope of contentment and any happiness. Her father's dependence upon her would not diminish, and her letter to the *Christian Remembrancer* truly reflected her own understanding of her commitment to him. There were few who could share this task with her. Ironically, even amusingly, in this rather sombre situation Arthur Nicholls's replacement as curate, a Mr de Renzy, was proving so unreliable and unsatisfactory that the Reverend Brontë's relief at Arthur's leaving was beginning to be tinged with regret. The 'obnoxious' and 'impertinent' Nicholls would appear in a different, more favourable light when compared to the infuriating de Renzy who thus, like George Smith, became an unwitting ally of the steady Arthur.

Chapter Seven

◆

'In Fact, Dear Ellen, I Am Engaged'

In the New Year of 1854, once Charlotte had finally responded to Arthur bombarding her with letters, they continued to correspond and to meet in secret. Four years earlier, Patrick Brontë had shown her the love letters her mother had sent him during their courtship; now the disobedient, wayward daughter had begun her own collection to tie with ribbon. It would not have escaped Charlotte's notice that the love letters her mother wrote were addressed to a poor curate, and an Irish one at that! How parents do torment their children and forget their own history!

There are many mysteries surrounding the story of Charlotte's courtship. Perhaps, as it was conducted in secret from her father, it is right that it remains so to us. There was one tantalising and amusing incident, one familiar to many a letter writer, when Charlotte wrongly addressed a letter to Arthur and it was delivered, correctly, to the address she had used – to Ellen Nussey. Sadly, no one has ever revealed the contents of what must have been an embarrassing but not uncommon mix-up. Ellen, *of course*, would never have read a letter not intended for her. It would not do to imagine otherwise.

Another mystery surrounds the 'secret' meetings that Charlotte and Arthur arranged. It is widely believed that they met in a lane, still known as 'Charlotte's Lane', at the edge of the township. If so, their meetings were more in keeping with the plots of Charlotte's novels than the actual courting couple's ages. Are we really to believe that Arthur could have stayed freely at nearby Oxenhope without the news travelling like the sparks of a moorland fire all over the parish? Were they never seen by other, perhaps younger, courting couples? Servants, let alone their masters and mistresses, will gossip, and Charlotte and Arthur can hardly have gone about in disguise. Even had they done so, her distinctive diminutive figure ranged alongside his tall stocky frame must surely have given the game away, for they were both familiar figures in the parish. Charlotte avowed that she became increasingly disturbed in thus deceiving her father, but it is more likely that she knew that the secret could not be kept from him, the Haworth gossips' network being what it was.

Be that as it may, through January and February Charlotte spent time getting to know Arthur better. By February she had begun to write to Ellen again, renewing the long-standing friendship. This time, however, she was more circumspect. She did not unburden herself in breathless haste; indeed, she hardly mentioned Arthur Nicholls until the following April, when she gave her friend a full account of all that had happened. Significantly, Ellen was *told* of Charlotte's decisions, not consulted about them. There is no reason to doubt Charlotte's account, for she was consistent in the tale that she told her other friends. However, there is no extant record from anyone else's point of view, it would be interesting to have Patrick Brontë's side of the story or, for that matter, Arthur's.

Charlotte's letter to Ellen provides as it were a mirror to her own thinking and feelings. Perhaps, for her, as for many people, writing letters was a way of setting out her own thinking:

. . . Mr Nicholls came on Monday, and was here all last week. Matters have progressed thus since July. He renewed his visit in September, but then matters so fell out that I saw little of him. He continued to write. The correspondence pressed on my mind. I grew very miserable in keeping it from Papa. At last sheer pain made me gather courage to break it – I told all. It was very hard and rough work at the time – but the issue after a few days was that I obtained leave to continue the communication. Mr N came in Jan; he was ten days in the neighbour-hood. I saw much of him. I had stipulated with Papa for opportunity to become better acquainted – I had it, and all I learnt inclined me to esteem and if not love – at least affection. Still Papa was very, very hostile – bitterly unjust.

I told Mr Nicholls the great obstacles that lay in his way. He has persevered. The result of this, his last visit, is, that Papa's consent is gained – that his respect, I believe is won, for Mr Nicholls has in all things proved himself disinterested and forbearing. He has shown, too, that while his feelings are exquisitely keen – he can freely forgive. Certainly I must respect him, nor can I withhold from him more than mere cool respect. In fact, dear Ellen, I am engaged.

(CB to Ellen Nussey, 11 April 1854)

Charlotte manages to say so much in so few words. In this succinct account, the short sentences and statements convey or imply the heartbreak and anguish which she had faced. When Charlotte tells us that her father was 'bitterly unjust', we believe her. It is a measure both of her anxiety and her determination that she confronted her father and won the day against his hostility and opposition. Whatever new course she was following had not been lightly undertaken. Can we really believe that she would have confronted her father if she had been less than certain about her hopes of happiness with Arthur? Ellen was not asked for advice or, indeed, to comment; she is bluntly and efficiently brought up to date. Charlotte seems to have known that she had to keep her own counsel and not dissipate her feelings by gossiping. Ellen is now clearly a spectator, no longer an active helpful confidante, nor is she given the opportunity to indulge in mischievous character assassination. That habit had to be broken.

The letter continues, shedding more light on the arrangements in train:

> *Mr Nicholls, in the course of a few months, will return to the curacy of Haworth. I stipulated that I would not leave Papa, and to Papa himself I proposed a plan of residence which should maintain his seclusion and convenience uninvaded and in a pecuniary sense bring him gain instead of loss. What seemed at one time impossible is now arranged, and Papa begins really to take pleasure in the prospect.*

What a victory had been won. What an organiser Charlotte Brontë yet again proved to be. If Patrick Brontë was an irascible and obstinate man then he had met his match in his daughter. Both men, holding diametrically opposing positions, were forced to bend to the tiny woman's will, neither offering, or perhaps daring to offer, alternatives. Charlotte made certain that Arthur would agree to move into the parsonage, and equally that her father would not only approve her marriage, but accede to changes she proposed to make to the household. Since she provided most of the money, and far more of it than Patrick Brontë could ever have foreseen, he could have had little objection to her plans. The peat store, quite a small room to the left of the cellar door, would be transformed into a study for Arthur. Papa would be undisturbed in his study as usual. For his part, Arthur was to undertake to care for his father-in-law-to-be for as long as the latter lived, and, as before, to provide the daily help in running the parish. A further, more contentious condition – in an age when most husbands had absolute control over their wives' personal affairs – was imposed on him when arrangements were made for Charlotte's money to be entailed, placing it effectively out of his control. Arthur agreed at once, thereby silencing any voices (including Patrick Brontë's) that might have been raised to protest that he was only marrying Charlotte for her money.

The letter to Ellen concludes with Charlotte judiciously careful not to make too much of her relationship with Arthur:

For myself, dear Ellen, while thankful to One who seems to have guided me through much difficulty, much deep distress and perplexity of mind, I am still very calm, very inexpectant. What I taste of happiness is of the soberest order. I trust to love my husband – I am grateful for his tender love to me. I believe him an affectionate, a conscientious, a high-principled man; and if, with all this, I should yield to regrets, that fine talents, congenial tastes and thoughts are not added, it seems to me, I should be most presumptuous and thankless.

Providence offers me this destiny. Doubtless then it is the best for me. Nor do I shrink from wishing those dear to me one not less happy.

Commentators have made much of this passage, pointing to it as a compromise, as proof that Charlotte was marrying where she did not love. Yet the balanced maturity of her statement, rather than the outpouring of a passion more suitable to a youngster swept off her feet, is in keeping with her years and her intelligence. Seen in the context of a newly resumed correspondence with someone who might once have expected to have been an intimate confidante in the daily progress of the relationship, Charlotte's letter seems well-judged, as well as appropriately restrained for reasons other than coolness about her husband and her future with him:

It is possible that our marriage may take place in the course of the Summer. Mr Nicholls wishes it to be in July. He spoke of you with great kindness, and said he hoped you would be at our wedding. I said I thought of having no other bridesmaid. Did I say rightly? I mean the marriage to be literally as quiet as possible.

Do not mention these things just yet. I mean to write to Miss Wooler shortly. Good-bye, There is a strange half-sad feeling in making these announcements. The whole thing is something other than the imagination paints it beforehand; cares, fears, come mixed inextricably with hopes. I trust to talk the matter over with you. Often last week I wished for your presence, and said so to Mr Nicholls, Arthur as I now call him, but he said it was the only time and place when he could not have wished to see you . . .

Could it be that the 'solemn' Arthur had made a joke about not wanting to share Charlotte with Ellen, the poor man having only just been allowed to be with her himself, and not liking the idea of a chaperone. The letter is a careful and gentle composition in which Charlotte is anxious not to cause Ellen any pain. Here we have the creator of Jane Eyre telling Ellen that love and marriage in life are very much 'other than the imagination paints'. This, as we have seen, is a lesson that Charlotte had recently learnt; the wild life of fantasy, of fiction, of dreamland is not the world of men and women in which we all live. Rochester and Jane with their two marriage services have no place in Charlotte's reality. No houses need to be burnt down, no men maimed. The bride-to-be need not expect to have to flee the church and spend nights on the moors under the stars rather than be bigamously married or become an adulteress. The sentence 'What I taste of happiness is of the soberest order' is seen by many commentators as a sad one for a woman about to be married. It seems less so, however, when we recall that she was a clergyman's daughter marrying a clergyman, and would have known and respected the Prayer Book exhortation that Christian marriage should be undertaken 'reverently, discreetly, advisedly, soberly and in the fear of God'. Charlotte and Arthur would both approach marriage as a sacramental act performed through the swearing of profoundly meaningful oaths before the altar. Seen in this light, Charlotte's letter is not one telling of her reservations, but rather one of apt hesitation before a solemn undertaking. Ellen, who if anything was even more 'proper' in her religious observance than Charlotte, would have appreciated the emphasis and respected it.

The invitation to Ellen to be bridesmaid is poignant. Perhaps there really were no others she would rather have had there, but how she would have liked her sisters to have been her bridesmaids. It is a measure of Charlotte's new acceptance of reality that nowhere in this letter does she speak of her isolation and the loss of her brother and sisters. This does not mean, however, that she did not have moments when she pondered what might have been. There must have been times when any of the Brontë girls imagined weddings with each other as bridesmaids, Branwell letting fly on the organ and Papa conducting the services. It would be an irresistible game for any young girls. The novelist Jane Austen and her sister Cassandra, also daughters of a parsonage, went as far in their play as entering their own names in the register of marriages kept in the vestry of their father's church. More than most, the daughters of clergy are well aware of weddings of all kinds. Sober her expectation might be, but already Arthur's affection and tenderness towards her were having a healing effect.

On the following day Charlotte wrote, as she had promised Ellen she would, to Margaret Wooler, her old schoolteacher and employer, in whom she had confided in place of the not-so-disinterested Ellen:

My dear Miss Wooler,

> *The truly kind interest which you have always taken in my affairs makes me feel that it is due to you to transmit an early communication on a subject respecting which I have already consulted you more than once.*
>
> *I must tell you then – that since I wrote last – Papa's mind has gradually come round to a view very different to that which he once took, and that after some correspondence, and as the result of a visit Mr Nicholls paid here about a week ago – it was agreed that he is to resume the curacy of Haworth, as soon as Papa's present assistant [de Renzy] is provided with a situation, and in due course of time he is to be received as an inmate into this house.*
>
> *It gives me unspeakable content to see that – now my Father has once admitted this new view of the case – he dwells on it complacently. In all arrangements his convenience and seclusion will be scrupulously respected. Mr Nicholls seems deeply to feel the wish to comfort and sustain his declining years. I think – from Mr N's character – I may depend on this not being a mere transitory feeling, but rather that it will be accepted steadily as a duty – and discharged tenderly as an office of affection.'*

(CB to Margaret Wooler, 12 April 1854)

How Arthur must have loved her. Nothing was too much for him to undertake 'tenderly', and history would prove the integrity of his promises, and confirm Charlotte's insight into his nature and her understanding of his worth. She was not mistaken when she thought she was marrying a good man.

The letter to Miss Wooler continues in a very different vein from that sent to Ellen with the same announcement:

> *. . . The destiny which Providence in His goodness and wisdom seems to offer me will not – I am aware – be generally regarded as brilliant – but*

I trust I see in it some germs of real happiness. I trust the demands of both feeling and duty will be in some measure reconciled by the step in contemplation – it is Mr Nicholls's wish that the marriage should take place this Summer he urges the month of July – but that seems very soon . . .

Ellen and I are – I think – quite friends again – thanks in a great measure to the kind mediating word [Miss Wooler's] which 'turned away wrath'.

C. Brontë

Papa, has just got a letter from the good and dear Bishop [of Ripon] which has touched and pleased me much. It expresses so cordial an approbation of Mr N's return to Haworth (respecting which he was consulted) and such kind gratification at the domestic arrangements which are to ensue. It seems his penetration discovered the state of things when he was here in Jany. 1853 – while his benevolence sympathised with Mr N. – then in sorrow and dejection. I saw him press his hand and speak to him very kindly at parting.

The Bishop's compassionate pastoral care must have brought much encouragement to all the players in this drama. It was most helpful of him to offer his blessing in a situation in which three people were trying their hardest to do what was best while coping with feelings that ran deep. Nor was Arthur Nicholls the only one of these three to have a forgiving nature. Patrick Brontë must have had a considerable battle with himself before he bowed to his daughter's wishes. It is to his credit that once he acquiesced and agreed the match he never repined, whatever that may have cost him. Both men honoured their part of the bargain, and thus began – or rather, re-began – an amicable relationship, although it was now a more personal one than formerly. There can be little doubt that Arthur Nicholls would have had considerable respect and admiration for his parson. Patrick Brontë's long ministry at Haworth had been a fearless, principled and caring one; the work achieved in the schools of the area alone was a matter for admiration. Moreover, apart from his marriage, there were many pleasures to be anticipated in Nicholls's re-appointment to Haworth. There was, too, some justice in the fact that one who had been so close to the Brontë family through its darkest days should now take his place as one of its members. It is to the credit of both men that in his will Patrick Brontë described his curate as 'My beloved son Arthur'.

In a further letter to Ellen, in which can be detected an increasing excitement, Charlotte, as practical and thrifty as ever, briefs her friend about her trousseau:

I suppose I shall have to go to Leeds. My purchases cannot be either expensive or extensive. You must resolve in your head the bonnets and dresses; something that can be turned to decent use and worn after the wedding-day will be best I think.

(CB to Ellen Nussey, 15 April 1854)

She goes on happily to tell Ellen of her father's change of attitude:

Papa's mind seems wholly changed about the matter, and he has said both to me and when I was not there, how much happier he feels since he allowed all to be settled. It is a wonderful relief for me to hear him treat the thing rationally, and quietly and amicably, to talk over with him themes on which once I dared not touch. He is rather anxious things should get forward now, and takes quite an interest in the arrangements of the preliminaries. His health improves daily, though this east wind still keeps up a slight irritation in the throat and chest . . .

My hope is that in the end this arrangement will turn out more truly to Papa's advantage than any other it was in my power to achieve. Mr Nicholls only in his last letter refers touchingly to his earnest desire to prove his gratitude to Papa, by offering support and consolation to his declining age. This will not be mere talk with him; he is no talker, no dealer in professions.

As confident as Charlotte was in her fiancé, it is difficult not to wonder exactly what were the 'other' arrangements that she thought it might have been in her 'power to achieve'. It is possible that one she considered might have been marriage to George Smith, who might not have been so ready to move into the parsonage of a northern moorland parish. Yet Charlotte had much to feel pleased about. Where most women might hope to please their husbands, in marrying Arthur she seemed to be set on bringing happiness to two men, for her almost a prerequisite.

To complete her personal announcements, Charlotte wrote almost at once to Elizabeth Gaskell, a letter which provides collaborative evidence of the progress of her courtship and of her expectations. To have three versions of the same event or announcement is a rare gift for biographers. In this case it allows us to be a little more confident in our assumptions about the writer's intentions.

My dear Mrs Gaskell, – I should have deferred writing to you till I could fix the day of coming to Manchester, but I have a thing or two to communicate which I want to get done with. You remember – or perhaps you do not remember – what I told you when you were at Haworth. Towards the end of autumn the matter was again brought prominently forward. There was so much reluctance, and many difficulties to be overcome. I cannot deny that I had a battle to fight with myself; I am not sure that I have even yet conquered certain inward combatants. Be this as it may – in January last Papa gave his sanction for a renewal of acquaintance. Things have progressed I don't know how. It is of no use going into detail. After various visits and as the result of perseverance in one quarter and a gradual change of feeling in others, I find myself what people called 'engaged'.

So far the story corroborates Charlotte's earlier letters to Ellen and Margaret Wooler, only hinting rather darkly that she had had a battle with herself about what she really wanted. The letter continues by telling us a little more about Arthur than had otherwise been admitted by anyone, least of all Charlotte:

Mr Nicholls returns to Haworth. The people are very glad – especially the poor and old and very young – to all of whom he was kind, with a kindness that showed no flash at first, but left a very durable impression. He is to become a resident in this house. I believe it is expected that I shall change my name in the course of summer – perhaps in July. He promises to show his gratitude to Papa by offering faithful support and consolation to his age. As he is not a man of fine words, I believe him. The Rubicon once passed, Papa seems cheerful and satisfied; he says he has been far too stern; he even admits he was unjust – terribly unjust he certainly was for a time, but now all this is effaced from memory – now that he is kind again and declares himself happy – and talks reasonably and without invective. I could almost cry sometimes that in this important action in my life I cannot better satisfy Papa's natural pride. My destiny will not be brilliant, certainly, but Mr Nicholls is conscientious, affectionate, pure in heart and life. He offers a most constant and tried attachment – I am very grateful to him. I mean to try and make him happy, and Papa too . . .

(CB to Elizabeth Gaskell, 18 April 1854)

Arthur Nicholls is seen here in a good light, he was well thought-of and popular in the parish. Charlotte continued this theme when she wrote to thank George Smith for his letter of congratulations, though she began and ended her own letter with terse and mischievous, if not spiteful, comments about his marriage:

> ... *It gave me also sincere pleasure to be assured of your happiness though of that I never doubted. I have faith also in its permanent character – provided Mrs George Smith is – what it pleases me to fancy her to be. You never told me any particulars about her, though I should have liked them very much ... My future husband is a clergyman. He was for eight years my father's curate. He left because the idea of his marriage was not entertained as he wished. His departure was regarded by the parish as a calamity, for he had devoted himself to his duties with no ordinary diligence ... There can, of course, be no reason for withholding the intelligence from your Mother and sisters; remember me kindly to them whenever you write ... I hardly know in what form of greeting to include your wife's name, as I have never seen her. Say to her whatever may seem to you most appropriate and most expressive of goodwill. I sometimes wonder how Mr Williams is, and hope he is well. In the course of the year that is gone Cornhill and London have receded a long way from me; the links of communication have waxed very frail and few. It must be so in this world. All things considered, I don't wish it was otherwise.*
>
> (CB to George Smith, 25 April 1854)

Charlotte's remarks to the effect that while she had been turning down Arthur Nicholls, and possibly other proposals, George (by implication the person for whom she had been saving herself) had unfeelingly proposed to someone else, are telling. Her references to Smith's marriage and wife are pointed, they could be summed up as – Glad you are happy, I hope it lasts with whoever it is you are married to, don't expect to hear from me again. Reconciled to marrying Arthur, as she told George Smith, 'All things considered, I don't wish it was otherwise'.

Casting off her London connections and hopes, Charlotte threw herself fully into enjoying a new future. With the storm clouds of her father's prejudices and anger blown away, she felt altogether happier, even boasting that her usual headaches had lessened. She was even able to joke with Ellen when a mutual friend had told her that she, Charlotte, looked poorly, 'rather ugly as usual'. Perhaps it no longer mattered now that she had acknowledged that at least one man found her desirable.

As soon as she had news of Charlotte's engagement, Mrs Gaskell set about gossiping with a vengeance, firing off letters in all directions. She was not sure that Mr Nicholls wasn't too stiff and High Church to allow Charlotte to be friends with dissenters like herself (a Unitarian); she did not think that he would allow Charlotte any real freedom; she feared for the latter's happiness. If this all seems rather extreme, Elizabeth Gaskell herself confessed that she found it odd that a result she had actively wished for had left her feeling angry and confused. This display of gossiping, and the irresponsible scattering of half-formed opinions, is a useful warning of this tendency in Mrs Gaskell to apply her novelist's enthusiasm for good stories, especially in the case of her biography of Charlotte. From brief acquaintance and scanty fragments of knowledge she would quickly propound 'certainties' dressed up as attractive and exciting yarns, not the least being her pillorying of Patrick Brontë as a wholly unsuitable parent.

While Charlotte was busily announcing her forthcoming marriage, Arthur Nicholls was still the curate at Kirk Smeaton, where he was to remain until he resigned the position in June that year. Either by chance or because of his parish obligations, Arthur managed to avoid being paraded by Charlotte among her friends, with the result that little is known of his comings and goings. Mrs Gaskell could not resist interfering by enlisting the help of friends in forwarding the match; she herself devoted a good deal of energy to trying to secure a better position for Arthur so that he would not be so clearly 'the poor curate'. One of the friends acting upon her bidding was the poet, biographer, historian and man of letters Monckton Milnes, who provides us with one of the few glimpses of Arthur, his nature and the state he was in during his exile from Haworth:

> . . . *I met Mr Nicholls . . . he is a strong-built, somewhat hard-featured man, with a good deal of Celtic sentiment about his manner & voice – quite the type of northern Irishman.*
>
> *He seemed sadly broken in health & spirits & declined two cures, which Dr Hook enabled me to offer him . . . he gave me the impression of a man whose ardour was burnt out. I was amused at his surprise at the interest I took in him and carefully avoided any mention of you. He spoke with great respect of Mr Brontë's abilities & character & of her simply & unreservedly.*
>
> (Monckton Milnes to Elizabeth Gaskell, 30 January 1854)

While there has been much conjecture about whether Charlotte had an Irish accent, there is clearly no doubt about Arthur's.

The story of the last months of the courtship is told by Charlotte and a number of other commentators. Early in May she stayed in Manchester as Mrs Gaskell's guest, a visit which furnished plenty of opportunity for gossip. In a letter to a friend, Catherine Winkworth wrote of meeting her there and of being encouraged by Mrs Gaskell to 'say something about the marriage' as she was shown into Charlotte's room. This she did, finding Charlotte more than ready to talk of the Reverend Nicholls, saying how the parishioners were delighted to think of him returning and how highly she regarded him. She also found herself able talk about the forthcoming marriage. Catherine Winkworth described a conversation that any woman whose mother had died early might feel a need to have: ' . . . then we talked over all the natural doubts that any thoughtful woman would feel at such a time, and my mother's early married life . . . she [Charlotte] said she felt greatly comforted.'

The conversation ranged over whether a woman could always be light-hearted before her marriage; how she had to adjust to a husband's ways; whether a reliable man was more attractive than an impulsive one; whether dullness was a thing to be feared in a husband. Much has been made of this reported conversation, which has often been cited as an account of Charlotte's anxieties at this time, although whether it can be trusted as authentic must remain conjecture.

Later in the same letter, parts of which have already been quoted, Catherine Winkworth provides a few further scraps of information about the, to her, mysterious Arthur; again, however, it comes at third hand:

He wrote to her very miserably; wrote six times and then she answered him – a letter exhorting him to heroic submission to his lot, &c. He sent word it had comforted him so much that he must have a little more, and so she came to write to him several times. Then her father wanted a curate, and never liked anyone so well as Mr Nicholls, but did not at first like to have him, sent for him, however, after a time. This was about Christmas. Miss Brontë had not then made up her mind; but when she saw him again, she decided that she could make him happy, and that his love was too good to be thrown away by one so lonely as she is . . .

He thinks her intellectually superior to himself, and admires her gifts, and likes her the better, which sounds as though he were generous. And he has very good family connections, and he gets on with her father, and all the parishioners adore him . . .

There is a strange consistency to all the brief accounts of Charlotte at this time which gives them something of the quality of a press release; it is not altogether surprising that this quickly became the 'official' version of whatever had taken place in Haworth. It is more than likely, however, that Mrs Gaskell was the source of all such versions, something which accounts for their succinctness and similarity.

While Arthur Nicholls was being discussed and dissected by Charlotte's friends, his replacement as curate at Haworth, was proving less than satisfactory. The truth was that Mr de Renzy was put out at being so summarily dismissed once Charlotte's father had agreed to take Nicholls back again, going about the parish to ' pour out acrimonious complaints to John Brown, the National Schoolmaster and other subordinates'; Charlotte wished 'he would be quiet'. De Renzy, however, was to be difficult and uncooperative until he left the parish, even taking extra holiday so that Arthur had to arrange for other clergy to conduct services while he and Charlotte were away on their honeymoon. As Arthur's favour in Patrick Brontë's eyes increased, the more disobliging and peevish de Renzy became. To be fair, the man might well have had cause to feel mistreated, caught up as he was in events that were nothing to do with him. As it was he found himself being encouraged to leave to make way for the 'triumphant' return of Arthur Nicholls, whom the fickle parishioners suddenly loved and missed greatly. De Renzy's revenge took the form of being difficult about the actual date of his leaving, and to cause no little consternation as arrangements were made for the wedding and honeymoon tour.

Nothing Charlotte planned was straightforward, not least because she was still having to juggle possibilities with her father's wishes. Having at last capitulated, he was all for an early wedding and Charlotte, though alarmed at the thought, agreed. De Renzy's obdurate insistence on his right to take a holiday before he finally left, however, meant more shuffling of the date. A letter to the faithful and long-suffering Margaret Wooler in June clearly shows Charlotte to have been in a considerable muddle:

My dear Miss Wooler,

Owing to certain untoward proceedings – matters have hitherto been kept in such a state of incertainty that I could not make any approach towards fixing the day; and now if I would avoid inconveniencing Papa – I must hurry. I believe the commencement of July is the furthest date upon which I can calculate – possibly I may be obliged to accept one still nearer – the close of June. I cannot quite decide till next week. Meantime

will you – dear Miss Wooler – come as soon as you possibly can – and let
me know your earliest convenience the day of your arrival. I have
written to Ellen N begged her to communicate with you and mentioning
an arrangement which I think might suit you both. On second thoughts
– if you saw her soon – she might write and save you the trouble of a
letter. I earnestly hope that nothing will happen to prevent your coming.
Your absence would be a real and grievous disappointment. Papa also
seems much to wish your presence. Mr Nicholls enters with true kind-
ness into my wish to have all done quietly and he has made such
arrangements as – I trust – will secure literal privacy. Yourself, E.
Nussey and Mr Sowden [officiating clergyman] will be the only persons
present at the ceremony. Mr and Mrs Grant [the friends at Oxenhope
with whom Arthur stayed] are asked to the breakfast afterwards. I know
you will kindly excuse this brief note – for I am and have been very busy
– and must still be busy up to the very day.

(CB to Margaret Wooler, 16 June 1854)

This letter was written only thirteen days before the wedding took
place on 29 June, and yet Charlotte was still uncertain of the actual day
of the ceremony, and was still having to juggle things. As in all her
letters of this month, she added a few words about how pleased she was
with Arthur now that she knew him better:

. . . and I must say that I have not yet found him to lose with closer
knowledge – I make no grand discoveries – but occasionally come on a
quiet little nook of character which excites esteem. He is always reliable,
truthful, faithful, affectionate; a little unbending perhaps – but still
persuadable – and open to kind influence. A man never indeed to be
driven – but who may be led . . .

One cannot help wondering what 'grand discoveries' Charlotte might
have had in mind. Surely not that Arthur was already married and kept
a mad wife in an attic!

The shadow of her stories might well have lain over her own
wedding arrangements. How could she not recall Jane Eyre hesitating
before putting the labels on her trunk the night before she is due to
marry the would-be-bigamous Rochester for the first time? Are we
to believe that, as she set out to choose the material for her wedding
and going-away dresses, she never for a moment remembered
Jane, Rochester and Adèle setting off by carriage on their identical
mission? It is not a storyteller's habit to forget such details, such ironic

similarities. When we consider how closely – in some respects, at least – Charlotte made her experience follow that of Jane Eyre, it is not too fanciful to imagine that Jane, or perhaps Lucy Snowe, must sometimes have appeared in their creator's memory. We have only to remember the innkeeper's description of Jane Eyre towards the end of that novel to see how closely Charlotte's work mirrored her own anxieties. Describing the governess who had bewitched Edward Rochester, the innkeeper of the Rochester Arms describes Jane as Charlotte habitually felt herself to be : ' . . . nobody but him [Rochester] thought her so very handsome. She was a little, small thing, they say, almost like a child.' (*Jane Eyre*, Chapter 36)

It is hard to imagine that such powerfully realised fiction which, in so many ways, echoed, and derived its power from Charlotte's own life, would not still inhabit some corner of the imagination that bred it, would not from time to time present itself momentarily to comfort or, more likely, to disconcert. The dreamland from which came the people and events of her stories could still be conjured up by their creator. Nothing in that fiction suggests that the path of love is smooth, or that wedding arrangements are easily managed, or, indeed, that weddings take place without a hitch or interruption. More than one or two ghosts, some from life and some from fiction, would hover around Haworth Parsonage as the solemn ceremony began. Moreover, even if the fictitious is set aside, it has to be seen that any wedding Patrick Brontë witnessed must have been haunted by thoughts of the early death of his beloved wife, the mother of his six children of whom only one was still living.

Being engaged to be married seems to have suited Charlotte Brontë. Letters setting out arrangements were dispatched in all directions, and she let nothing check her as her plans advanced. A note of optimism and confidence reappears in her letters to friends. Charlotte enjoyed being in control, as she had enjoyed organising her sisters, and she now relished the defeat of her father's opposition to her marriage. Since Papa was bowing to her wishes and Arthur would do anything she said, she found herself in a strong position. Never one to conform, she was once more in her element, in control, readily informing her friends that Arthur agreed wholeheartedly with her plans, supporting her in every way. Tiny she might be, but she was a powerful, confident manager, something not altogether surprising in so skilful a novelist. In her adult published work she created more than three hundred and fifty fictitious people in over eighty different settings, with the result that she was nothing if not a good planner. Besides, she had rehearsed being in love in her novels; indeed, she had arranged a few weddings in her stories, and there are at least nine in her juvenile writing.

Charlotte had also become increasing solicitous towards others. At least one letter to Ellen shows her trying out wifely consideration, and although she had always been ready with advice about health to people, she now displays heights of concern that seem to be nothing less than a rehearsal of Charlotte the caring partner and caring daughter:

Dear Ellen,

I wonder how you are, and whether that harassing cough is better; but I am afraid the variable weather of last week will not have been favourable to improvement. I will not and do not believe the cough lies on any vital organ. Still it is a mark of weakness, and a warning to be scrupulously careful about undue exposure. Just now, dear Ellen, an hour's inadvertence might derange your whole constitution for years to come – might throw you into a state of chronic ill-health which would waste, fade, and wither you up prematurely. So, once again, TAKE CARE. *If you go to* —— *, or any other evening party, pack yourself in blankets and a feather bed to come home, also fold your boa twice over your mouth, to serve as a respirator* . . .

(CB to Ellen Nussey, 22 May 1854)

Charlotte's concern here seems almost jocular, although other letters show it to have been seriously meant. In her letter she goes on to tell Ellen of her worries about Arthur's health. It appears that the strain of the last months – his exile in Kirk Smeaton; his absence from Charlotte; his having to face Patrick Brontë – all meant that he had lost weight and had so debilitated an appearance that Charlotte became alarmed:

. . . .*Mr Nicholls comes tomorrow. I feel anxious about him, more anxious on one point than I dare quite express myself. It seems he has again been suffering sharply from his rheumatic affection. I hear this not from himself, but from another quarter. He was ill while I was at Manchester and Brookroyd [with Mrs Gaskell and Ellen Nussey, respectively]. He uttered no complaint to me, dropped no hint of the subject. Alas! he was hoping he had got the better of it, and I know how this contradiction of his hopes will sadden him. For unselfish reasons he did so earnestly wish this complaint might not become chronic. I fear, I fear. But, however, I mean to stand by him now, whether in weal or woe. This liability to rheumatic pain was one of the strong arguments used against the marriage. It did not weigh somehow. If he is doomed to suffer, it seems that so much more will he need care and help . . . I look forward to tomorrow with a mixture of impatience and anxiety. Poor fellow! I want to see with my own eyes how he is . . .*

There is nothing of the lukewarm fiancée in these concerns. Arthur Nicholls duly visited and his anxious Charlotte saw for herself the true extent of his 'illness', speedily sending on the news to Ellen, and thereby renewing her habit of breathlessly reporting all her latest information to her friend:

. . . Mr Nicholls has just left me this morning . . . At first I was thoroughly frightened by his look when he came on Monday last – it was wasted and strange, and his whole manner nervous. My worst apprehensions – I thought were in the way of being realized. However, inquiry gradually relieved me. In the first place – he could give his ailment no name. He had not had one touch of rheumatism – that report was quite groundless – he was going to die, however, or something like it, I took heart on hearing this – which may seem paradoxical – but you know, dear Nell – when people are really going to die – they don't come a distance of some fifty miles to tell you so.

Having drawn in the horns of my sympathy – I heard further that he had been to Mr Teale [a doctor in Leeds] – and was not surprised to receive the additional intelligence that that gentleman had no manner of complaint whatever except an over-excited mind – in short, I soon discovered that my business was – instead of sympathising – to rate him soundly. He had wholesome treatment while he was at Haworth – and went away singularly better. Perfectly unreasonable however on some points – as his fallible sex are not ashamed to be – groaning over the prospect of a few more weeks of bachelorhood – as much as if it were an age of banishment in prison. It is probable that he will fret himself thin again in time but I shall not pity him if he does – there is not a woman in England but would have more sense – more courage – more sustaining hope than to behave so . . .

(CB to Ellen Nussey, 27 May 1854)

Clearly Charlotte was not only on top of things, but was enjoying herself greatly. There can be little doubt that she was finding fulfilment in her new role. Like her heroine Jane Eyre, she longed to be needed by a lover. Once sure of herself she lets her sense of humour have free rein, Arthur's attention-seeking hypochondria receiving short shrift in the same letter: 'Man is an amazing piece of mechanism when you see – so to speak – the full weakness – of what he calls – his strength. There is not one female child above the age of eight but might rebuke him for the spoilt petulance of his wilful nonsense.'

Charlotte was now very busy indeed. Her father's moods swung from depression to cheerfulness – on one day he complained that he had gone deaf, then, on the next, a Sunday, he preached twice. Wedding cards – cards announcing that the marriage had taken place – had to be ordered and printed, more of them than had at first been thought because of Arthur's 'string of clerical acquaintances'. Ellen was sent shopping and served her friend well, patiently getting all the things in Leeds that were not available in Haworth. While Arthur fretted in Kirk Smeaton Charlotte stage-managed the whole event, organised a wedding breakfast, and did her best to keep the date of the ceremony a secret. She had set her heart on the quietest possible wedding.

And so the long story of Arthur Nicholls's persistence drew to a conclusion. His perseverance, his amenable nature and his unswerving devotion to Charlotte had finally won the day, although it was little wonder that he had found the waiting tedious. Nothing she asked of him would be too much. He and her father were now reconciled, his surplice would once more hang in the vestry of St Michael and All Angels, he would once more be taking duty to relieve the old man of the responsibility. His books could be moved into the little study his wife-to-be had prepared for him at the back of the parsonage. His copies of *Jane Eyre*, *Shirley* and *Villette* were coming home.

Chapter Eight

'Our Honeymoon Will Shine Our Life Long'

'The whole thing is something other than the imagination paints it.'

(Charlotte Brontë)

'Our honeymoon will shine our life long: its beams will only fade over your grave or mine.'

(Edward Rochester in *Jane Eyre*, Chapter 38)

With Mr de Renzy at last prepared to leave, Charlotte was able to name the day for her wedding: Thursday, 29 June 1854 at eight o'clock in the morning – not, perhaps, the most auspicious time, for that is precisely the hour of Rochester's proposed bigamous marriage to Jane Eyre. The service would be held in the parish church. Mr Sowden, a clergyman friend of Arthur's would marry them by special licence (so no banns would need to be read); Ellen Nussey, Margaret Wooler and, of course, Charlotte's father, would be there to witness the marriage. The whole thing was to be kept secret from the parishioners until after it had taken place. The newlyweds would then leave for a honeymoon tour of Ireland where Charlotte would meet her new relatives. Whether there were to be an organist or bellringers at the wedding can only be guessed, although if there were, it is difficult to believe that the whole thing could have been kept secret.

The day before the wedding Miss Wooler and Ellen Nussey came to stay at the parsonage to make final arrangements with the bride. Arthur went to stay with his friends the Grants in Oxenhope. Trunks were packed in readiness. Did Charlotte hesitate as she put the labels bearing the name 'Mrs Arthur Nicholls' on the trunk, as she had imagined Jane Eyre doing with her own labels before her marriage to Rochester, the marriage that was so dramatically halted?

. . . there were my trunks, packed, locked, corded, ranged in a row along the wall of my little chamber; to-morrow, at this time, they would be far on their road to London: and so should I (D.V.) – or rather, not I, but one Jane Rochester, a person whom as yet I knew not. The cards of address alone remained to nail on: they lay four little squares, in the drawer. Mr Rochester had himself written the direction, 'Mrs Rochester, —— – Hotel, London,' on each: I could not persuade myself to affix them, or to have them affixed. Mrs Rochester! She did not exist: she would not be born till to-morrow, some time after eight o'clock a.m.; and I would wait to be assured she had come into the world alive before I assigned to her all that property.

(Jane Eyre, Chapter 25)

Perhaps Charlotte had a similar moment of doubt; after all, she had arranged for her own marriage to take place at the same time in the morning as Jane's. It is possible, too, that she would have remembered Lucy Snowe's anxieties at the ambiguous end of *Villette*, where she had compared marriage itself with tempest, and where neither the heroine nor the reader knows whether Paul Emmanuel will survive the storm at the end of the book, and thus return to marry Lucy. But perhaps her stories and her dreams never crossed her mind.

The eve of Charlotte Brontë's wedding was not to be without its drama, however. Her father could always be counted on to provide surprises worthy of any of her plots. Now, at a late hour, according to Mrs Gaskell, he announced that he would not be able to be in church for the service next morning. The story goes that he did not feel equal to attending the ceremony, a decision which exposed him to much criticism. Here was the selfish, petulant, and unreasonable old father once more making things as difficult as possible for his daughter. It was an image that fitted the impression Mrs Gaskell had formed of him from her one brief visit. Yet if this caricature was a gift to a novelist, it was nevertheless unjust. What did the prospect of giving his daughter away in marriage hold for the old man ? He had already 'given away', to the grave, his wife and five of his children. The ceremony would be performed over the vault in which his wife's body lay beside those of his son and three of his daughters. It is perhaps unreasonable to have expected him to have 'given away' Charlotte, who was the staff of his old age, the remnant of the family. Her marriage service would rehearse and recall, in potent words, all he had hoped for in his own marriage. At his great age – seventy-seven, an astonishing age in the mid-nineteenth century, especially for someone from a hard peasant background – he knew that he ran the risk of losing Charlotte. Should she conceive, being thirty-eight years old, small, and never of robust health, the outcome might well prove fatal. 'Forsaking all other' was heavy with meaning for the old clergyman, the very sacrament of matrimony being for him, a priest, a most solemn undertaking and ceremony. Each moment of this particular service, each exhortation and explanation, would be a bitter reminder of his suffering. This apparent selfishness is somewhat mitigated when it is remembered that the words of the service were for him no ritual mumbling, but sincere supplications. He would be reminded that matrimony signified:

> *the mystical union that is betwixt Christ and his Church . . . and*
> *therefore is not by any to be enterprised, nor taken in hand unadvisedly,*
> *lightly or wantonly, to satisfy men's carnal lusts and appetites, like brute*
> *beasts that have no understanding, but reverently, discreetly, advisedly,*
> *soberly, and in the fear of God.*

The order of service continues by setting out the causes why marriage was ordained, each one having particular resonance for Patrick at the end of his life as a widower:

> *First, it was ordained for the pro-creation of children, to be brought up*
> *in the fear and nurture of the Lord.*

Had he not fathered six children, the sole survivor being at the altar rail? Is it any wonder he had qualms, selfish or otherwise? The Prayer Book concludes its exposition of reasons celebrating what Patrick Brontë believed all his life was the greatest virtue of all:

> *. . . it was ordained for the mutual society, help and comfort, that the one*
> *ought to have of the other, both in prosperity and adversity.*

Had he attended the marriage, Patrick would have arrived at the full realisation that he would be losing his last child were he to answer the conducting priest's question: 'Who giveth this woman to be married to this man?' If anything was important to the Reverend Brontë it was *words*. He was a poet, a preacher, a writer; next to his faith – indeed, it could be argued at least equal to it – was his belief in the mysterious power of words. This was something he had instilled and encouraged in his children, and the last of them, Charlotte, shared that passion. Given this reverence for words – words as comforters, as the means of continuing and advancing civilisation – neither he nor Charlotte would see the marriage service as anything other than solemn and profoundly meaningful. After all, Charlotte's great novel *Jane Eyre* takes the Prayer Book marriage service as its pivotal point. She knew only too well the power of the question; 'if either of you know any impediment why ye may not be lawfully joined together . . . ' For Rochester, as for his creator, this would have to be answered 'at the dreadful day of judgement when the secrets of all hearts shall be disclosed.'

The service is disturbing enough for any 'normal' family, but for Patrick Brontë there would have been an understandable , perhaps even unbearable, poignancy. It is said that once the service was over he was the life and soul of the wedding breakfast back in the parsonage. Perhaps Charlotte's father knew his own strengths and weaknesses better than anyone.

On the eve of the wedding, however, his announcement that he would not be present in the church caused some consternation. If he would not be there then who could give Charlotte away. It may have taken Charlotte, Ellen and Margaret Wooler a moment or two to realise that the Prayer Book does not define that person in any way, that any relation or friend could undertake the duty. Patrick Brontë, of course, would have known this, would have conducted many weddings where someone other than father or relation had given away the bride. He knew full well he was not causing any 'impediment' to the marriage by not being there. On the contrary, his absence might well prove a blessing, for he probably realised that he could not trust himself, that he could not be sure his emotions would not get the better of him. Better, then, to stay away, than to risk wrecking his daughter's wedding.

Thus it was that at eight o'clock on the morning of Thursday, 29 June 1854, in the Church of St Michael and All Angels, Haworth, without her father present, Miss Charlotte Brontë married the Reverend Arthur Bell Nicholls. The Reverend Sowden officiated, Miss Margaret Wooler gave the bride away, and together with Miss Ellen Nussey signed the register as witness to the marriage. There is, however, doubt about who else was in the church. Some believe that John Redmond, the parish clerk, was there, as well as the sexton, John Brown, and Arthur's friends, the Grants, from Oxenhope. As we have seen, elaborate plans had been laid, at Charlotte's insistence, to keep the wedding discreet. The marriage was conducted by special licence, which suggests that banns of marriage had not been publicly announced beforehand. On the eve of the wedding Arthur sent a message that he had arrived at the Grants, and on the following morning, just before eight o'clock, a village boy was set as lookout to watch for the approach of Arthur and Sowden. The lookout was then to hasten with this news to the ladies in the parsonage, who would set out for the church. All went to plan. The boy's reward was to be taken out of school lessons to have his breakfast in the parsonage after the bride and groom had left.

Charlotte Brontë's wedding dress was of soft white muslin with green embroidery, and with it she wore a white bonnet decorated with small flowers, leaves and a veil. The dress has not survived, but the bonnet and veil, as well as the bride's going-away outfit, are kept at the Haworth Parsonage Museum. The going-away dress, a full skirt with a tightly waisted top was originally of light grey with silver stripes, although, after more than 140 years it now appears as a faded brown. One of the dresses that Rochester bought for Jane Eyre before her wedding was of 'pearl gray silk'. It does seem, therefore, that Jane was not completely absent from Charlotte's thoughts, that she may well have rehearsed many of her own choices in her fiction. Nor is it conceivable that the question asked of bride and groom during the marriage service as to whether they know of 'any impediment' to their being married could have passed, in Charlotte's and Arthur's case, without recollection of that electrifying moment in *Jane Eyre* when Rochester's brother-in-law, Mason, and his lawyer interrupt and then halt the service. Sowden would have read out the charge word for word in the Prayer Book as it is in *Jane Eyre*:

> *'I require and charge you both (as ye will answer at the dreadful day of judgement, when the secrets of all hearts shall be disclosed), that if either of you know any impediment why ye may not lawfully be joined together in matrimony . . . '*

He would have then paused. We know, as did Charlotte and Arthur, that Patrick Brontë was not in the church. Even so, could they have been absolutely sure at that moment (or indeed at any other) that he would not suddenly and unexpectedly interrupt the service and seek to prevent the marriage? He had opposed the match for long enough before that Thursday morning, and it is possible that he could have stayed away because he feared that he might have spoken up at that precise point in the ceremony. We are told he stayed at home, but whether Arthur and Charlotte would have been so confident at the time that he would remain there is another matter. There is always a sense of relief when a marriage has been carried out. That surely would have been the case in this wedding, considering all the obstacles that had been overcome. The principal obstacle, Patrick Brontë, stayed in the parsonage and thought his own thoughts, thoughts which will ever remain closed to scrutiny.

And so Charlotte Brontë, the creator of the unassuming, invisible governess Jane Eyre, and the exasperating and self-isolating Lucy Snowe, was herself married. Mr Currer Bell was finally cast aside, replaced by the new Mrs Arthur Nicholls. All Charlotte's protestations that she would remain single all her life, would live out her life as an old maid, were proved false. She had yearned for support, had eagerly sought love and affection, and it is clear from her novels that she looked for physical comfort, not merely intellectual companionship. It is true, however, that at times she had been misled into thinking that shared intellectual interests were necessary for a fulfilling relationship. She had had to struggle with herself against this fallacy, realising that she was chasing a chimera, that she was allowing her dream of a relation-ship to inhibit the forming of a genuine attachment. It was when she stopped deluding herself, stopped chasing a fantasy of what life could be, that she recognised the possibility of happiness with Arthur Nicholls. Arthur was a realist. He professed a deep love for Charlotte, as he also admired and respected her intellect and ability as a novelist, deferring to her great gifts. If he was no dream lover, no romantic ideal, he was nevertheless a man offering to care for her in sickness and in health. The reticence about her feelings for Arthur found in letters to her friends may not be wholly truthful, may in fact be misleading. It is conceivable that her pronounced hesitations were in the nature of disclaimers, so long had she purveyed the idea of solitude and protested that she would never marry. She was no breathless seventeen-year-old but a woman of thirty-six when she had to begin explaining what appeared to her friends to be a complete change of attitude. To have appeared passionate, exhilarated, would hardly have been in keeping with her intelligence, her lifelong habits or her sense of correctness. It is not necessary, therefore, to read her letters to friends as if they were statements sworn in court. Writers – good ones, at least – have a well-developed sense of audience, and Charlotte wrote as she wished to be represented to her readers.

Whatever the outcome of the marriage, Charlotte Brontë had found the courage to exchange life as she knew it for the unknown, to follow Shakespeare's precept for true love in *The Merchant of Venice*, 'To give and hazard all she hath'. The fictitious courtships and marriages of her stories were now replaced by the reality, very different, as Charlotte admitted, from those events in the imagination. Almost continuously, she balanced her romantic visions of life against the actuality, arguably the price she had to pay for her creative gift. As children, the Brontës worried their friends, and Tabitha Aykroyd, the housekeeper, with the heady wildness of their imaginations; indeed, Tabby thought their wits would addle if they were not careful. It does seem that Charlotte's instinct for story, for dramatic scenes and the creation of lovers and the analysis of their relationships, spilt over into her everyday life. It had taken her a long time to see clearly the difference between dreams of romance and marriage and the real event.

The one advantage that Arthur Nicholls had over all her fictional lovers was his humanity, his physical presence. The absent and 'safe' bedmate Ellen was to be replaced by the dangerous man Arthur. In *Jane Eyre* Charlotte had written of 'the experimental' kiss.

Now the rehearsed experimental would be replaced by the real. All she was ever to say of this realisation was that she had never been so happy in her life. Charlotte found in marriage the comfort for which she had yearned since long before the death of her sisters, perhaps since her first infatuation with Heger. This comfort was not in the mind or intellect but in the embracing arms of a husband and lover, what Charlotte and her father always believed to be 'the best earthly comfort'.

When, at thirty-eight years of age, the shy and retiring, if formidable, literary genius was ready to set aside certainties for unknowns, ready to follow life's plot rather than shape a plot in fiction, she chose Arthur Nicholls – poor Irish curate that he was – 'to have and to hold'. It was a choice she was never to regret until her dying day. She knew that marriage was 'other than the imagination paints it', and she was ready to know it and enjoy it for what it was.

Mrs Arthur Nicholls, Post Office, Kilkee, County Clare, Ireland

The Reverend and Mrs Nicholls spent their honeymoon in Wales and Ireland, setting off from Haworth by carriage and pair for Keighley railway station. Thus began a tour which was to last more than a month and which, as well as travel by carriage, included train journeys, sea crossings and at least one journey on horseback.

From the beginning, Mrs Nicholls's life was very different from Charlotte Brontë's. She travelled to Ireland to meet her new relatives.

In marrying Arthur she had become once more part of a large and closely knit family, a family as keen to meet the celebrated author as she was to have brothers- and sisters-in-law. She had found in marrying Arthur one of the things that had attracted her to George Smith, for in that relationship Charlotte came to value George's mother and sisters highly. She was to find a new family of young and old whose company she could enjoy. Arthur's widowed aunt, Mrs Bell, who had brought him up in a fashion not unlike the way the Brontë children had been brought up by their Aunt Branwell, was to prove a delight to Charlotte, being a sophisticated, cultured and most kindly woman. For these and many other reasons the honeymoon tour would prove to be an interesting journey for the new Mrs Nicholls, adding much to her life and experience, and proving the worth of the risk that she had taken. Besides being newly married she was travelling to her father's homeland as well as her husband's. She was travelling with an Irishman, a proud graduate of Trinity College, Dublin, who knew that city and the Irish people well.

For Charlotte, their tour would not be without its surprises, not all of them pleasant. Ireland had not fully recovered from the devastating potato famines and cholera epidemics of the middle and late eighteen-forties, during which it is estimated that the population was depleted – either by death or emigration – by some 2 million. These had been followed by the clearances and evictions by landlords – many of them absentee landlords living in Britain – which had left so many poor families homeless and starving. The year 1848 had seen a rebellion in the cause of throwing off the rule of the British government, which led in time to the foundation of the Irish Republican Brotherhood or the Fenian Movement which in turn led to the setting up of secret military organisations. There was still a certain amount of unrest in 1854, when Charlotte and Arthur made their visit. Charlotte was interested in revolution. Much of her early juvenile writing had been about rebellions, while her father had written about 'the rebels' in his story 'The Maid of Killarney'; moreover, a part of her fascination with Heger had been fired by his involvement with the uprising in Brussels. The social unrest and fear of rebellion arising from the Chartist Movement and, earlier, the Luddite riots in Yorkshire, and which had provided her with material for her one substantial 'social' novel, *Shirley*, meant that she had more than a passing interest in such things. The circumstances of the poor of Haworth would have prepared her in some measure for what she would see in Dublin and the rest of Ireland. Even so, the reality of Dublin, with its decayed Georgian squares and tenements where extreme poverty abutted directly upon the more affluent part of the city, would provide a telling contrast between poverty in England and that in Ireland. Dublin had seen the provision of extensive soup kitchens – where the poor ate with spoons chained to the tables – as it tried to cope with the many dispossessed unskilled workers who moved into the city as they lost their livelihoods and their homes in the country. At times the 'civilised' parts of Dublin were virtually under siege from this great wild throng of the poor.

On the first day of their honeymoon Charlotte and Arthur travelled as far as Conway in North Wales, where they spent their first night together. Charlotte had a cold, 'predictably', she would have said, having once grumbled that she always seemed to take her Haworth headaches and colds away with her. Cold or no cold, honeymoon or not, Charlotte put duty first, finding a moment to write a short letter thanking Ellen, and through her Miss Wooler, for the help they had given at the wedding. Charlotte was positive and enthusiastic, apparently determined to enjoy herself:

Dear Ellen,

I scribble one hasty line just to say that after a pleasant enough journey – we have got safely to Conway – the evening is wet and wild, though the day was fair chiefly with some gleams of sunshine. However, we are sheltered in a comfortable inn. My cold is not worse . . . give my kindest and most grateful love to Miss Wooler whenever you write . . . Yours faithfully and lovingly

C.B.N.

(Charlotte Bell Nicholls [CBN] to Ellen Nussey, 29 June 1854)

Mrs Nicholls noted the gleams of sunshine, said they were comfortably sheltered, and did not let the 'wet and wild' weather spoil her mood. She was pleased, too, to be in the ancient walled town of Conway with its spectacular castle, the subject of one of the most celebrated paintings *The Bard* by her favourite artist, John Martin. Here Charlotte's life was coming together. The romantic dreams of her childhood, her reading of the fourteenth-century Welsh Bard David ap Gwilym and the medieval Welsh tales of the *The Mabinogion*, here seemed to become reality. Given her profound intellectual curiosity and her love of history, she must have been delighted to find herself in a place so redolent of a romantic, if often violent, past. The journey would have ended with the train passing through Robert Stephenson's tubular rail bridge just before entering Conway station, and she and Arthur would no doubt have admired Thomas Telford's suspension bridge just below the castle walls; both bridges being of revolutionary design. Her father, with his keen scientific bent, would have been glad to have her impressions of these engineering marvels.

The next four days were spent touring North Wales. The drives through the passes of Snowdonia delighted her, ' one drive indeed from Llanberis to Beddgelert surpassed anything I remember of the English Lakes.' Clearly Mrs Nicholls in Wales was ready to be happier than Miss Brontë had been in the Lakes. The wildness of the country would have appealed to her far more than the more sedate Lakeland scenes; besides, in her husband she had a somewhat more congenial companion than the fawning Sir James Kay-Shuttleworth, who had whirled her about the Lake District in his coach. Honeymoons tend to cast a pleasant light over landscape, especially a landscape steeped in legends and familiar stories.

On the 4 July the couple set off from Conway along the coast to Bangor by the comparatively new – and spectacular – coastal railway, which at times hugged the mountainside as it skirted the sea. After a few days they continued to Holyhead on the Isle of Anglesey, where on 4 July they boarded a packet boat bound for Kingstown (now Dún Laoghaire), for the port of Dublin. They would have crossed the Menai Straits by another – the first and finest – of Robert Stephenson's great tubular bridges, which had been opened during the years that *Jane Eyre* became a bestseller. The revolutionary bridge and the revolutionary novel had each intrigued the public; both are unique, and both remain famous to this day.

'I Must Say I Like My New Relations'

Charlotte reported that the sea crossing to her husband's homeland was, fortunately, 'calm and the passage good'. On landing, the honey-moon couple were met by three of Charlotte's new relations, Arthur's older brother, Alan, and two cousins, Joseph and Mary Anne, all of whom must have been as curious to meet the famous author as they were keen to welcome her to the family. At once Charlotte had to reconsider her situation. It is impossible to know what she had expected of Arthur's family, but it is clear from a letter to Miss Wooler (though, perhaps significantly, not to Ellen) that she was surprised at the family's standing and their gentle courteousness. Clearly all the talk of her demeaning herself by marrying Arthur had misled her. The fancy

'London' notions of the lionised – albeit reluctantly – Currer Bell had perhaps encouraged condescension on her part.

Arthur would have enjoyed the opportunity of introducing her to his brother Alan Nicholls who was the manager of the Grand Canal at Dublin, no mean position. The waterway, which ran westwards from the capital to the eastern border of County Galway, was an important and very successful enterprise which, as well as freight, carried passengers in large boats equipped with first- and second-class accommodation, and even ran a fly service with three horses pulling a smaller craft at 10 miles an hour by day and 6 at night. The canal had hotels at intervals along its length and competed well with the new railways for the transportation of goods as well as people. Alan Nicholls, who named one of his daughters Charlotte Brontë Nicholls, was to die an extremely wealthy man. Joseph Bell was a student at Trinity College, with which the family, including Arthur, had long been associated. He accompanied Charlotte and Arthur on a tour of the college, during which they visited the famous library and the chapel, as well as the museum. Charlotte, the one-time governess, must have cherished her visit to this seat of learning. She must also have thought of her father's college, St John's, far away in Cambridge and about which she had been told so much. Mary Anne, the third of the family trio, 'a pretty lady-like girl with gentle English manners', delighted Charlotte by her pleasant nature. For Charlotte, Ireland was proving a considerable change from Haworth and from England in general. It is interesting that nothing was known of Arthur's family or his upbringing until Charlotte, having 'known' him in the parish for nine years, had been forced to take notice of him. Until then, he had patiently borne the gibes about his inferior status.

The time spent sightseeing in Dublin was cut short. Charlotte's cold persisted, and they fairly quickly accomplished the seventy or so miles westwards to Banagher in County Offaly, situated in the middle of the country, and almost the furthest point of the Grand Canal from Dublin, a journey that could only partly be accomplished by rail. Banagher was the village where Arthur had lived with his Aunt and Uncle Bell in order to receive an education at the latter's school, the Royal School, which was kept in the grounds of Cuba House where the family lived. The house was a solid building in the Palladian manner set four-square in its own estate, although by 1854 it had seen better days and was not in the best repair. Charlotte, however, was not in the mood to find fault; on the contrary, she was ready to be pleased, to find everything about her honeymoon tour delightful – even if she was a little startled by all she encountered.

Aunt Harriet Bell, who was then fifty-three years old, the head of the family since her husband's death in 1839, had cared for ten children – her own or, like Arthur, those of relations – in Cuba House. Now she took the ailing Charlotte under her wing and promptly nursed her back to good health. This mature woman, renowned for her kindliness and charm, was a world away from the stiff and rather formal Aunt Branwell who had overseen Charlotte's childhood at Haworth. Harriet Bell soon lost all her nervousness at meeting the famous author, and the two women had wonderful conversations by the fireside, in the course of which Charlotte learnt that in marrying Arthur she had in fact done rather well for herself:

> *I cannot help feeling singularly interested in all about the place [Cuba House]. In this house Mr Nicholls was brought up by his uncle Dr Bell, it is very large and looks externally like a gentleman's country seat – within most of the rooms are lofty and spacious and some – the drawing room – dining room &c. handsomely and commodiously furnished. The passages look desolate and bare – our bedroom, a great room on the ground floor would have looked gloomy when we were shown into it but for the turf-fire that was burning in the wide old chimney. The male members of the family – such as I have seen seem thoroughly educated gentlemen. Mrs Bell is like an English or Scotch Matron, quiet, kind and well-bred – it seems she was brought up in London.*
>
> *Both her daughters are strikingly pretty in appearance – and their manners are very amiable and pleasing. I must say I like my new relations. My dear husband appears in a new light here in his own country. More than once I have had deep pleasure in hearing his praises on all sides. Some of the old servants and followers of the family tell me I am a most fortunate person for I have got one of the best gentlemen in the country. His aunt too speaks of him with a mixture of affection and respect most gratifying to hear. I was not well when I came here – fatigue and excitement had nearly knocked me up – and my cough was become very bad – but Mrs Bell has nursed both with kindness and skill, and I am greatly better now. I trust I feel thankful to God for having enabled me to make what seems a right choice – and I pray to be able to repay as I ought the affectionate devotion of a truthful, honourable, unboastful man.*
>
> (CBN to Margaret Wooler, 10 July 1854)

Could Charlotte be showing off a little here ? If we take her letters about her courtship as a whole, it is apparent that she faced a dilemma. She had consistently underplayed her feelings for Arthur, perhaps to protect the sensibilities of the spinster friends to whom she was writing. She had always appeared to be lukewarm about her fiancé and about her impending marriage. Now she had to make the transition to enthusiasm without losing credibility, perhaps be a little reluctant to admit how wrong she had been, how she had misjudged Arthur. Certainly the letter to Miss Wooler does seem to be something of an exercise in face-saving. Her delight is tempered by a touch of humility: 'it seems I have made a right choice'. This is a sober mature statement and typical of Charlotte Brontë. After all, once, when on a visit to London, she was asked whether she liked the city. She hesitated and then replied 'Yes, and No'. She could and did describe loneliness and suffering, her own as well as her characters', without qualification; about happiness, however, it was her habit to be a little more circum-spect. There was a streak of what can only be called 'incredulity' in her nature, a persistent preoccupation with the idea that good things 'could not be for me'. It is marked how slow, for example, her heroines are to realise that their wish for happiness can find fulfilment, that they can indeed be desired and even loved by other people. Charlotte invested her heroines with her own diffidence, almost as if she had convinced herself with her own words that happiness was not for her. Once married to Arthur, however, she had to unpick those words and admit to her sense of happiness. Though her happiness with Arthur may have been complete from the start of their marriage, she may have been understandably hesitant about putting her good fortune into words. Throughout the time of their marriage she professed nothing but contentment with her husband, and happiness such as she had never before known.

It was not in Charlotte Brontë's nature to take anything for granted, unless it was her sense of her own ugliness and her fear that she was destined to live the lonely life of a single woman. Life, and the grief she had experienced, had taught her never to be sure of anything; never complacent. Nor should the opposition to her marriage that her father displayed be overlooked, for the pressure he put upon her forced her to set her will against his, to make a deliberate choice to marry and thereby override whatever objections he put in her way. That had been no easy choice for her. Other than Charlotte and Arthur, Margaret Wooler was perhaps the only person who really understood the decision that her friend had been forced to make. Charlotte had stayed with Miss Wooler during the courtship months and clearly had discussed her dilemma with her, at the time when she had stopped writing to her erstwhile intimate friend and confidante, Ellen Nussey. She had known she was choosing for her father's future happiness as well as her own. While this may seem ridiculous today, Charlotte's circumstances meant that she was not making a simple choice in her own and Arthur's interests, for there was a third party in mind whom she felt obliged to consider. Miss Wooler would have understood the complexity of Charlotte's choice.

In her acknowledgement of Arthur's modest, unboastful nature, Charlotte appears also to be accepting that she and others had misjudged him. For so long she had only seen him as 'another curate', typecast for ridicule and teasing, and otherwise ignored. Charlotte and her sisters had been expert at dismissing their father's curates as figures of fun, only tolerated as necessary in helping their father do his parish work. Curates were quite simply never to be taken seriously; after all, the best of them, William Weightman, had proved to be merely a flirt, sending all three sisters a Valentine card at the same time. Once married, however, Charlotte seems to have realised the extent to which she had misjudged Arthur Nicholls. Her letters now were attempts to convey this realisation in moderate tones to those to whom she had long protested Arthur's inadequacies. Patrick Brontë may well have known his curate better than anyone. He may even have known more than he was prepared to admit. His own origins in Ireland had been far less promising and gracious than Arthur's. Arthur had been a student of Greek, Latin and Hebrew, had obtained a diploma in theology as well as his degree, and was from a good family which boasted other clergymen and teachers among its number. Arthur had all the qualifications and advantages that Patrick lacked and had struggled so hard to achieve.

For his part, Arthur had endured a considerable amount of unfair adverse publicity. Charlotte, seeing him among his family, quickly realised and eagerly admitted her good fortune.

What could have been better for her than to be welcomed into her husband's large family circle, with young women and successful gentlemen about her? Arthur's younger brother, James, was, at twenty-eight, the headmaster of the Royal School, in which Charlotte must have taken an interest, given her own teaching experiences, although there could have been no greater contrast between the Pensionnat Heger École de Demoiselles in the rue d'Isabelle in Brussels and the modest, if well-known, boarding school for boys in the depressed, post-famine village of Banagher. The comparison would not have escaped her, nor would the contrast between Aunt Harriet Bell and Madame Zoë Heger have passed unnoticed. Here Charlotte was once more lodged in a house with a school. Did she ever recall the dormitories of the Pensionnat Heger when she visited the dormitories of her brother-in-law's school? After all she had comparatively recently been re-creating dormitories in *Villette*. Banagher was a far cry from the Palais Royal area of Brussels, although its parish church would have been a more familiar place of worship to her than the great medieval Cathedral of St Michel et Ste Gudule. She was, however, once again a Protestant in a largely Catholic country. Even so, in Banagher as part of her husband's family she felt as much at home as she had been made to feel an alien in Brussels a decade earlier. Here she was healed by Aunt Bell's attention and a good man's love; in Brussels she had fed on sorrow, loneliness, exclusion and frustration. In Ireland she was warmed and welcomed at a family hearth, finding the comfort which she had needed and she had so longed for – and which had been denied – in Belgium, a comfort that is absent from any of the Brontë sisters' novels. The impossibility of her infatuation with the married Heger had been replaced by marriage to Arthur, to which the only impediments had been her tardiness in recognising his love, and her father's opposition. More than any heroine in her novels, Charlotte Brontë, casting off the masculine disguise of the pen name in which she had taken refuge as a means of fighting off the bitter grief at her sisters' deaths, found a home for herself, found refuge in the arms of a lover. The novelist who had made 'the lonely orphan' – the single woman wrapped in solitude – the theme of all her adult writing, had found in a real marriage a fulfilment more substantial than any metaphorical artistic conclusion. She had found the happiness her heroines had so eagerly and bitterly sought; the affection of a decent man and the companionship of his family. Time had redeemed her sadness in a quite surprising way. Nothing in Charlotte's account of her honeymoon denies the happiness she had found, her sense of good fortune. An incidental unexplored aspect of Charlotte's visit to Banagher was its proximity to Birr and the seat, at Birr Castle, of the Earls of Rosse. It was to Birr that the women in Arthur's family had travelled to avail themselves of copies of Charlotte's novels.

The Earl of Rosse had been connected with the Royal School at Cuba House, on at least one occasion acting as a visiting examiner. At the time of Charlotte's visit, the school was falling into decline and the Earl of Rosse was actively trying to find alternative accommodation for the school, it is thought in the town of Birr itself, where there was more likelihood of pupils. Banagher had suffered much during the famines and the associated epidemics and, in many ways, it was a depressed town with a falling population. The link with Birr Castle is of interest for other reasons. The Earl had been born in Yorkshire and his wife was a Heaton from Bradford, of which parish Patrick Brontë was the perpetual curate at Haworth. It hardly seems credible that Lady Rosse would have no curiosity or knowledge of her Yorkshire neighbouring curate's talented daughter. Charlotte Brontë's fame and Mr Currer Bell's identity were by this time well-established.

On the whole, little is known of the honeymoon tour other than its ports of call. Once Charlotte had recovered from her cold she and Arthur went south, following the course of the River Shannon downstream from Banagher, making for the coast. We do not have all the details of how the trip was made, however, although it must have been by a mixture of horse-drawn carriage of some kind and rail. Arthur Nicholls, in a letter to the brother of the clergyman who married them, tells that they 'took the Shannon on their way to Limerick', probably by steamship.

Fortunately, Charlotte's impulse to write letters was not diminished by her marriage, and equally fortunately several of what we may call her 'honeymoon' letters have survived. Each letter told its own story. As usual, Charlotte tailored what she wrote to each particular recipient. As might be expected, her letters to Ellen Nussey and Margaret Wooler are the most candid. Perhaps it is fitting at this point to remind ourselves that these were all private letters, despite their having been treated as public property since Mrs Gaskell's memoir of Charlotte was published.

Given that Charlotte assiduously destroyed letters sent to her – Arthur Nicholls was to state that he had never seen so much as a scrap of Ellen Nussey's handwriting – she doubtless did not expect her own to have survived in such numbers.

The honeymoon tour continued from Banagher to Limerick, thence via Tarbert to the little seaside resort of Kilkee, on the coast of County Clare north of the Shannon estuary. From here on 18 July, after twenty days of marriage, Charlotte wrote to Miss Wooler's sister, Catherine, who had been one of her teachers years earlier. The letter shows what good spirits the couple were in:

Your kind letter reached me in a wild and remote spot – a little watering place on the South west Coast of Ireland. Thank you for your kind wishes. I believe my dear husband to be a good man, and trust I have done right in marrying him. I hope too I shall be enabled always to feel grateful for the kindness and affection he shews me . . .

. . . if I had time I would tell you what I saw in Dublin – but your kind letter reached me in a parcel with about a dozen more, and they are all to be answered – and my husband is just now sitting before me stretching his patience to the utmost, but wishing me very much to have done writing, and put on my bonnet for a walk. From Dublin we went to Banagher where Mr Nicholls' relations live . . . I was very much pleased with all that I saw – but I was also greatly surprised to find so much of English order and repose in the family habits and arrangements. I had heard a great deal about Irish negligence &c. and I own that till I came to Kilkee – I saw little of it. Here at our inn – splendidly designated 'the West-End hotel' – there was a good deal to carp at if one were in carping humour – but we laugh instead of grumbling – for out of doors there is much indeed to compensate for any indoor shortcomings; so magnificent an ocean – so bold and grand a coast – I never yet saw. My husband calls me – Give my love to all who care to have it and believe me dear Miss Catherine, – your old pupil,

C.B.Nicholls

(CBN to Catherine Wooler, 18 July 1854)

There is a lightness of tone here that skittishly displays Charlotte's happiness. Her references to 'her husband' glow with the warmth and pride that can only derive from real pleasure. It is as though she is putting the words into the air to savour them as something wonderful, words she had long thought she would never be able to say except in a novel.

One of the letters in the parcel that Charlotte received in Kilkee was from Catherine Winkworth, the writer whom she had met at Mrs Gaskell's home months earlier, and with whom she had talked about her forthcoming marriage. Late in July, by which time the couple had reached Cork, she wrote back:

Yes – I am married – a month ago this very day I changed my name . . . after a short sojourn in the capital – went to the coast – such a wild ironbound coast – with such an ocean view as I had not yet seen and such battling waves with rocks as I had never imagined.

(CBN to Catherine Winkworth, 27 July 1854)

In her letter to Catherine Wooler Charlotte speaks of her husband calling to her, arguably an echo of Rochester's supernatural cry for Jane towards the end of *Jane Eyre*. Now in the letter to Catherine Winkworth she is describing something very similar to the scene from Thomas Bewick's *A History of British Birds* that the little Jane pored over in her window seat at the start of the same novel. Consciously or unconsciously, the novelist is at work, the true love story stated in terms that connect it to the fiction.

The letter continues with what has become a famously quoted description of a test which Arthur passed with flying colours. Much has been made of Charlotte's fear that she and Arthur were not of 'congenial tastes', that he was no intellectual or, in Charlotte's words, 'not a poet or a poetical man'. Clearly she had not seen the entries in his commonplace book. It may be that she meant that he was no Branwell, neither was he an Emily or an Anne. Charlotte Brontë may have thought her childhood 'ordinary', but in fact the opposite was the case. What she understood as 'congenial' was a creative imagination that would take fire on the instant, pluck characters, situations and events out of the air, or throw off a lyric or a sonnet at the drop of a hat in between executing a watercolour and devising the plot for an epic novel. The letter to Catherine Winkworth describes some of her fears of incompatibility of tastes:

> *my husband is not a poet or a poetical man – and one of my grand doubts before marriage was about 'congenial tastes' and so on. The first morning we went out on to the cliffs and saw the Atlantic coming in all white foam, I did not know whether I should get leave or time to take the matter in my own way. I did not want to talk – but I did want to look and be silent. Having hinted a petition, licence was not refused – covered with a rug to keep off the spray I was allowed to sit where I chose and he only interrupted me when he thought I crept too near the edge of the cliff. So far he is always good in this way – and this protection which does not interfere or pretend is I believe a thousand times better than any half sort of pseudo sympathy. I will try with God's help to be as indulgent to him whenever indulgence is needed.*

At heart, this passage describes a common anxiety about 'give and take'. Both Charlotte and Arthur had well-established habits and ways of coping with daily living. In her case, Charlotte had deep-rooted patterns of work and reflection; she knew how essential to her writing were landscapes, scenes and events, as too was the opportunity to absorb their influence. Her letter is eloquent of her relief that, so far, Arthur had been sensitive to this side of her character. Such reassurance is needed in all relationships where people are not to suffocate each other or deny separate sensibilities. On their return to Haworth Arthur gave his own account of the cliff-top wave-watching in a letter to George Sowden, in which he admirably displays 'congenial tastes':

> . . . *we also diverged to Kilkee, a glorious watering place, with the finest shore I ever saw – Completely girdled with stupendous cliffs – it was most refreshing to sit on a rock and look out on the broad Atlantic boiling and foaming at our feet . . .*

(ABN to George Sowden, August 1854)

The conclusion of Charlotte's letter from Cork contains the most intriguing story of the whole honeymoon. From Kilkee, the couple had made their way southwards to Killarney in County Kerry. While there, they had taken the trek through the famous tourist attraction known as the Gap of Dunloe, even today a substantial journey over rough terrain. This Charlotte did on horseback. There is no evidence of her ever having ridden before, and the road through the gap is steep and winding, climbing over stony ground to a narrow pass at the head of valleys.

For Charlotte, brought up on the paintings of John Martin and the poems of Wordsworth the very idea of climbing a mountain pass was in itself dramatic enough. The outing proved as exciting as she could have wished:

> *We saw and went through the Gap of Dunloe. A sudden glimpse of a very grim phantom came on us in the Gap. The guide had warned me to alight from my horse as the path was now very broken and dangerous – I did not feel afraid and declined – we passed the dangerous part – the horse trembled in every limb and slipped once but did not fall – soon after she (it was a mare) started and was unruly for a minute – however I kept my seat – my husband went to her head and led her – suddenly without any apparent cause – she seemed to go mad – reared, plunged – I was thrown on the stones right under her – my husband did not see that I had fallen – he still held her – I saw and felt her kick, plunge, trample round me. I had my thoughts about the moment – its consequences – my husband – my father – When my plight was seen, the struggling creature was let loose – she sprung over me. I was lifted off the stones neither bruised by the fall nor touched by the mare's hoofs. Of course the only feeling left was gratitude for more sakes than my own.*

(CBN to Catherine Winkworth, 27 July 1854)

There are elements of this narrative which recall Rochester's first
meeting with Jane Eyre, when his horse, Mesrour, stumbles as if terri-
fied by a spirit and throws him. Then, too, there is the scene in *Villette*
when Miss Marchmont tells of how her lover, Frank, his foot caught in
a stirrup, is dragged to his death by his horse. And perhaps it is not too
fanciful to reflect on the honeymooning Charlotte falling beneath the
hoofs of a mare, when in *Jane Eyre* she has her heroine vow that

> . . . *to gain some real affection from . . . any . . . whom I truly love, I
> would willingly submit to have the bone of my arm broken, or to let a
> bull toss me, or to stand behind a kicking horse, and let it dash its hoof at
> my chest –* . . .

(Jane Eyre, Chapter 8)

Not for the first time, events in Charlotte Brontë's life proved as
dramatic as any she had invented for her novels. The incident in the
Gap of Dunloe has all the strange qualities of a rite of passage. The
danger was real; the part of the trail where this happened is many miles
from habitation, and had Charlotte been seriously, or even slightly,
injured there were no rescue services to pluck her off the mountain
track. She had every reason to worry about her husband and her father,
for any injury would have had most serious implications. Furthermore,
it is significant that for the first time in her life she placed concern for
her father second. Non-Poet or Un-Poetical though he might be,
Arthur was already the focus of her affection and her anxiety.

The thought of Charlotte Brontë on horseback, being thrown and
taking it all in her stride seems so out of character, but perhaps that is
what her determination to marry also displayed: that Charlotte Brontë
was no ordinary person and that she possessed considerable strength.
There is, too, a curious irony in the idea of Charlotte the new wife
being subjected to an ordeal by horse's hoofs, that seems almost too
appropriate. The 'glimpse of a very grim phantom' at the top of a
mountain pass is so like many of John Martin's paintings that it must
have seemed very familiar to her, the whole incident very much what
she would have expected to happen in such a place. She had always
been one to take risks; she had once been rowed out to a ship in the
Thames and insisted she be allowed on board, and she had travelled
unchaperoned to and from Brussels when she had returned there
without Emily. The long and steep path through the Gap of Dunloe
was there to be climbed. The safety of the fireside chair was not
Charlotte Brontë's first choice.

Leaving Killarney, the couple travelled south to Cork, and from there back to Dublin. By this time Charlotte was beginning to long to be home, for news of her father's health had not been good. On the day after she received that news she wrote from Dublin to Martha Brown at the parsonage, telling her that they intended to be in Haworth on Tuesday, 1 August 'at about seven o'clock in the evening'. On the same day she wrote to Ellen Nussey, telling of their impending return:

> *We have been travelling about . . . I shall make no effort to describe the scenery through which we have passed. Some parts have exceeded all I ever imagined. Of course much pleasure has sprung from all this, and more, perhaps, from the kind and ceaseless protection which has ever surrounded me, and made travelling a different matter to me from what it has heretofore been.*
>
> *Still, Nell, it is written that there shall be no unmixed happiness in this world. Papa has not been well, and I have been longing, longing intensely sometimes, to be at home. Indeed, I could enjoy and rest no more, and so home we are going.*
>
> (CBN to Elizabeth Nussey, 28 July 1854)

On 1 August, as Charlotte had predicted, they were safely back in the parsonage, where they found that Patrick Brontë had indeed been ill. He soon recovered once his daughter was back home – not the first father so to behave.

Chapter Nine

~

'It Is a Solemn and Strange and Perilous Thing For a Woman to Become a Wife'

The honeymoon over, Charlotte's letters now provide insights into her adjustment to married life. Her life was now very different. How could it be otherwise? In writing to Ellen she renews a candour that suggests the former intimacy with her friend. Once married Charlotte appears able to write in her old vein, whereas during the courtship, she seems to have understood that Ellen would have been neither a helpful nor an encouraging correspondent. The two of them had perfected the art of character assassination over so long a period, and had kept alive the idea that they were destined to be old maids, that Charlotte may well have thought it necessary to keep her distance while she soberly considered Arthur Nicholls's offer. In her new status, she sought to renew and continue her friendship, on the best possible terms:

> Since I came home I have not had an unemployed moment. My life is changed indeed – to be wanted continually – to be constantly called for and occupied seems strange; yet it is a marvellously good thing. As yet I don't understand how some wives grow so selfish – As far as my experience of matrimony goes – I think it tends to draw you out of, and away from yourself . . .
>
> Dear Nell – during the last 6 weeks – the colour of my thoughts is a good deal changed: I know more of the realities of life than I once did. I think many false ideas are propagated perhaps unintentionally. I think those women who indiscriminately urge their acquaintance to marry – much to blame.
>
> (CBN to Ellen Nussey, 9 August 1854)

Charlotte here deploys her novelist's skills in writing succinctly and appositely about the change in her life. 'The marvellously good thing'

187

– to be needed and called for – was always to her a Holy Grail. She now triumphantly, though with a touch of moderation, announces her happiness; she is at last, 'wanted continuously'. As might be expected Charlotte reflects on how her life has changed and is perceptive in asserting that matrimony 'draws you out of, and away from yourself', something which she eagerly sought after her years of isolation following her sisters' deaths. She is, too, frank about the true meaning of marriage – 'the colour of my thoughts is a good deal changed: I know more of the realities of life than I once did.' It was no easy thing for the artist in Charlotte to forsake her dreamland and take the risk of accepting an imperfect relationship in the real world. Here the woman Charlotte was casting off the comfortable fiction of the man Currer Bell. Her new signature, C.B.Nicholls, sustains something of the ambiguity of her identity as a novelist, since, conveniently, the 'B' could as easily stand for Brontë as Bell. In accepting Arthur's name she had subsumed her 'Bell' into his, possibly even returning it to its origins. There is telling evidence of what it cost her to take the new name in several letters where she signs herself 'C. Bron–', has then to cross out her incomplete maiden name and replace it with Nicholls. The change was not an easy one for her.

Charlotte concludes her letter to Ellen with still more advice:

I can only say with deeper sincerity and fuller significance – what I always said in theory – Wait God's will. Indeed – indeed Nell – it is a solemn and strange and perilous thing for a woman to become a wife. Man's lot is far – far different.

Again, her theme is that of reality superseding theory, though there is a hint at the physical implications of marriage in the phrase the 'strange and perilous' in this context. A postscript to the same letter tells how much her husband has thrived on the 'strange and perilous' experience of the first six weeks of married life:

Have I told you how much better Mr Nicholls is ? He looks quite strong and hale – he gained 12 pounds during the 4 weeks we were in Ireland. To see this improvement in him has been a main source of happiness to me, and to speak truth – a subject of wonder too.

It is somehow odd to think of a clergyman solemnly weighing himself before and after a holiday. Once more, however, Charlotte is advertising her happiness with the choice she has made, both in marriage and in her husband.

The people of the parish were evidently very pleased to have Arthur back among them, to such an extent that the Reverend and Mrs Nicholls held a large tea party in the Sunday School Room to thank them for the 'hearty welcome and general goodwill' shown to them. Some *500* of Haworth's inhabitants were invited to tea and supper, including the 'Sunday and day scholars and Teachers – the church ringers, singers'. Sadly, there is no account of this occasion by one of the parishioners, for the idea of almost a quarter of the population of this poor, slum-like, depressed township sitting down to supper and drinking toasts stretches the imagination. A party for 500 was not something a poor curate could ever hope to provide, so that the advantage of Charlotte's income as a writer is immediately evident, the money that had allowed her to have rooms in the parsonage enlarged, properly curtained and newly wallpapered; that gave her the opportunity, if she chose, to defy her father and insist on having her own way. Like her predecessor, Jane Austen, she valued the praise that her novels won, but she also thoroughly enjoyed the freedom that the royalty payments gave her as a women in a society where single women without private means were left desperately dependent. The money Charlotte made from her writing was an astonishing sum for its day. The £500 she was paid for *Villette* (and, as has been said, she had hoped for £700) must be compared with a schoolmaster's £70 a year and her father's stipend of £160–£190. There can be no doubt that in this respect alone, Arthur had made a good match.

Charlotte delighted in the parish tea-and-supper party, particularly proud that a toast was drunk to her Arthur describing him as a 'consistent Christian and a kind gentleman', which she took as a great compliment. It is difficult not to wonder what the Reverend and Mrs Nicholls provided in the way of drink for so many of the parish, since it is not customary to drink toasts in tea. Nor do we know whether Patrick Brontë attended, and if he did, whether he raised his glass to Arthur. Or was he once again indisposed?

Back in the parish, re-established in a familiar setting and with work which he had always enjoyed, Arthur could feel well pleased. Against the odds, he had married his adored Charlotte, and he had the respect of parishioners he knew well. It must have seemed a long time since he had kept vigil across the churchyard from his lodgings, gazing at Charlotte's window. There is no reason to doubt that he and Patrick Brontë were now, if not on the best of terms, at least reconciled to making the new family situation work. For his part Arthur Nicholls had always argued that he and the parson were on perfectly amicable terms, and that he quite understood the latter's objections to his daughter marrying his curate. It is easy to forget that he would have known nothing of Patrick Brontë's attacks upon his character, having no access to the letters that research has afforded history. Charlotte, in her accounts to her friends, has coloured our perception of the courtship and particularly emphasised her father's opposition, but she would have hardly shown her husband letters that vilified him.

The organising Charlotte could be well satisfied. Not only had she married a decent man, she was also able to 'feel comforted to think this marriage has secured Papa good aid in his old age'. Indeed, she had not even had to move house or change bedrooms. She did, however, find herself very busy, feeling sometimes, when her husband bid her to take a walk on the moors, that she could just as well write letters instead. This was not really a grumble, however, nor should it be hastily assumed that marriage had stopped her writing, that her husband allowed her no time for herself. There were, as in any marriage, considerable adjustments to be made on all sides. Patrick Brontë had to accommodate a change to his routines in his own house where he had held sway for more than thirty years. The disciplined, dutiful daughter now had two men in the parsonage whose needs she had to consider. These were not minor adjustments for the household, nor would new routines be established overnight. Patrick Brontë and Charlotte had lived together for five years since the death of Anne, and however haphazard and troubled their lives had been they had found a modus vivendi. Having shared so much, there was a strong bond between them, as there was with Tabitha Aykroyd, who had cared for all the children in turn, and with Martha Brown. Every step Charlotte had taken in her writing and in coping with her fame had been shared with her father. No friendship of hers had really threatened that bond or their unity. It is understandable that for his part Patrick Brontë could see no reason why that situation should ever have been altered. His daughter's marriage was the biggest challenge he had to face in his old age, and his thoughts and feelings, as his increasing physical tiredness left him more and more the victim of his circumstances, can only be guessed at. His eyesight was once again failing and his health uncertain, while he must also have been increasingly frustrated by a loss of his powers and of his authority. He took advantage of whatever strength he could muster, however, and with Arthur's help in running the parish he found he had the energy to preach again. It is not hard to see how necessary it was for him to hold on to his own sense of competence and of value in what was still his parish. The celebratory tea-and-supper party for the parishioners with which the Nichollses had marked their return must also have been an expression of relief in the township, after the chaos of the unfortunate de Renzy's short but ill-fated sojourn, that a familiar pattern was to be restored. Arthur Nicholls's excellent management of the schools and his smooth running of parish affairs had been as greatly valued as they had been missed. De Renzy had had a hopeless task, not least because his parson was far too set in his ways to be helpful to a new man. The parishioners in Haworth, never an easy flock, would have been deeply suspicious of any newcomer, and consequently delighted to have the old team back in business. Doubtless there was much truth in the parish saying that in Mr Brontë they had a fine parson who got on with his own affairs and didn't meddle with theirs.

'I Hardly Like Coming in Contact With All the Mrs Parsons'

The world that Charlotte Nicholls tried to keep in balance consisted of what she called the 'Mrs Parsons' – she had her own 'parson' father and 'parson' husband, quite enough parsons for her – and her friendships with Ellen Nussey and Margaret Wooler. In the case of Ellen, Charlotte planned to invite her to stay at the parsonage so that she could get to know Arthur Nicholls, while he and Charlotte teasingly tried their hand at matchmaking her with yet another parson, the Reverend Sutcliffe Sowden, who had married them. There are plenty of such light-hearted passages in the letters Charlotte wrote in the early days of her marriage; taken with her assurances that she was now enjoying much better health, they suggest that married life suited her:

> *I really like Mr Sowden very well. He asked after you. Mr Nicholls told him we expected you would be coming to stay with us in the course of 3 or 4 weeks – and that he [Arthur] should then invite him over again as he wished us to take sundry rather long walks – and as he should have his wife to look after – and that she was trouble enough – it would be quite necessary to have a guardian for the other lady. Mr S. ——— seemed perfectly acquiescent.*
>
> (CBN to Ellen Nussey, 9 August 1854)

Like all newlyweds, both she and Arthur enjoyed joking about their new titles, she writing often about 'her husband', he offering gentle jokes about his 'wife'. His plea that his wife would be enough for him to look after is perhaps a fair one; after all, she had fallen from a horse while on honeymoon. Nothing came of the matchmaking, however, for Ellen was as much the dedicated spinster as Charlotte was not. Indeed, time would show that Ellen had never really liked Arthur very much, nor did she keep faith with Patrick Brontë after Charlotte's death, and she was to have harsh and spiteful things to say about them both.

To Margaret Wooler, Charlotte wrote warmly about her marriage. Yes, her father was in reasonable health; yes, Arthur was still putting on weight, and joking that his good health was beginning to worry him a little. She also believed that she was coming to terms with her new status:

> . . . *now that I am married I do not expect to be an object of much general interest. Ladies who have won some prominence (call it either* notoriety *or* celebrity) *in their single life – often fall quite into the background when they change their names; but if true domestic happiness replace Fame – the exchange will indeed be for the better.*
>
> . . . *My own life is more occupied than it used to be; I have not so much time for thinking: I am obliged to be more practical, for my dear Arthur is a very practical as well as very punctual, methodical man. Every morning he is in the National School by nine o'clock; he gives the children religious instruction till half-past 10. Almost every afternoon he pays visits amongst the poor parishioners. Of course he often finds a little work for his wife to do, and I hope she is not sorry to help him.*
>
> *I believe it is not bad for me that his bent should be so wholly towards matters of real life and active usefulness – so little inclined to the literary and contemplative. As to his continued affection and kind attentions – it does not become me to say much of them but as yet they neither change nor diminish.*

(CBN to Margaret Wooler, 19 September 1854)

Once again we see Charlotte confessing that she needed help in keeping herself firmly in touch with reality, that her 'practical' and 'methodical' Arthur was thus an ideal partner for her. It is conceivable that abandoning the lure of fantasy, of the imaginary worlds of her creative imagination, had been the price she had to pay in her private life. Was she so beguiled by her images of perfection, so mesmerised by the satisfying patterns supplied in fiction – denouements that are so rare and elusive in life – that she had long overlooked the true demands of domestic happiness in her hunger for romantic epics? Her considerable inventiveness must have had an effect on her outlook and habitual way of thinking. Rather than sharing her life with another such powerfully creative mind – as she had already done with her sisters – she seems to have realised that for her everyday life she needed a partner with a different bent. The marriage was full of promise; her greatest sadness and the cause of most of her depression, her solitude, was no more. She cheerfully writes, in delight not regret, that her life is now busy, that she is needed, that she has plenty to do. No more does she mention the silence settling in to entrap her in a home that has become like a prison. There is a sense of bustle in her life, an atmosphere in which she thrived. Her desperate cries of loneliness, her need occasionally to run from the parsonage, have been replaced by exultant statements of how little time she has for anything, and of the pleasure she takes in her husband's good health. It is wrong to wish her back to a tormented, painful isolation and to the lonely struggle to create more novels for posterity. We should celebrate her happiness and rejoice in her enjoyment of marriage rather than grieve over the incomplete manuscripts that might have been completed if Charlotte had remained a spinster. Those biographers who find her life, and especially her married life, 'drab' and uneventful are missing the point. To call her courtship 'tepid' and refer to her marriage and death as 'not really exciting' betrays a certain type of scholar's myopic, ivory-tower detachment from his fellow men and women. Life is not, as the poet W.H. Auden said of poetry, 'always on its high horse'. We do not need rope-ladder elopements and leaps from blazing battlements to make 'real' life exciting. A courtship that is tepid to one may be exhilarating to another; equally, it is nonsense to describe a person's actual historical death as not really 'exciting'.

One view of Charlotte's marriage would suggest that her choices and her courage made her life exciting enough. As has been said, marriage in the mid-nineteenth century meant pregnancy; at Charlotte's age and with her medical history, to take such a risk was a very brave undertaking. The outcome, her death within a year of her marriage, makes her story exceedingly tragic. Her father saw it as a tale of extreme folly, concluding much as he had feared it would. For her part, Charlotte found it all exciting, as her letters show. The frequent references to 'my husband', 'my dear boy', 'Arthur – as I now call him', and her appropriate modesty about his attentions – 'it does not become me to say much of them' – provide ample evidence of a happy wife.

Charlotte, in an era when the majority of women died before reaching her age, had in her maturity thrown caution to the wind, taken a husband, and found him to be affectionate, considerate and consistently kind. Every letter she wrote after marriage, even those from her sickbed, spoke of how much she enjoyed the attentions, affection and kindliness of her 'boy' Arthur. Her marriage in real life was quite as good as any she had invented; indeed her courtship and her relationship with her man were far more satisfying than those she had contrived for Lucy Snowe in *Villette*. A sense of comfort and lightness is evident in her letters, for although the poor curate may not have been a Tolstoy, nor even a Boswell, he was without doubt a good husband to her. She was well content with life with the man who had refused to take no for an answer.

Whatever the 'perils' were that Charlotte told Ellen Nussey lay in store for any woman when she married, she embraced them and enjoyed the comforts that followed. This is not as surprising as it may at first seem. If she was anything, the author of *Jane Eyre* and *Villette* was clearly a sensualist. Blood flowed from the very beginning of *Jane Eyre*, so that it was little wonder that her contemporary readers flinched – and then read on avidly. Patrick Brontë was, by all accounts, a full-blooded impetuous man, accepting of physical relationships, and all the evidence of the writing by his children, from tumbling, puppy-like play with words to mature sustained stories, endorses the physical side of their lives. Can we really believe that a creature like the sot Arthur Huntingdon in *The Tenant of Wildfell Hall*, to say nothing of Heathcliff in *Wuthering Heights* and Bertha Mason in *Jane Eyre*, could have been created by cold, withdrawn people. The overwhelming evidence, from their verse as well as their prose, is of passionate engagement, of romantic longings, of a powerful understanding of the physical basis of relationships. Even the so-called 'gentle' Anne wrote of violence with shocking effect. In the main, there is nothing decorous or refined in Brontë novels; time and again we are shocked by such violent scenes as the brutal flattening of young birds by a governess or the hanging of a dog by its collar. The sisters, and Charlotte least of all, would never have traded their 'country' honesty and fire for 'town' courtesies. While we may not today label *Jane Eyre* or *The Tenant of Wildfell Hall* 'depraved', nevertheless we still find them, together with the brutality and dark morality of *Wuthering Heights*, deeply shocking. The acceptance of violence and the celebration of the flesh-and-blood, whatever their artistic effect, show the Brontë sisters facing up to the physical realities of life. The briefest comparison with the novels of Jane Austen clearly shows how far their works are removed from polite convention and social courtesies. The reception by the reading public in the middle of the nineteenth century registered this fact; the novels were, without exception, seen as quite shocking. It was not only adultery that shocked readers however – it was the recognition of 'blood' as a life-supporting force.

Caresses, Kisses and Babies

Jane Eyre is a novel that begins with blows and ends with caresses. The most piteous of Jane's deprivations throughout her life, and particularly as a child, is the lack of cuddles and kisses. The effect of this is conveyed in the story by her sense of imprisonment within her own physical sexuality. How often, and how powerfully, she longs to throw open doors and windows to escape from confinement, something that she shares with Rochester's wife, the mad Bertha Mason, whose imprisonment makes a cruel and eloquent juxtaposition, showing us, as it does Jane, both sides of the wedding veil, as well as the implications of marrying Rochester. There are times when Jane Eyre must almost suffocate, again like Bertha, within her own tormenting emotions. Her flight to the open moorland, during which she first sleeps in and then rises from a coffin-shaped bed in the heather under the open sky, is a crucial point in the novel. In Charlotte's case, Arthur's courtship, his indefatigable and continual urging of his suit, offered her a similar release from the fate of becoming steeped in what she called the 'soured vinegar shrillness' of the ageing single woman. Arthur's insistence seems to have made her curious about the challenge that marriage offered, and about its implications. Not for the first time, Charlotte used her letters, especially those to particularly chosen correspondents, to sound out what a married future might hold for her. To this end she had exchanged letters with, and was to have quite a lot to do with, a newly married couple, Amelia and Joseph Taylor.

Amelia Ringrose had married Joseph Taylor, the brother of Mary Taylor, an old schoolfriend of Charlotte and of Ellen Nussey who had emigrated to New Zealand. Charlotte's correspondence and friendship with Amelia is important for the insight it provides into her attitude towards and curiosity about small children. Two subjects now appear quite frequently in her letters at this time: the adjustments that women had to make when they married, and the implications of having children. Through her friendship with Mrs Gaskell she had first come to see that it was possible to be a writer and a mother, that it was not necessarily a choice of either the one or the other. With Catherine Winkworth, whose sister had recently married (though she herself was single), she had discussed the necessary adjustments women who were married had to make. Here Charlotte was able to reflect on how a woman was required, or would need, to humour a man's wishes, like and dislikes. In this respect it seems that she was particularly worried that Arthur was not her intellectual equal. He was, after all, not a Brontë, would be no adequate substitute for Branwell, Emily or Anne. George Smith the publisher would much more readily have fitted that bill.

Charlotte's correspondence with Amelia Ringrose in the year 1854, by then Mrs Joseph Taylor, and indeed her friendship with the family, meant that a baby was now part of her world. We should not, however, overlook the fine portrayal of a child at the beginning of *Villette*. Any sympathetic reading of these passages offers an unsentimental and loving portrayal of a child. The child Charlotte noticed and knew was born to the Taylors in the autumn of 1851 and, having been a sickly baby, caused her parents to fuss over her, something which in turn incurred Charlotte's scorn. The child, though christened Emily Martha, was nicknamed 'Tim', an abbreviation for Timon of Athens, presumably because there were times when she seemed to hate the world and everyone in it. Charlotte, with no children of her own (as Amelia Taylor once pointed out when criticised), was always ready to be critical of the parenting of others, announcing that whereas she had formerly believed that the earth revolved round the sun, she now knew that it revolved round 'some babies'. From time to time she reported that she liked the baby best of the family, though she added that with its doting parents she would not 'like to be in its socks!' It may be that in observing the pregnancy and the subsequent parenting Charlotte wondered whether she would ever have the opportunity to raise her own child, a child that would not necessarily be seen as the centre of the universe. As she grew to toddle and find words, Tim endeared herself, if questionably, to Charlotte by persisting in calling her 'Granny' ('Aunt' was then the accepted mode of address by a child to a close female friend of the family), thereby neatly reminding us of the novelist's age at the time of her courtship and marriage. The late thirties was the average age for a grandmother in the poor township of Haworth, though few women there survived to see their grandchildren born. With good humour and perhaps not a little irony, Charlotte accepted the given style of 'Grandma' in letters to Ellen. Tim features frequently in Charlotte's letters, she being particularly cross when a holiday with the Taylors in Scotland was abruptly curtailed because the doting parents had thought the child was poorly and therefore at risk away from home. The single 'Grandma' was none too pleased to find that life could be ruled by so small a child.

Could Charlotte, in being courted and being made to consider the possibility of marriage, also be contemplating the implications of having children. As has been said, no marriage in the mid-nineteenth century would have been undertaken without thought being given to child-bearing. Marriage, as the Book of Common Prayer made abundantly clear, was 'first ordained for the procreation of children'. Those words must have had a particular resonance for Patrick Brontë; indeed, the marriage agreement which he and Charlotte had drawn up provided for her children, were there to be any, to inherit in precedence over her husband. Thus children had been considered and even provided for, nor can the fact that Charlotte might have wished to have children be completely discounted. Yet there is a tendency to believe that simply continuing to be a successful author would be enough to satisfy her. Her stories show a quite different emphasis, however. The impulse in her novels – except, that is, for *Villette* – is towards marriage and motherhood (it is, for instance, easy to overlook the first Mrs Rochester's children). Charlotte does not shirk the physical consummation of marriage: the conjugal fulfilment. Even in her first novel – though in fact the last to be published – *The Professor*, children grace the cottage that is the Crimsworths' newfound paradise. By transference from author to fictional character, all three Brontë sisters have what might be termed surrogate babies in their novels, as well as surrogate lovers; a count of the number of children that Ellen Dean cares for in *Wuthering Heights* proves the point. Even so, while 'parenting in theory' is never far from the central themes of every novel by each of the Brontë sisters, comment about real babies only appears with any frequency in Charlotte's letters at around the time of Arthur's persistent courtship, suggesting that children were now being looked at and thought about in a way that was new to the parsonage. After her marriage we learn from Charlotte that Tim was quite taken with Patrick Brontë's white whiskers, while thoroughly disliking Arthur's black ones, telling him in no uncertain terms that he should go and shave them off. It does seem that at least one child was present in Charlotte's mind in a way that none had ever been before. Knowing the story of *Jane Eyre*, such tenderness and interest in children should come as no surprise. The tenderness of Bessie in that novel, her embraces and kisses, her enduring love for the orphan Jane, provide a fine example of motherly affection that never falters nor fails. Moreover, her marriage is, as has already been mentioned, of the best kind, her husband perhaps the only thoroughly good-hearted man in the whole story. It is not without significance that Bessie's married name is Leaven. Bessie receives more kisses from Jane than any other character, the little girl clinging to her on being sent away to school: 'I was taken from Bessie's neck, to which I clung with kisses' (*Jane Eyre*, Chapter 5).

Charlotte Brontë's use of kisses in her novels is as sparing as Shakespeare's in his plays. The kiss is seen as sacramental, a sharing of the breath that is the soul, a token of mutual love. Kisses that lack this mutuality are held to be the kisses of Judas. Jane Eyre is clear about this when Rochester, after his marriage to Bertha Mason has been discovered, stoops to kiss her:

> But I remembered caresses were now forbidden. I turned my face away, and put his aside. 'What! – How is this?' he exclaimed hastily. 'Oh, I know! you won't kiss the husband of Bertha Mason? You consider my arms filled and my embraces appropriated?'
>
> (*Jane Eyre*, Chapter 27)

The kisses of Jane's cousin St John Rivers provide the most comprehensive comment Charlotte put into print:

> One evening, when, at bedtime, his sisters and I stood round him, bidding him good-night, he kissed each of them, as was his custom; and, as was equally his custom, he gave me his hand. Diana, who chanced to be in a frolicsome humour . . . exclaimed –
>
> 'St John! you used to call Jane your third sister, but you don't treat her as such: you should kiss her too.'
>
> She pushed me towards him. I thought Diana very provoking, and felt uncomfortably confused; and while I was thus thinking and feeling, St John bent his head; his Greek face was brought to a level with mine, his eyes questioned my eyes piercingly – he kissed me. There are no such things as marble kisses or ice kisses, or I should say my ecclesiastical cousin's salute belonged to one of these classes; but there may be experiment kisses, and his was an experiment kiss. When given he viewed me to learn the result; it was not striking: I am sure I did not blush; perhaps I might have turned a little pale, for I felt as if this kiss were a seal affixed to my fetters.
>
> (*Jane Eyre*, Chapter 34)

It would be a brave man who bent to kiss Charlotte Brontë after reading that. Were Arthur's kisses seen as experiments? He must surely have known that much was expected of him – after all, few men are provided with so many hints of their wife's thoughts about passion and true love. We shall never know to what extent Charlotte's fiction seduced him, but we can understand the challenge he faced in making his proposal of marriage. Rather than his nervous behaviour on that occasion being anything to do with fear of Patrick Brontë, might it not have been temerity at offering himself as a lover to a woman famous for writing passionate love stories, the creator of Rochester and Bertha Mason, the explorer of the 'experiment kiss'. Charlotte Brontë's professed happiness, once married, rather suggests that Arthur's kisses, unlike those of St John Rivers, were far from such cold experiment. Clearly Charlotte Brontë had more than a passing interest in kisses, which could suggest that Arthur was a lucky man.

Conclusion

❧

'As to My Husband, My Heart Is Knit to Him'

As we have seen, the early months of marriage were happy ones for Charlotte and Arthur. A new peace had been found with Patrick Brontë, the old man sitting back with relief as Arthur once again ran the parish. No need now for him to look for lodgings in the parish, or send messengers to find out when his daughter was coming home or, for that matter, where she was.

The Reverend and Mrs Nicholls were now busy people. Charlotte wrote to several of her friends telling them she had never been more occupied, both active and needed about the home and the parish. It was a change for her in common with the whole adjustment of marriage, an adjustment that was as far-reaching for Arthur as it was for Charlotte. She at least stayed in her own home, while her husband must have sensed that he was moving into a powerfully charged house; must, too, have had memories of his own about the family's past and his involvement with Charlotte's brother and sisters. It is, perhaps, likely that he and the servant Martha would have exchanged a few knowing looks, after all the gossip that had flown between the parsonage kitchen and his lodgings in her parents' house. Nor is it easy to imagine that Martha was not as keenly interested in the recent developments as she had been with every detail of the courtship. After all, on more than one occasion she had seen her mistress flee up the stairs rather than meet Arthur. In fact, he and Martha seem to have enjoyed a good relationship, despite her earlier misgivings, even dislike, for he watched over her affairs until her death, invariably treating her with respect.

During their first happy months together, the couple were visited by Arthur's clergy friends, whose wives Charlotte perhaps understandably wished to keep at a little distance, by Sir James Kay-Shuttleworth and his wife, and by one of Arthur's cousins from Ireland. Throughout all this time Charlotte continually spoke and wrote of her good fortune in her choice of husband. She was happy as she had never been, both she and Arthur claiming that no cross word had ever come between them, nor had there been any dispute with her father. Sir James Kay-Shuttleworth, who had long cultivated Charlotte as a celebrated author, now set about wooing her parson husband, offering him the living of Padiham in Lancashire, of which he was the patron. It must have been pleasing for Charlotte to see her husband being courted and offered promotion, even though it was very likely her fame that drove Sir James on. Things looked rosy for the newlyweds, for although Arthur stuck to his promise that until Patrick Brontë died Haworth would be his home, the patronage and respect of Sir James, with his many connections, as retired First Secretary of the Committee of the Council of Education, would be a feather in the curate's cap and promised well for the future.

In January 1855 the sought-after Reverend and the famous Mrs Nicholls visited Sir James and Lady Kay-Shuttleworth at Gawthorpe Hall, where they stayed for a few days. Charlotte had been a guest there in her spinster days, but how different and exciting this visit must have been, now that she was accompanied by her husband. She must, too, have been much more relaxed, where before she had been intimidated. The fine house had undergone recent improvements during which the architect Sir Charles Barry (who from 1840 until his death in 1860 was responsible for much of the rebuilding of the Houses of Parliament after the disastrous fire in 1834) had converted it from a fairly ruinous Tudor mansion to an imposing building equipped with all the most modern features such as piped water. Exasperatingly, Charlotte, who had seen the house both before and after the improvements, left no record of her feelings about the transformation.

It was while at Gawthorpe that Charlotte caught cold, it is thought from walking through wet grass in thin shoes. Her cold persisted after her return to Haworth, and as January passed she fell into a sickness that gave cause for concern. At the end of the month a doctor was called who surmised – as did the parsonage servants and Charlotte herself – that she was pregnant. There was hope that her 'illness' would pass, that persistent nausea would ease and there would be a happy outcome to her present indisposition. Earlier, prolonged attacks of nausea and sickness had forced her to cancel a planned visit to stay with Ellen Nussey:

I very much wish to come to Brookroyd – but the fact is I am not sure whether I shall be well enough to leave home. At present I should be a most tedious visitor. My health has been really very good ever since my return from Ireland 'till about ten days ago, when the stomach seemed quite suddenly to lose its tone – indigestion and continual faint sickness have been my portion ever since. Don't conjecture – dear Nell – for it is too soon yet though I certainly never before felt as I have done lately. But keep the matter wholly to yourself – for I can come to no decided opinion at present. I am rather mortified to lose my good looks and grow thin as I am doing . . .

(CBN to Ellen Nussey, 19 January 1855)

Although Charlotte clearly thought that she might be pregnant, as did the other members of the household, modern biographers and their medical advisers have expressed their doubts, often accompanied by somewhat distasteful speculation. Any evidence lies with Charlotte Nicholls's remains in the Brontë vault in Haworth, fortunately over-built in 1879 by the foundations of the church that replaced the building Patrick Brontë knew, where its secret may be well kept.

Charlotte's health rapidly declined. In mid-January she had remade her will, removing the barrier against Arthur inheriting the accumu-lated money from her writing and leaving him her estate. Writing to Amelia Taylor at the end of that month, however, she is still optimistic and making light of her illness:

. . . 'till about a fortnight since I have scarcely had an ailment since I was married – but latterly my health has been a good deal disordered – only however by indigestion – loss of appetite and such like annoyances.

Papa continues much better – and Arthur is well and flourishing. His cousin has been here and the visit was a real treat – he is a cultivated, thoroughly educated man with a mind stored with information gathered from books and travel – and what is far rarer – with the art of conversing appropriately and quietly and never pushing his superiority upon you. His name is James Adamson Bell and he is a clergyman.

(CBN to Amelia Taylor, 21 January 1855)

How proud Charlotte was of her in-laws. How much Patrick Brontë must have enjoyed the enlightened conversations with a fellow Irishman and clergyman. What a change the marriage had brought and what promise it all held for life in the parsonage! It is evident that Charlotte had found fulfilment in her marriage, a happiness which, despite her success as a novelist, had always seemed to evade her grasp. The letter continues: 'It is an hourly happiness to me dear Amelia to see how well Arthur and my Father get on together now – there has never been a misunderstanding or wrong word.'

The next weeks saw Charlotte bedridden and Arthur writing three times on her behalf to Ellen. Dr McTurk, the physician from Leeds who had attended her sister Anne, examined her and, while he thought her illness would last a while, felt 'there was no immediate danger'. On 14 February, St Valentine's Day, Arthur wrote to Ellen once more:

> *It is difficult to write to friends about my wife's illness, as its cause is yet uncertain – at present she is completely prostrated with weakness and sickness and frequent fever – all may turn out well in the end, and I hope it will; if you saw her you would perceive that she can maintain no correspondence at present.*
>
> (ABN to Ellen Nussey, 14 February 1855)

From her sickbed, Charlotte managed to write a few letters in pencil. All of them tell of the great comfort her husband was to her in her illness: 'No kinder, better husband than mine, it seems to me, can there be in the world. I do not want now for kind companionship in health and the tenderest nursing in sickness.' A letter to Ellen written at the end of February restates her happiness with Arthur while confessing her illness:

> *My dear Ellen,*
>
> *I must write one line out of my weary bed . . . I am not going to talk of my sufferings, it would be useless and painful – I want to give you an assurance which I know will comfort you – and that is that I find my husband the tenderest nurse, the kindest support – the best earthly comfort that ever woman had. His patience never fails, and it is tried by sad days and broken nights . . .*
>
> (CBN to Ellen Nussey, February 1855)

In her final letter to Ellen, Charlotte tells her friend that she is 'reduced to greater weakness' and that she cannot talk, 'even to my dear, patient, constant Arthur, I can say but few words at once.' Two letters to Amelia Taylor are among the last Charlotte was able to write. Still she writes of her love for her husband and his love for her:

> *Let me speak the plain truth – my sufferings are very great – my nights indescribable – sickness with scarce a reprieve – I strain until what I*

vomit is mixed with blood. Medicine I have quite discontinued. If you can send me anything that will do me good – do.

As to my husband – my heart is knit to him – he is so tender, so good, helpful, patient . . .

(CBN to Amelia Taylor, February 1855)

And later:

I'll try to write a line myself . . . The medicines produced no perceptible effect on me but I thank you for them all the same.

I would not let Arthur write to Dr Hemingway – I know it would be wholly useless. For 2 days I have been something better – owing to the milder weather.

. . . Oh for happier times! My little Grandchild [Tim] – when shall I see her again?

(CBN to Amelia Taylor, February 1855)

Charlotte's condition now rapidly deteriorated. Her father wrote to Ellen Nussey the letter he must have dreaded having to write, and which he had so often had to write before about members of his family. At seventy-eight, faced with the greatest personal disaster he could imagine, he remained composed and dignified:

My Dear Madam,

We are all in great trouble, and Mr Nicholls so much so that he is not sufficiently strong and composed as to be able to write. I therefore devote a few moments to tell you that my Daughter is very ill, and apparently on the verge of the grave. If she could speak she would no doubt dictate to us while answering your kind letter, but we are left to ourselves to give what answer we can. The Doctors have no hope of her case, as fondly as we a long time cherished hope that hope is now gone, and we have only to look forward to the solemn event with prayer to God that He will give us grace and strength sufficient unto our day.

Will you be so kind as to write to Miss Wooler, and Mrs Joe Taylor [Amelia, the mother of Tim] and inform them that we requested you to do so, telling them of our present condition? – Ever truly and respectfully yours,

P. Brontë

(PB to Ellen Nussey, 30 March 1855)

What it must have cost the old man to write that letter can scarcely be imagined. The very next day Arthur pulled himself together and sent his saddest letter to Ellen:

> *Mr Brontë's letter would prepare you for the sad intelligence I have to communicate. Our dear Charlotte is no more. She died last night of exhaustion. For the last two or three weeks we had become very uneasy about her, but it was not until Sunday evening that it became apparent that her sojourn with us was likely to be short. We intend to bury her on Wednesday morning.*
>
> (ABN to Ellen Nussey, 31 March 1855)

So the story ends – all the happiness curtailed, the possibility of a child of her marriage to Arthur and her father's chance of a grandchild, together with our only hope of a descendant of that gifted family – all snatched away. Patrick Brontë, as he must have feared, was to be the sole survivor of his own family. He would find solace in his son-in-law's companionship. Arthur kept his word, caring for the old man until his death in 1861, living in male seclusion for six years in the sadly empty parsonage, keeping the promise he had made to his beloved Charlotte.

On Patrick Brontë's death the fickle trustees of the parish, for their own inscrutable reasons, declined to appoint the widower Arthur Nicholls as their next parson. He put the contents of the house up for sale and left for Ireland, where he kept mementoes of his life in Haworth and shrank from the publicity associated with his marriage to one of the greatest novelists in the English language. Perhaps his dearest legacy from his wife was her sustained gratitude for the happiness that he had brought to her in what were to be the last few months of her life, a time when she had been 'So happy', when she had truly set all aside for the love of a good man.

Epilogue

❧

'My Dear Son Arthur'
(Patrick Brontë in his will)

In all the accepted versions of the story of the Brontë family, Patrick Brontë's grief at the loss of his only surviving child seems somehow to have overshadowed Arthur's loss of his wife, his beloved Charlotte. Moreover, if she was indeed pregnant, as she and he seemed to believe, he had also lost their unborn child. Patrick Brontë, who had outlived his wife and all six of his children, was left without hope of a grandchild. The line of what was to become one of the most famous families in the history of literature was at an end. But while the literary world of the nineteenth century would mourn the death of Currer Bell, little heed was given to the feelings of Arthur Nicholls, the son-in-law, the patient admirer, the once rejected suitor, the husband and lover.

Patrick Brontë wrote that at the time of Charlotte's death Arthur was too overcome with grief to put pen to paper. How deep that grief must have been. All who had known Charlotte as Mrs Nicholls had been pleased to see her so happy, to see the lonely woman content with her curate husband and their life in Haworth. Now it was the curate who was condemned to loneliness. Shut up with his father-in-law in the parsonage, he honoured his promise, staying with the forlorn old man until his death, aged eighty-four, in 1861. Once it became clear to Arthur Nicholls, however, that the trustees of St Michael and All Angels, were not going to appoint him to succeed his father-in-law as perpetual curate in charge of the parish, he felt his work in Haworth was over. He would serve no other clergyman as curate.

As the contents of the parsonage came under the auctioneer's hammer in October 1861 – thereby scattering the precious relics of this extraordinary family far and wide – the Reverend Arthur Bell Nicholls made for Ireland, to settle in Banagher, from whence he had come. Martha Brown, the servant who had shared so much of the Brontë family's history, accompanied him, as did Patrick Brontë's last dog, Plato. Among the widower's possessions were letters, drawings and paintings, and an assortment of writings by his wife, her sisters and their ill-fated brother, memorabilia that it gave him pain to handle. In 1864, ten years after his marriage to Charlotte, he married his cousin, Mary Bell, whom Charlotte had admired for her gentle manners and lively spirit when they had met during their honeymoon visit to Ireland. There were no children of Arthur's second marriage, and it is said that at his death in 1906 the second Mrs Nicholls placed George Richmond's famous portrait of Charlotte Brontë by her husband's coffin.

The history of Arthur's grieving and of his life without Charlotte, the account of his attempts to protect her memory from distortion and sensational conjecture, is another story, and one which deserves, one day, to be told.

Select Bibliography

Barker, Juliet, *The Brontës* (Weidenfeld and Nicolson, 1994)

Chapple, JAV and Pollard, A, *The Letters of Mrs Gaskell* (Manchester University Press, 1966)

Chitham, E, *The Brontës Irish Background* (Macmillan, 1986)

Flintoff, E, *In The Steps of the Brontës* (Countryside Books, 1993)

Gardiner, J, *The World Within: The Brontës at Haworth* (Collins and Brown, 1992)

Lintoff, S, ed., *Brontë and Brontë: The Belgian Essays* (Yale University Press, 1996)

Lock, J and Dixon, W T, *A Man of Sorrow* (Nelson, 1965)

Maynard, J, *Charlotte Brontë and Sexuality* (Cambridge University Press, 1984)

Pinion, FB, *A Brontë Companion* (Macmillan, 1975)

Shuttleworth, S, *Charlotte Brontë and Victorian Psychology* (Cambridge University Press, 1996)

Winnifrith, T, *A New Life of Charlotte Brontë* (Macmillan, 1988)

Wise, TJ, *The Brontës: Their Lives, Friendships and Correspondence* (Blackwell, 1933)

Smith, Margaret, *The Letters of Charlotte Brontë* Vol 1 (Oxford University Press, 1995)

The Transactions of The Brontë Society, published periodically by The Brontë Society, The Parsonage Museum, Haworth. Members of the Society, which is international and open to all, receive this journal free of charge.

Picture Acknowledgements

The publishers would like to thank the following for their permission to reproduce photographs and illustrations in the plate section.

Brian Wilks pp. 1, 2 (below), 3, 6 (below), 7.
© The Brontë Society pp. 2 (above), 4, 5 (both), 8 (both).
National Library of Wales, Cardiff p. 6 (above).

Index

Thackeray, William, 67–8, 96, 114, 130–1

Villette
Bretton family, 115
characters in, 77
child, portrayal of, 196
love scene, 51–2
love's loss and fidelity, depicting, 54
Martineau's view of, 67
message of, 130
patient loyalty and constancy, evocation of, 53–4
proofs, Charlotte reading, 84

publication, 85
reception of, 85
review of, 144
story of, 37–8
Thackeray's view of, 67–8
writing of, 36, 127, 129–30

Weightman, William, 22, 79, 179
Williams, William Smith, 104–9, 116
Winkworth, Catherine, 85, 138, 159, 182–3, 196
Wooler, Catherine, 181
Wooler, Margaret, 141, 144, 153, 160–1, 166, 169, 174, 178–9, 181, 191–2